THE LEGAL ASPECTS
OF
PRISONS AND JAILS

THE LEGAL ASPECTS OF PRISONS AND JAILS

By

PENELOPE D. CLUTE, B.A., J.D.

Plattsburgh, New York

With a Foreword by

Perry M. Johnson, B.S., M.S.

Director, Michigan Department of Corrections
Lansing, Michigan

CHARLES C THOMAS • PUBLISHER
Springfield • Illinois • U.S.A.

Published and Distributed Throughout the World by

CHARLES C THOMAS • PUBLISHER

Bannerstone House

301-327 East Lawrence Avenue, Springfield, Illinois, U.S.A.

© *1980, by* CHARLES C THOMAS • PUBLISHER

ISBN 0-398-04005-2 (cloth)
ISBN 0-398-04006-0 (paper)

Library of Congress Catalog Card Number: 79-26394

Printed in the United States of America
V-R-1

Library of Congress Cataloging in Publication Data

Clute, Penelope D
    The legal aspects of prisons and jails.

    Includes index.
    1. Prisons--Law and legislation--United States.
2. Prisoners--Legal status, laws, etc.--United States.
I. Title.
KF9730.C55   344'.73'035   79-26394
ISBN 0-398-04005-2
ISBN 0-398-04006-0 pbk.

to my parents from whom I learned the value of
doing things in the correct way.

FOREWORD

WHEN I began working in corrections years ago, the subject of a prison administration's relationship to the courts was of little concern, because courts had very little to say about how prisons should be run or about the rights of prisoners. This is not to suggest that prisons were lawless places, but rather that the laws were largely interpreted and administered by prison officials without input from the courts. The dramatic change in judicial policy towards prisons and prisoner complaints that occurred in the late 60s and early 70s caught corrections administrators in this country unprepared. As the courts abandoned the "hands-off doctrine," decisions emanating from federal courts appeared to those in the corrections profession as confusing and, at times, conflicting. Few correctional systems contained the resources necessary to evaluate this expanding body of case law; therefore, they were unable to comprehend the full significance of these developments. It is not surprising, therefore, that many corrections professionals expressed frustration and helplessness in adapting their practices and procedures to comply with the expanding application of constitutional law. Much has been written about these changes but, unfortunately, most of it has been written by lawyers speaking to other lawyers and has left those of us who are not attorneys still struggling in the quagmire. What has been needed is a common sense explanation of corrections law, written in terms that a nonlawyer could understand. *The Legal Aspects of Prisons and Jails* fills the void very nicely.

If correctional administrators have been frustrated and confused by the new activism of the courts in the corrections area, there is another group that has been even more affected in the day-to-day performance of their jobs. I am speaking of the correctional officers who work inside the walls and fences of our prisons, coming into daily contact with a prison population increasingly more sophisticated about its constitutional rights. These officers are asked to cope with the numerous problems inherent in dealing with people who are locked up and prevented from establishing normal human contacts. They are also asked to do that task within an increasingly legalistic framework that they sometimes cannot understand. This lack of understanding creates resentment and antagonism towards the courts, and unfortunately, at times, towards the prisoners. Such antagonism is not only fruitless, it is also counterproductive. Yet we cannot blame the line officers for this when we have failed to inform these men and women in a clear and comprehensible manner of the effects mandates, issued by the courts, have on their jobs. We must strive to dissipate this antagonism between correctional officers and the courts and help those officers to come to the realization that it is possible to operate a prison or jail effectively and efficiently within these constitutional mandates.

When the author of this book served on my staff with the Michigan Department of Corrections, one of her tasks was educating our correctional officers on the various legal issues that affected their daily job performance. She proved to be a very competent attorney, but beyond that she was able to communicate her legal knowledge with clarity and simplicity to those not trained in the law. She was an excellent teacher, whose communication and rapport with our correctional officers made her an invaluable resource. I am very pleased that she has committed her ideas and information to writing so that it can be widely utilized to perform the same educational tasks she so ably performed during her time with our department. *The Legal Aspects of Prisons and Jails* should prove to be a welcome resource for the corrections practitioner, as well as to the students of correctional curriculum.

Perry M. Johnson

PREFACE

THIS book originated in my work with the Michigan Department of Corrections and took shape while teaching a course to corrections officers in New York. The genuine eagerness to know what the law required impressed me; the failure of the legal system to communicate an understanding of its decisions to those charged with implementing them disturbs me.

The constant interest and need to know of the corrections personnel I worked with, particularly the hearing officers in Michigan, inspired this work. I sincerely hope it will be of value to them.

The assistance of Jude C. Chamberlain, a New York Department of Correctional Services corrections officer, in reviewing and commenting on the chapters in progress was much appreciated.

P.D.C.

CONTENTS

THE LEGAL ASPECTS
OF
PRISONS AND JAILS

Chapter One

INTRODUCTION AND PURPOSE

PERSPECTIVE

ALTHOUGH both statutes and cases make up the general law of our society, the short history of litigation regarding corrections has been almost entirely constitutional case law. The typical statutes pertaining to prisons and jails are general in terms, granting broad authority to corrections administrators.

Because corrections administrators traditionally were vested with total power over their institutions and charges, the prisoners' efforts have been directed towards limiting that authority and asserting their individual rights. This has been done almost entirely through the United States Constitution. Thus, *The Legal Aspects of Prisons and Jails* means the Constitutional aspects, administering prisons and jails within the Constitution; and the subject of this book is the Constitution in the correctional setting.

Most of what has been written on the subject of law and corrections has been written from the prisoner's point-of-view, challenging any restriction and seeking the expansion of the legal frontier of prisoners' rights. This approach is necessarily limited to defining the extremes and perimeters of the subject. It leaves unanswered a multitude of legal questions raised by the day-to-day administration of a correctional system.

The purpose here is to treat this subject from the corrections administrator's point-of-view. Of course, the current state of the law will be covered, but it will be interwoven with explanations or recommendations regarding its applicability to real-life situations. The implementation of the legal principles will be emphasized.

In concentrating on the description and implementation of legal requirements, we hope to provide a tool for corrections administrators. This different perspective does not change the status of the law, but it does affect the usefulness of the information. Corrections personnel need to know how to implement the increasing number of court decisions affecting them. The law pervades their work; they are expected to follow it; they are entitled to understand it. The corrections administrator needs a framework for analyzing policy and practical issues having legal ramifications.

Used as is, this text will provide a comprehensive guide for measuring actions and policies against legal requirements. It will serve as a ready manual or handbook of appropriate legal principles and standards affecting corrections administration. It is designed to be used for short in-service training courses or as a ready, on-the-job desk reference.

For college use and lengthy professional training sessions, this text should be supplemented with actual case decisions. The end of each chapter provides a list, with full citations, of illustrative cases analyzing and applying the principles discussed in that chapter. The reading of full case decisions is strongly recommended, as it provides the reader with the complete context and rationale of a decision. Only then are the nuances and the impact of the varying factual circumstances appreciated. The resultant holding of the case, then, is no longer read in a vacuum, but comes much more alive and provides better assistance in planning future policies and courses of action.

After two decades of continuous prison litigation, many of the constitutional principles are clearly drawn; in others, the trend is discernible, as are the limits. The corrections administrator need not remain in a reactive, defensive position, but can use the understanding of the law to examine current policy and practice, make needed adjustments, and prevent future litigation and liability.

THE CONSTITUTION IN THE PRISON SETTING

General Approach

Frequently the subject of law and prisons is labelled "prisoners' rights" or "correctional law." This indicates a particular, well-defined area of law, distinct from all others. It conjures up the image of a person, newly convicted, arriving at a prison and being told to turn in his clothes, personal belongings, and constitutional rights. He moves a few feet down the hallway and is handed prison clothing and prison rights.

This is not the way it happens. There are no special, different rights that prisoners have. As the United States Supreme Court stated in *Wolff v. McDonnell,* "There is no iron curtain drawn between the Constitution and the prisons of this country." Instead of viewing "prisoners' rights" as a peculiar subject unto itself, it is much more helpful to see it as part of constitutional law generally. For, the same rights that apply outside prison also apply inside; the basic principles are identical.

Background

A brief sketch of the meaning and origin of our constitutional rights will help to explain this. When the American colonists created their own independent government, they did so within the framework of a written constitution. The Constitution is the means by which the colonists transferred their power to govern to their representatives.

It gives a great deal of authority to elected officials and a great deal of power over the citizenry. But, the Constitution, in addition to creating a government with extensive powers, also is the document by which the people *drew the line* on government intervention in their lives. Constitutional rights are not something that the government has given to us, but something we have kept and prohibit government from taking away. The basic human rights that the colonists retained, after giving up much of their freedom to create an organized society, are contained in the Bill of Rights — the amendments to the United States Constitution.

Constitutional rights are not an all-or-nothing situation, neither in the free society nor in prison. For example, a person does not have an absolute right to make a public speech anywhere, anytime, about anything. It may be regulated by time, place, and manner, as through permit requirements, so as not to interfere with traffic control, etc. If the speech incites violence, it may be stopped. But it cannot be prevented ahead of time simply because it *might* lead to violence, nor can all public speeches be prohibited altogether. Similarly, it is not correct to say that prisoners have no rights, nor do they have absolute rights.

Both in free and prison society, rights can be "interferred with" or restricted if the government can establish a proper justification. The appropriateness of the justification will depend upon the individual circumstances of the particular case. Each case or set of facts must be examined individually. These facts are then measured against the applicable legal rules or principles.

In our society we speak of "rule of law" rather than "rule of men," that the legal rights and principles governing us remain constant regardless of who is in power. The law, nevertheless, is a vibrant, living thing, seeking an accommodation between society's competing interests in control and in individual freedom. This perpetual tension and competition is symbolized by the portrayal of justice as someone holding a scale or balance. Law, or justice, weighs the competing interests and strives to strike a balance between them. Whether the balance tips in favor of control or for individual freedom in a particular case depends upon the weight of the differing interests under the facts of the specific situation.

The principles of constitutional rights and their limitations, which will be discussed in this book, remain constant. However, as the particulars of each case are analyzed and weighed, the results may differ. The varying facts may tip the balance in one direction, justifying a restriction on the exercise of rights, while the facts of a similar case may tip in favor of the individual, invalidating a restriction. This occurs in free society as well as in prison.

The Prison Setting

The basic guidelines for applying constitutional rights in prison are, first, prisoners *do* have constitutional rights; second, even the most fundamental constitutional rights may be restricted; but, third, they may be restricted only to the degree justified by "important or substantial government interests" and no further. The courts have recognized that, for prisons, these interests are security, order, and rehabilitation.

In restricting rights, the government cannot merely claim that the restriction is justified, but must show a specific justification. This will vary depending upon the facts and circumstances of the particular situation.

Thus, questions are to be answered whenever a prisoner asserts a violation of rights, or an official must make a decision concerning the prison environment:

1. Is a constitutional right involved? (Not everything is a right.)
2. Is or should the exercise of the right be restricted?
3. What is a proper reason for restricting the exercise of the right?

The following chapters will examine specific constitutional rights and various justifications for their restriction. They will clearly illustrate that the *facts* make all the difference, and the facts are always different.

The Role of the Courts

In reading constitutional law, the role of the courts must be kept firmly in mind. A court does not go out looking for problems, but decides only those disputes that are brought before it. When examining a challenged action, policy, or rule, a court does not decide whether that action, etc., was wise, but merely whether it violated a constitutional right.

A judge does not second-guess an administrator, but measures that administrator's actions against constitutional standards. These standards are *minimum* requirements; once they are met, the policy choices are left to the administrator and are not reviewable by courts. Thus, constitutional cases generally deal with extremes, with the outside limits of legally permissible action. Unless there is a specific statutory or rule violation, those actions that fall within the constitutional boundaries will be left untouched by courts, even if they are considered to reflect poor policy or judgment.

The Balancing Test

Whether a constitutional right may properly be restricted or interfered with is always a question of balancing the individual's interest in exercising the right versus the government's interest in restricting it. This often translates into balancing the likelihood and severity of the harm resulting from exercising the right against the degree of governmental intrusion or interference with an individual and the importance of the right involved. It is always a balancing test; always a question of degree; always dependent upon the particular facts of the case. Again, it is often not an all-or-nothing situation. Frequently, minimal interference with the exercise of rights may be constitutionally acceptable where a greater degree of interference would be prohibited. This balancing will be illustrated repeatedly in the pages to follow.

The perspective the courts bring to weighing the balance of interests is somewhat different from that often encouraged by the parties to the lawsuits. The prisoner, more often than not, feels entitled to absolute rights and attacks any semblance of restriction. Corrections officials have traditionally taken a firm stance in the other direction, insisting upon the administrative discretion to run prisons as they see fit. The security consciousness of corrections officials frequently results in their taking precautions against all possible problems. Security is their business and they must always be "security-minded," ever-vigilant to the potential for disruption. In keeping with this view, at times measures are taken and rights restricted on the basis that something *might* happen.

A court, however, must require specific justification for a regulation or restriction of a constitutional right. A restriction is legitimate if it is necessary for security, order, or rehabilitation, but that necessity can be shown only by documented facts. If the feared problem has never occurred, it is possible that its remoteness — the unlikelihood of harm — will weigh against the legitimacy of the restriction.

The Role of the Corrections Administrator

An administrator familiar with the constitutional principles applicable to corrections, and aware of the accountability demanded by the public and courts of administrators in all fields, can use this knowledge to operate more effectively.

Learning not only the legal decisions, but also their principles and rationale, enables a corrections official to draw appropriate lines; to distinguish fact situations to which a given principle applies from those not pertinent. Legal considerations become an integral part of all policy decisions and planning.

Issuing rules or specific guidelines for employee action is a most effective means of ensuring compliance with legal requirements. In addition, written departmental policy and rules promote consistency and employee accountability. In rule-making, the administrator's role is similar to a legislature. The rules, like statutes, regulate conduct, control discretion, and protect rights.

Many corrections personnel who conduct hearings on disciplinary charges, or make decisions concerning classification or program placement, perform functions similar to judges. The effectiveness of these adjudications is also greatly facilitated by careful rule-making. The decision-making must be made within the framework of the rules according to the criteria and procedures set forth. Thus, the adjudicatory function is also made more consistent, comprehensible, and accountable.

WHAT IF I'M SUED?

First Things First

This topic is of overwhelming concern to today's employees. Treating it at the beginning of this text will serve the dual purpose of quickly answering common questions and providing a "setting" or backdrop for studying the issues in the following chapters. The common question lurking in the back of an employee's mind is, "Can the prisoner sue me?" But the more appropriate question is, "Can the prisoner win?"

An ever-increasing number of corrections employees are being sued by prisoners. The lawsuits generally claim that the defendant employee violated the prisoner's constitutional rights and may request a large amount of damages (even hundreds of thousands of dollars) as the remedy for this violation.

Certainly, it is most unpleasant to have a lawsuit hanging over your head. No matter how unfounded you know the claims to be, you cannot be certain of the outcome. Or maybe the prisoner's claims are true, but you did not realize that your action violated the Constitution, so you don't know what to expect. There are several points to be aware of that may help ease your mind.

First, yes, the prisoner can sue; anyone can bring a lawsuit. It simply involves writing a "complaint" and sending it to court and to the person being sued. No one screens the suits first to decide whether to allow it; everyone has the right of access to the courts. Consequently, the fact of being sued says nothing about who will win, it simply means that someone, the plaintiff, is making a legal complaint to the court about your, the defendant's, actions. Most suits never go to trial, and a great many are thrown out, or dismissed, at very early stages.

Second, if you are sued you will want to know whether you must hire your own attorney. Most states and many local units of government have statutes or rules guaranteeing that they will provide counsel for employees who are sued for an action taken within the course of their employment. If the employee belongs to a union, the union may provide an attorney. The laws in this regard differ in each state and locality, however, so the particular provision must be checked to determine its coverage. Some laws also provide that any judgment for money damages will be paid for by the employer.

Third, in determining whether the case is a proper one, the judge will decide several questions similar to those noted earlier:

1. Is there a constitutional right involved?
2. If so, was the right interfered with or restricted?
3. If so, was a proper justification established for the interference or restriction?

4. If not, what should the remedy be?

Liability or Immunity?

This book is largely devoted to exploring the first three questions, so now we will discuss only the last, the appropriate remedy. Even though the prisoner may request money damages, the court will award them only in rare cases, where it determines that the defendant clearly acted in bad faith by maliciously or intentionally violating the prisoner's rights.

Most suits against prison officials are brought in federal court under a federal statute known as Section 1983 (42 USC §1983). This allows a lawsuit against any person who acts "under color of law" to deprive another person of federally protected rights. Several remedies are authorized, including issuing an injunction to stop the illegal practice and ordering money damages.

Commonly, the prisoner's suit is complaining of an action that the employee took in accordance with standard departmental practice or procedure. For example, the prisoner may be challenging the fact that he was strip searched even though there was no suspicion that he possessed any contraband, as a violation of his Fourth Amendment rights; or asserting that her right of access to the courts was denied because the law library is only open four hours a day; or claiming that First Amendment rights are violated by restrictions on personal clothing. In each case the individual employee who conducted the search, or supervised the law library, or seized the contraband clothing may be sued even though he or she was simply following orders. The suit is really attacking the policy or procedure as unconstitutional, not just an isolated act of the employee. Even so, the employee was acting "under color of law" (department policy) and may be personally sued under §1983. If the employee works for state government, the prisoner must sue the employee personally, because the Eleventh Amendment to the United States Constitution prohibits suits by individuals against states. Municipalities and other local units of government may be sued, however.

In these cases, if the court finds that a constitutional right was restricted without proper justification, the usual remedy will be to enjoin the enforcement of the unconstitutional policy or procedure. That is, the court will prohibit continued use of the present policy and require the department to act in accordance with the Constitution. Even if the prisoner has requested damages and the court agrees that rights were violated, it will generally not order the defendant to pay damages.

Damages are ordered only when the court finds that, at the time of the violation, the defendant (employee) acted in bad faith. That is, the defendant knew that the action taken was not proper or knew it was in violation of the prisoner's rights.

When bad faith is found, the defendant is "liable" for damages. However, when there is no evidence of bad faith, the defendant will have "immunity." This immunity applies only to damages, to the remedy; it does not protect one from being sued. Immunity, then, is a defense to damages that comes into play only when the plaintiff's rights have been violated. The question of liability or immunity does not even come up until after it is decided that there was a violation of rights.

In deciding whether immunity applies, two broad categories of employee action must first be distinguished: (1) *Duties* — many times an employee had a duty to perform the particular act complained of. The employee had no choice, but was simply following required procedure. For example, it was the defendant's job to read all outgoing prisoner mail under a procedure requiring that all mail be read. If the duty was performed in good faith and following the department requirements, the employee will not be liable for damages even if the requirement was unconstitutional (as it was in this example since it included reading attorney-client and other mail entitled to confidentiality). (2) *Discretionary acts* — in other situations, an employee is authorized to use judgment and make choices regarding the appropriate course of action. When a discretionary action is found to be unconstitutional, the employee-defendant will be immune from damages if the employee, (a) actually had authority to exercise discretion, (b) acted in good faith, *and* (c) had reasonable grounds for the action taken, in light of the circumstances known at the time of the action.

If any one of these three factors is missing, the employee may be liable. For example, if the employee really was not authorized to use discretion in the situation, and exceeded the bounds of authority, item (a) is not met. To fulfill item (b), "good faith," the defendant must have acted both sincerely with the belief that he or she was doing right *and*, in fact, not have acted in disregard of clearly established constitutional rights. The determination of item (c), whether there were reasonable grounds, will be made on the basis of the circumstances known to the defendant at the time of the challenged action; a different view afforded by hindsight will not be used to second guess the defendant's judgment at the time.

Conversely, an employee who performs his or her job within departmental guidelines and does not knowingly violate a prisoner's rights should be immune from a damage remedy, even if it is later determined that the employee's actions were unconstitutional.

CONCLUSION

The following chapters will explore the application of specific constitutional rights in the correctional setting. As each is discussed, you may wish to keep in mind the general principles set forth in this chapter and apply the guidelines for determining liability in the specific contexts as they are covered.

It is hoped that the corrections employee and the student will find this book a useful compass to orient themselves in what has often appeared to be a realm without guideposts — the Constitution in the correctional setting.

RECOMMENDED CASES

Principles of Liability/Immunity

Scheuer v. Rhodes, 416 US 232 (1974) (high executive officials)
Wood v. Strickland, 420 US 308 (1975) (school boards)
Procunier v. Navarette, 434 US 555 (1978) (prison guards)
Butz v. Economou, 438 US 478 (1978) (administrative hearing officers)
Alabama v. Pugh, 438 US 781 (1978) (Eleventh Amendment bars suit against state and Board of Corrections)
Monell v. Department of Social Services of City of New York, 436 US 658

(1978) (municipalities may be sued under §1983)
Alyeska Pipeline Service Company v. The Wilderness Society, 421 US 240
    (1975)
Knell v. Bensinger, 522 F.2d 720 (7th Cir 1975)
Duckett v. Ward, 458 F.Supp 624 (SDNY 1978) (liable for unconstitutional
    disciplinary procedures)

Damages

Carey v. Piphus, 435 US 247 (1978) (once proof of injury, damages can
    include mental and emotional distress)
Cavey v. Levine, 435 F.Supp 475 (D Md. 1977) *aff'd* 580 F.2d 1047 (4th Cir.
    1978) (warden personally liable for compensatory and punitive
    damages)
Hutto v. Finney, 437 US 678 (1978) (bad faith — attorney fees)
Mack v. Johnson, 430 F.Supp 1139 (ED Pa. 1977) (unconstitutional
    disciplinary procedures)
Reiser v. District of Columbia, 563 F.2d 462 (DC Cir. 1977) (parents of rape
    murder victim win damages against District of Columbia for releasing
    and later not revoking parolee with long history of sexual assault)
Taylor v. Clement, 433 F.Supp 585 (SDNY 1977)
Negron v. Ward, 458 F.Supp 748 (SDNY 1978)
Carter v. Noble, 526 F.2d 677 (5th Cir. 1976) (jail haircut; bad faith)

Chapter Two

FREEDOM OF SPEECH AND ASSOCIATION

GENERAL PRINCIPLES

THE First Amendment to the United States Constitution states, "Congress shall make no law respecting an establishment of religion, or prohibiting the free exercise thereof; or abridging the freedom of speech, or of the press; or the right of the people peaceably to assemble, and to petition the government for a redress of grievances."

This chapter will treat the second and third clauses of the Amendment, while freedom of religion will be discussed in the next chapter.

Government restraint on these freedoms in the "outside world" is a rare instance, invoked only when there is said to be a "clear and present danger" to society. First Amendment freedoms are very cherished in this country, so much so that they are frequently referred to as "preferred rights." Except in very limited circumstances, people who are not in prison have the freedom and mobility to say what they wish, associate with whomever they choose, and purchase whatever publications they please. These rights are jealously guarded, and people are quick to challenge any governmental interference.

Many cases, texts, articles, and other discussions concerning freedom of speech and the press are available to the student wishing to explore the history and development of those constitutional rights. This volume is limited to the exercise of those rights in prison and will cover only those cases which deal specifically with the prison context. Suffice it to say that even in the "free society" the freedoms of speech, press, and association are not absolute. When exercise of those rights is so threatening as to present a "clear and present danger" of violence or overthrow of government, authorities may intervene. Although there may be debate over whether the facts of a particular case establish a "clear and present danger," there is no dispute that there is a point at which these freedoms may be interfered with.

It is also important to know that not all "speech" is protected; the Supreme Court has held that obscenity does not fall within the meaning of First Amendment speech, and thus, can be prohibited. The definition of what is "obscene" then becomes very important. There have been many cases on the subject with particular reference to films and magazines. Legal principles have been developed. These must be followed by a governmental unit seeking to ban pornography or otherwise restrict allegedly obscene material. Not everything distasteful is obscene; lawmakers and police officials do not have complete discretion to prohibit material that they personally deem offensive. Only speech that meets the legal definition of obscenity is stripped of constitutional protection.

FREEDOM OF SPEECH

A prisoner's access to the outside world is obviously limited; the prisoner generally has no ability to leave until paroled, and the outsiders who come into a prison are few. A prisoner's main means of communication is in writing letters to family, friends, courts, attorneys, and the media. It is in letters that prisoners have the opportunity to exercise their freedom of expression; they can communicate ideas to others and receive ideas in return. This expression or exchange of ideas is the substance of the guarantee of free speech. The purpose of that constitutional guarantee is to ensure the "marketplace of ideas."

Not surprisingly, the freedom of speech cases in the prison context have centered primarily around mail regulations. Traditionally, although allowing limited correspondence, prison officials restricted whom a prisoner could correspond with, the number, length, and content of letters, and read all incoming and outgoing mail. Typical regulations forbade prisoners to discuss officials, policies, or conditions in prison, or other inmates; or to make obscene, lewd, vulgar, slanderous, or threatening statements. In many cases, the prisoner would not be informed that objectionable incoming mail had been received. If the prison censor decided a letter violated any of the regulations, it would either be returned to the sender or destroyed.

Prisoners have also challenged hair and clothing regulations as unconstitutional interference with freedom of expression in terms of their right to choose their personal appearance. In addition, there have been cases asserting prisoners' right of access to the media and journalists' right of access to prisoners.

Mail

Personal Mail

TRADITIONAL APPROACH. While the tradition of the prisons was to closely restrict and censor prisoner correspondence, the tradition of the courts was to maintain a "hands off" policy towards all issues of prison administration. It is this attitude that has undergone fundamental change since the late 1960s. Its modification was signalled in the lower federal courts for several years before being confronted in the United States Supreme Court.

Perhaps this long history of noninvolvement lulled prison administrators into a false sense of insularity. As the judicial attitude changed and the constitutional principles were articulated, many officials were caught by surprise. The initial court decisions were viewed as irrational and aberrational, out of tune with the proper view of separation between court and state prisons. Consequently, many officials did not respond to these decisions by re-evaluating their policies and practices in light of newly defined constitutional standards. They did not view these decisions as the sign of changing times.

It is true that the change from "hands off" to imposing the obligation on administrators to justify certain regulations was a dramatic one, but it is also logical and reasonable with inherent limitations. The transition and its rationale are explained by the United States Supreme Court in *Procunier v. Martinez*:

> Traditionally, federal courts have adoped a broad hands-off
> attitude towards problems of prison administration. . . . this

attitude springs from complementary perceptions about the nature of the problems and the efficacy of judicial intervention. Prison administrators are responsible for maintaining internal order and discipline, for securing their institutions against unauthorized access or escape, and for rehabilitating, to the extent that human nature and inadequate resources allow, the inmates placed in their custody. The Herculean obstacles to effective discharge of these duties are too apparent to warrant explication. Suffice it to say that the problems of prisons in America are complex and intractable, and, more to the point, they are not readily susceptible of resolution by decree. Most require expertise, comprehensive planning, and the commitment of resources, all of which are peculiarly within the province of the legislative and executive branches of government. For all of those reasons, courts are ill-equipped to deal with the increasingly urgent problems of prison administration and reform. Judicial recognition of that fact reflects no more than a healthy sense of realism.

. . . . But a policy of judicial restraint cannot encompass any failure to take cognizance of valid constitutional claims whether arising in a federal or state institution. When a prison regulation or practice offends a fundamental constitutional guarantee, federal courts will discharge their duty to protect constitutional rights.

Courts' hands will stay off prisons so long as regulations do not interfere with constitutional rights. But when a rule restricts the exercise of a constitutional guarantee, the courts have a duty to examine that rule and balance the reasons for it against its effect on the rights involved. As we shall see in case after case, where a rule does not infringe on the exercise of constitutional rights, its wisdom, effectiveness, etc., will not be evaluated by the courts; the administrators will not be second-guessed. However, where the effect is to restrict constitutional rights, administrators will have the burden of justifying the need for the restriction in terms of the specific harm that is to be prevented. This is the approach that is universally followed by federal courts today. For lack of better terminology, we will call this the "Rights Approach."

RIGHTS APPROACH. Many federal courts around the country have grappled with challenges to prison censorship regulations. Without a precedent from the Supreme Court or other uniform standard to follow, they developed "a variety of widely inconsistent approaches." These were primarily attributable to differing views regarding the status of prisoners' rights. The Supreme Court decided to hear one of these cases on appeal in order to establish the proper standard for reviewing constitutional challenges to prison mail censorship.

The absence of a standard, the Court said, was detrimental to both sides: First Amendment interests were not consistently protected and "on the other hand, the uncertainty of the constitutional standard makes it impossible for correctional officials to anticipate what is required of them and invites repetitive, piecemeal litigation on behalf of inmates."

To everyone's surprise the Supreme Court, in deciding *Procunier v. Martinez,* found that it was unnecessary to determine the extent of rights retained by prisoners, whether the prisoner had a First Amendment right to uncensored mail. This is because censorship of mail affects the nonprisoner correspondent as well. Letters are a form of communication and are intended to be read by someone; there are two parties involved. Whether or not prisoners have First Amendment rights, it is clear that the nonprisoner sender or receiver does.

By recognizing that "the First Amendment liberties of free citizens are implicated in censorship of prisoner mail," the Court immediately rejected arguments that the mail could be censored because inmates had no right in this area. Instead the Court traced a series of nonprison cases that dealt with governmental restrictions on expression that were imposed incidental to other legitimate governmental interests. These included issues of free speech in schools and the violation of the Selective Service Law by burning a draft card (*see* Appendix for full text of *Martinez* with discussion of these cases).

The Court noted that each of the nonprison cases referred to involved a regulation whose purpose furthered a legitimate governmental interest, e.g. orderly school administration, prevention of violence, identification of draft registrants, but whose effect was to infringe upon First Amendment freedom of speech. In weighing the validity of these incidental restrictions the Court developed a four-part test: "a governmental regulation is sufficiently justified if it is within the constitutional power of the Government; if it furthers an important or substantial governmental interest; if the governmental interest is unrelated to the suppression of free expression; and if the incidental restriction on alleged First Amendment freedoms is no greater than is essential to the furtherance of that interest." United States v. O'Brien, 391 US 367, 377 (1968).

The Court then transferred this test into the prison context and applied it to mail censorship regulations. The first factor is readily satisfied; since government is charged with operating prisons, that responsibility obviously includes some degree of regulation of all activities, including the handling of mail.

In terms of the second and third prongs, the Court found that the governmental interests at stake in maintaining penal institutions are "the preservation of internal order and discipline, the maintenance of institutional security against escape or unauthorized entry, and the rehabilitation of prisoners." These purposes are legitimate in themselves and are unrelated to suppressing free speech. Censorship to detect escape plans or criminal activity would clearly be justified to protect these interests.

Is there any problem then? Do not the governmental interests in security, order, and rehabilitation authorize reading all incoming and outgoing prisoner mail? No, because there is a fourth prong: Officials may infringe upon First Amendment freedoms *only to the extent necessary* to further the security, order, or rehabilitation; they must use the least restrictive alternative to achieve their goals.

Two target areas are revealed in this test for reviewing mail regulations: First, regulations that authorize censorship for the purpose of restricting speech instead of those necessary for security, order, or rehabilitation are invalid. Examples are provisions struck down in *Martinez,* which prohibited statements that "unduly complain," "magnify grievances," express "inflammatory political, racial, or religious, or other views," or were deemed "defamatory" or "otherwise inappropriate." These regulations are clearly aimed directly at the content of the letters, the speech, and have, at most, incidental connection with the legitimate interests in security, order, and rehabilitation.

Second, even if the purpose of the rule is to further one of the recognized governmental interests, if it is broader than necessary to achieve that purpose, it is invalid. Thus, if the danger is escape plans, to read all mail of all inmates on the chance that there might be escape plans goes too far. That would be the most, not least, restrictive measure.

LEAST RESTRICTIVE ALTERNATIVE. Since security and order are such all-pervasive concerns in administering a prison, a wide variety of regulations are legitimately related to these interests. The toughest part of the test for corrections officials to meet is the "least restrictive alternative" aspect. At some point regulations, even though related to security concerns, are too remote from the likelihood of probable harm to be constitutionally acceptable. This is the area on which the courts will concentrate, and administrators should as well.

Of course, what is the "least restrictive" or "no more intrusive than necessary" depends upon the facts of the case. In reviewing a rule, the wording of that rule and the extent of interference it authorizes will be evaluated against the specific dangers the officials say the rule is intended to prevent. For example, smuggling drugs and money into prison is a common problem and one that is legitimate for administrators to prohibit. The court will not stop there, however, but will examine the techniques the officials have chosen.

Censorship connotes reading the contents of a letter and excising portions or refusing to deliver it. However, actually reading the mail is unnecessary to the discovery of contraband. If there is money or drugs in the envelope, it can be found by simply "inspecting" the envelope by opening and looking in or shaking the contents out. A rule that authorized *reading* mail for the discovery of contraband enclosures would be broader than necessary and invalid. Inspection protects the freedom of speech interest as well as the institutional security interest. An even less intrusive method by which some kinds of contraband can be detected is through x-ray or manipulation of unopened envelopes. Then only if something suspicious is felt need the envelope even be opened.

Another circumstance that is critical in determining propriety of the regulation is its applicability to outgoing as well as incoming mail. The dangers that might be presented by letters sent out of the prison appear to be fewer than those presented by incoming mail. Rules, like those in *Martinez*, that prohibit complaints about prison conditions or inflammatory racial views were justified by officials as necessary to prevent flash riots. The Court held that although preventing riots is certainly a legitimate governmental interest, whether that is furthered by forbidding such statements in letters going *out of prison* is highly questionable and goes much too far in restricting First Amendment rights.

Similarly, inspection of all incoming mail may well be the least restrictive alternative for detecting contraband, but since the likelihood of contraband being smuggled out of prison is much more remote, routine inspection of all outgoing letters may be unwarranted. To detect some threats to security, such as escape plans or extortion schemes, it is necessary to actually read, not just inspect, the letters. Since this is a severe intrusion on freedom of speech, it should not be done on a random or routine basis. The better practice is to authorize reading the contents only when there is some specific reason to believe that the particular inmate or correspondence in question may contain the forbidden plans.

Procedural Protections. The Court in *Procunier v. Martinez* also held that whenever officials decided to censor or withhold delivery of a letter, they must follow "minimum procedural safeguards." These safeguards are necessary to protect the correspondents from arbitrary governmental action, to provide a means for ensuring that the decision is based upon adequate information, and the parties involved are aware of the decision. Thus, the Supreme Court agreed with the lower court's requirement that in every case the "inmate be notified of the rejection of a letter written by or addressed to him, that the author of that letter be given a reasonable opportunity to protest that decision, and that complaints be referred to a prison official other than the person who originally disapproved the correspondence."

This is basic due process, discussed at greater length in Chapter Seven. It requires notice of the governmental action and the opportunity to be heard. It does not require a "hearing" as such, but simply some mechanism for complaining to an official with authority to review the initial decision. There are a variety of ways to implement these safeguards, ranging from a notice form with space for returning any complaints, to an interview with the inmate, to a more formal hearing with both the affected inmate and outside correspondent. Whichever procedure is selected, the meaningfulness of the process must be maintained. This necessitates a specific explanation of *why* the letter was rejected and real consideration by the reviewing official of any response from the inmate or correspondent.

DISCRETION. Another objectionable aspect of the rules struck down in *Procunier v. Martinez* was that the broad terms, such as "defamatory" or "otherwise inappropriate," gave complete discretion to the mailroom censors to use their own subjective opinion in rejecting letters. There were no real guidelines or standards for determining what violated the rules.

The need for articulated standards is essential to meet the test defined by the Supreme Court. Administrators must be able to identify the specific interest at stake and show how the particular rule is necessary to further the security, order, or discipline of the prison. What is the threat sought to be prevented? To properly implement and administer this process, it is necessary that guidance be given to the employees screening the mail so that all decisions will be in accord with the required constitutional principles.

The key is in writing policy and rules that identify the potential harm and provide guidelines for targeting-in on only the objectionable material. Distinctions between incoming and outgoing mail are essential. It is equally important that an all-or-nothing view of rights be avoided. A careful balancing of individual versus governmental interests must be made to arrive at those restrictions limited only to objectionable portions of the communications. This will necessitate designing varying degrees of intrusion, with actually reading the content only in extreme cases.

In summary, to meet the standards set forth in *Procunier v. Martinez*, mail regulations must be (a) specific enough to control administrative discretion and avoid inviting personal prejudice; (b) directly related to a legitimate governmental interest in security, order, or rehabilitation; and (c) the least restrictive means reasonably available to achieve the governmental interests.

Legal Mail

Correspondence between prisoners and attorneys, courts, and governmental officials carries more constitutional protection than personal mail because it involves other rights in addition to the freedom of speech, i.e. right to counsel, access to the courts, and redress of grievances. Consequently, only rarely may such mail be interfered with or read by corrections officials.

Although both prisoners and corrections officials agree that attorney-client mail may not be read by prison employees, there has been some dispute over the proper procedure to both safeguard the attorney-client relationship and satisfy the institution's security concerns. In *Wolff v. McDonnell,* the United States Supreme Court approved a procedure, already agreed to by state officials, whereby mail from attorneys would be opened by officials only in the presence of the prisoner-addressee *if* the envelope is clearly marked as originating from an attorney, and the attorney has earlier notified the prison officials of his or her identity and the client's. The envelope and letter are then inspected to determine if any contraband material is included.

It is significant to note that the Supreme Court did not fashion this procedure, but was simply reviewing the constitutionality of one already agreed to by the state. (The prisoners asserted that even merely opening the mail in their presence violated their constitutional rights; the Court rejected this contention.) Thus, the Court did not hold that the elements of this procedure were constitutionally required, but rather that they were not violative of the Constitution. As a matter of fact, the Court concluded by noting, "we think the State, by acceding to a rule whereby the inmate is present when mail from attorneys is inspected, has done all, *and perhaps even more* than the Constitution requires" (emphasis added.) The suggestion is clear that other procedures might be equally constitutionally acceptable.

The issue here is limited to the *inspection* of incoming mail; reading and censorship is definitely prohibited without clear evidence of abuse of the protected status of legal mail. If the letter is opened out of the prisoner's presence and inspected, however, it is quite impossible to convince the prisoner that the letter was not read. Although obtaining the prisoner's confidence is not constitutionally required, avoiding this suspicion will lend to the smoother operation of the institution. Thus, some of the alternative methods of inspecting for contraband, short of opening the envelope as discussed under *Personal Mail,* may be a better solution.

Publications

CONTENT. Typically, prisons have lists of publications that may not be received by inmates. As a rule, the prohibited publications are those considered to have an inflammatory effect on the prison population. These may be politically or racially militant or sexually oriented. Officials may ban books and magazines they think are obscene, especially those devoted to homosexual themes.

Since the decision in *Procunier v. Martinez,* lower courts have consistently applied its standards to publications as well as personal letters. Although no case regarding prison censorship of books, magazines, or newspapers has reached the Supreme Court, the interests involved are clearly the same as in personal correspondence. Certainly, the administrators have continuing interests in ensuring the security and order of their institutions and the rehabilitation of the inmates. Whether or not the prisoners have a First Amendment right to receive the publications, the publishers have First Amendment guarantees of freedom of expression and freedom of the press, which are interfered with by prison censorship policies. Consequently, the same standards should apply to any restrictions: That they (1) further a substantial governmental interest; and (2) be the least restrictive means available to further that interest.

When lower courts have examined publication restrictions under these tests they have frequently found the same defects of vagueness and overbreadth that rendered the rules reviewed in *Martinez* invalid. Rules that prohibit any nude photographs, "material of a sexual nature," or "of inflammatory or discriminatory nature" exclude more than is necessary to protect the institution's security, order, and rehabilitation interests.

Officials have the burden of justifying their censorship and that justification must be specifically rooted in the legitimate governmental interests so that receipt of the material in question would present a tangible threat to prison security or order or to the prisoner's rehabilitation. Whether the administrators' justification is constitutionally sufficient depends upon all the facts and individual circumstances of the case.

Guidelines narrowly drawn to prevent violence will certainly be upheld, as will those that prohibit the depiction of the manufacture of explosives, weapons, or drugs. In regard to sexually oriented material, some courts have held that prison officials must apply the obscenity standard set by the Supreme Court and not their own. Other courts have taken a middle ground attitude allowing censorship of sexually oriented publications when officials have reviewed the particular issue and have made a specific, factual determination that the publication is detrimental to prisoner rehabilitation because it would encourage deviate, criminal sexual behavior.

Material that advocates prisoners' legal rights or criticizes law enforcement, prison policies, or personnel may not be censored, but material that actually incites disobedience to those authorities may be prohibited.

Because of the preferred status of First Amendment rights, the starting point is a general presumption of free access to publications. Any restriction must, therefore, be specifically justified in terms of security, order, or rehabilitation *and* be the least intrusive means necessary. Since any publication that is available to a prisoner is readily available to a purchaser "outside" without governmental interference, there is no question that prison censorship regulations interfere with First Amendment rights.

The "least restrictive alternative" requirement imposes an obligation to make individual, not categorical, decisions. Not only must the prohibition of a publication be specifically justified in terms of a tangible threat, but only that portion of the publication containing the objectionable material may be excluded. That is, if only one article, or photograph, or page, etc. threatens security, order, or rehabilitation, then only that portion may be censored. The rest of the publication must be delivered to the prisoner.

Of course, the procedures set forth in *Martinez* of notice and opportunity to protest must be followed whenever a publication is censored, or delivery refused.

SOURCE. Another common institutional requirement is that publications may only be received directly from the publisher. Such a rule regulates only the source or manner of obtaining books and magazines. It does not censor or regulate the content in any way.

Thus, although it effectively prohibits purchase of used books, its impact on First Amendment guarantees is very remote. If family or friends wish to bring books for an inmate, they can do so by ordering from the publisher and requesting that the material be mailed to the prison instead of home. There may be inconvenience and higher cost, especially if the purchaser was unaware of the rule, but the problems can be accommodated within First Amendment protections.

On the other hand, the rule is directly related to the security of the institution in the interest of prohibiting contraband. Books can ideally conceal money, drugs, coded plans, etc., and would be extremely time-consuming to thoroughly inspect upon arrival. Although some lower courts have struck down the publisher-only rule as not being the least restrictive method of safeguarding the security interests in question, the United States Supreme Court has upheld the rule as a "reasonable response" to the security issues.

PROBLEMS

1. Can the institution censor or refuse to deliver personal mail in the following situations?
    a. The letter is from a segregated prisoner to a reporter and falsely represents the conditions of the institution?

   b. The letter is to a former prisoner and discusses a desire to escape?

   c. Incoming mail to a particular prisoner contains cards and pamphlets from an organization advocating racial supremacy? Does it make a difference if only one such card is in the letter?

2. Institution policy allows outgoing legal mail to be sealed by the prisoner. A prisoner in segregation addresses a sealed letter and writes "attorney mail" on the envelope. Should the staff send it out without opening it?

3. A prisoner is known to be representing himself on appeal, but sends and receives letters to attorneys. Must these letters be specially handled as legal mail?

4. It is a common corrections policy to prohibit publications depicting homosexual acts. What is the specific justification for this policy in terms of the three legitimate governmental interests? Write a rule concerning these publications that would meet the test of *Procunier v. Martinez.*

5. Your department's policy regarding publications states that "a prisoner may receive any book, periodical, or other publication that does not present a threat to the order or security of the institution or to prisoner rehabilitation."

Prisoner Jones has a subscription, approved by the institution, to a reputable hunting and fishing publication. The February issue featured an article containing a diagram of a disassembled rifle. No such article appeared in the March or April issues, but a similar article on an automatic handgun appeared in the June issue. The February issue was not delivered to Mr. Jones, and he has received no issues since May. The institutional mail room notified him that the magazine was now on the "prohibited publications list" as a threat to institutional security. Mr. Jones has appealed this action to you, the institution head. How will you decide his case?

Personal Appearance

Grooming

Prisoners have frequently asserted that grooming and clothing regulations, especially those restricting the length of head and facial hair, infringe on their First Amendment rights. The cases are similar to those that challenged the constitutional validity of regulations limiting hair length and style of male high school students.

Appearance regulations may vary depending upon the level of security classification and type of facility, but even the most liberal ones generally limit the hair length of male prisoners to the collar. If beards are permitted, they may be limited to a one-inch growth or the partial, goatee style.

School hair cases have held that the style of an individual's head and facial hair is not sufficiently communicative (as a form of speech) to warrant protection under the First Amendment, but it does constitute a "personal liberty" under the Fourteenth Amendment. Further, such cases have held that any restrictions must be based on a justifiable state interest.

Federal courts have applied a similar rationale, first to pretrial detainees, then to convicted prisoners. In general, they have found it reasonable for prison authorities to regulate hair and beards when it is shown that the regulations are based on security or public health reasons.

The primary security reason is the need for prisoners to be readily identifiable. As beard and hair grow, the inmate may only remotely resemble the picture taken upon his entry into the prison. Similarly, a prisoner with long hair, a beard, and a new ID picture to match can drastically change his appearance by cutting and shaving, thus greatly enhancing an escape plan. Shorter hair also minimizes the opportunities to conceal contraband. Lice hazard is the most common public health reason given for limiting hair length.

Clothing

The requirement of uniform prison clothing is common and has not been found to run afoul of the Constitution. As with hair regulations, clothing restrictions can readily be justified by security and health reasons. The wearing of personal clothing presents security problems in preventing ready distinctions between staff and prisoners and in facilitating escape. Additional security threats are presented by the existence of new objects for theft and argument among the prison population.

Even recognizing these problems, however, the corrections administrator may be well-advised to once-again avoid an all-or-nothing approach. Although not constitutionally required since First Amendment rights are not involved, the "least restrictive alternative test" provides a reasonable guideline for balancing the competing interests and allowing some degree of self-expression. For example, personal clothing could be allowed for visits; for honor block residents; or individual shirts allowed with uniform pants.

Equal Protection Considerations

RELIGION. Personal appearance or clothing items sometimes have religious significance, such as hair length for American Indians, beards for Jews and Muslims, and prayer rugs, kufis, and other items essential to proper religious observance. The cases are contradictory as to whether prison officials are prohibited from regulating the appearance of those who assert a religious justification, but generally their authority to do so in a reasonable way has been upheld. It would be reasonable to regulate the time and place of religious apparel, but not to prohibit them altogether except under unusual circumstances. For example, a general population prisoner may be limited to wearing religious apparel during religious services and in his own cell.

However, at least between religions holding similar beliefs, treatment must be uniform. Therefore, if one religious group, e.g. Jews, is allowed to grow beards, members of other religions holding the same tenet, e.g. Muslims, must be permitted the same privilege, or else a violation of equal protection may be found.

SEX. The law is beginning to examine the differential treatment of male and female prisoners. Substantial reasons must be given for different treatment programs, opportunity for community placement, etc., for those in women's institutions. Grooming regulations may eventually come under the same scrutiny. As already stated, the rationale given and accepted for limiting the length of men's hair pertain to the need for identification, contraband, and health problems. Do not these same problems exist with female prisoners? If so, then their hair length should be limited just as the males' (e.g. no longer than the collar); if not, how can it be shown that the same security threats are not present with women? Or maybe the threats are the same, but are not as great as previously supposed, leaving the men's regulations highly questionable.

Access to the Media

The United States Supreme Court has examined prison regulations limiting prisoners' access to the media. Both journalists and prisoners challenged department rules prohibiting personal interviews with specific inmates; the journalists asserted the freedom of the press and the public's right to know what goes on in prisons, while prisoners claimed infringement upon their freedom of speech.

The Court no longer avoided the question of whether prisoners had First Amendment rights; it held that "a prison inmate retains those First Amendment rights that are not inconsistent with his status as a prisoner or with the legitimate penological objectives of the corrections system." This very broad formulation must be applied in specific cases to reach determinations whether, under those circumstances, the exercise of First Amendment rights is "inconsistent" with penological objectives.

Although broad, the statement is significant in the highest court's recognition, for the first time, that a prisoner does have rights; they are not all lost by virtue of conviction. Further, the existence of rights in a particular case depends upon balancing them against the correctional interests. It is in the balancing process that the facts influence the outcome; lines are drawn and distinctions are made.

Even recognizing that the First Amendment rights of both the journalists and the prisoners were involved, the Court still found the restriction on personal interviews to be reasonable and justified by legitimate state interests of deterrence, rehabilitation, and internal security. In reaching this conclusion, the

Court emphasized that the plaintiffs' First Amendment rights were not completely curtailed by the interview prohibition because several alternative means of press access to information were available, such as: unlimited written correspondence; access to tour and photograph the prison facilities, during which randomly selected inmates could be interviewed; and the availability of recently released prisoners to provide information on prison conditions. The existence of the alternative modes of access is critical.

Once these mail and visit options are provided to the general public, moreover, additional means need not be given the press. The Court reiterated an earlier decision holding that, "The First Amendment does not guarantee the press the constitutional right of special access to information not available to the public generally." The First Amendment rights of the press are no greater than those of the public.

This principle was relied upon again to uphold a sheriff's refusal to allow a television crew access to the jail for an exposé on allegedly intolerable conditions; the Constitution did not require granting the journalists' request for special access.

Policies pertaining to media access should carefully balance the journalists' and prisoners' First Amendment rights against the institution's need to preserve security, order, and discipline. If personal interviews are permitted, safeguards should be included to ensure that there is no coercion of prisoners to grant interviews, and that prisoners are fully and specifically informed of the likely uses of the information they provide. A written waiver signed by the prisoner consenting to be interviewed or photographed is advisable, both to protect the prisoner and the department. An inmate who does not wish to be interviewed or photographed should not be subjected to it.

FREEDOM OF ASSOCIATION

The First Amendment is generally read to include the freedom of association, as well as that of expression. The private citizen finds no governmental interference with his or her choice of friends, clubs, or unions. The prison context is far different, however. Courts have accepted prison administrators' statements that potential security and discipline problems presented by gatherings of prisoners justify prohibiting group meetings, including meetings of prisoner "unions" and group visits.

Visits

PERSONAL. Corrections facilities traditionally have placed numerous restrictions on a prisoner's visits, frequently restricting the number and length of visits per month and limiting visitors to immediate family members or others approved by the facility. Despite the presence of "association" issues, courts have not found a constitutional right to visit. This may be because, since a prisoner usually may "associate" by writing, denial of visitation is not a complete denial of association. Visiting regulations that have some rational basis, are uniformly applied, and are nondiscriminatory are generally upheld. Although reasonable regulation of visitation has not violated constitutional rights, a total prohibition on all visitation for one or more inmates might well run afoul of constitutional safeguards, unless clearly justified by security conditions.

Once visiting is allowed, it may not arbitrarily be terminated; there must be a specific reason for the denial, such as the visitor attempted to smuggle contraband. Courts have not required a hearing procedure for termination of visits, but a procedure similar to that required in *Procunier v. Martinez* for denial of mail is advisable to guard against arbitrary terminations. A simple form providing written notice to the visitor and prisoner informing them of the reason the visit was denied or terminated and allowing them to respond will be sufficient. Any response should then be considered by officials in evaluating the reasons for, and length of, the termination (a sample form is in the Appendix).

Of course, the absence of a constitutional right to visits does not imply that it is wise to severely restrict visitation. Corrections administrators have long recognized the importance of regular visitations by family and friends. Maintaining these ties assists the prisoner's transition back to the community and provides a needed outlet to the pressures of prison living, facilitating the control of the institution. The trend is away from the more restrictive authorized visiting lists to open visiting with anyone who is not on an unauthorized visitors list. That is, anyone is authorized to visit until that person is placed on the unauthorized list because of illegal conduct or violation of the rules.

RELIGIOUS OR LEGAL. The administrator's discretion to regulate religious and legal visits is more limited. This is because the First Amendment guarantee of freedom of religion and Sixth Amendment right to assistance of counsel come into play. An institution may not interfere with a prisoner's right to visit with his or her attorney or minister without specific justification based on one of the legitimate governmental interests of security, order, or rehabilitation. For example, a particular attorney could be denied admission to the institution if he or she had been found bringing in contraband.

Not only must religious and legal visits be allowed, absent specific justification for denial, they must be given special treatment because of the constitutional protection surrounding the religious and attorney-client relationships. Consequently, the prison officials may not intrude on the confidentiality of these visits. To eavesdrop on visits or telephone calls between a prisoner and his or her minister or attorney is in violation of the constitution. Only the most extreme circumstances, such as specific information that the minister or attorney was participating in an escape plan or passing contraband, would justify such action.

The requirement that religious and legal visits receive special treatment naturally applies only after it is determined that the visitor is a *bona fide* minister or attorney. (An investigator or other paraprofessional working under the supervision of an attorney must be treated the same as the attorney.) If this is not established, those claiming entitlement to a religious or legal visit may be denied. Difficult problems are presented for administrators by "mail-order" ministries. Some religions will ordain anyone for the proper fee. Does this mean that a prisoner's friends and spouse can obtain an unlimited number of confidential visits simply by becoming mail-order ministers? It is possible that the officials' hands are tied due to the freedom of religion guarantee. Nevertheless, it is suggested that a more realistic and reasonable approach is to try to determine whether the person claiming a religious visit is a bona fide minister in the sense not only of having a paper ordination, but actually practicing that ministry. Such an investigation may be impossible for corrections officials to undertake.

However, keeping in mind that it is the "priest-penitent" and attorney-client *relationships* that are being protected, officials may be able to gather facts in particular cases that indicate that the visitor is not the prisoner's pastor or lawyer, but simply a friend or spouse who also happens to be ordained or admitted to the bar. These visitors need not be accorded special treatment despite their professions. Of course, because of the presumption of constitutional protection, an administrator should curtail apparent religious or legal visits only after gathering sound factual support.

"Unions" and Other Prisoner Organizations

The right most visibly and dramatically curtailed by the fact of incarceration is the freedom of association. Prisoners are behind walls and fences, isolated from the rest of society. Some outside organizations are welcome in prison, principally the Jaycees and Alcoholics Anonymous. These are seen as being rehabilitative and promoting responsible, law-abiding conduct. However, the barricades are usually raised to more political organizations, particularly self-help associations for prisoners. This was the type of group involved in *Jones v. North Carolina Prisoners' Labor Union, Inc.*, a United States Supreme Court decision defining inmates' associational rights.

Prisoners had incorporated an organization with the stated purposes of establishing collective bargaining with the administration to improve working conditions, changing department policies and practices, and presenting grievances to the officials. There were no dues or membership obligations; a prisoner could become a member by simply considering himself one. The North Carolina Department of Corrections allowed "membership," but adopted regulations prohibiting solicitation of membership, group meetings, or bulk mailings to members.

The prisoners sued, asserting that the rules violated their First Amendment rights and denied them *equal protection* of the laws since the Jaycees and Alcoholics Anonymous were allowed to have group meetings. The corrections officials responded that the very existence of the union presented potential dangers to institutional order and discipline. Regardless of whether the union members intended to use illegal means to achieve their purposes, "the creation of an inmate union will naturally result in increasing the existing friction between inmates and prison personnel. It can also create a friction between union inmates and nonunion inmates."

Administrators believed that, if allowed to grow, the department would be unable to control it, "even if its activities became overtly subversive to the functioning of the Department." Union leaders would become very powerful influences on the inmate population. "Work stoppages and routines are easily foreseeable. Riots and chaos would almost inevitably result."

Since there had been no "showing that these beliefs were unreasonable," the Court found that the prison officials had established that their regulations concerning union activities were in furtherance of legitimate state interests in security and order.

The Court then examined the prisoners' rights involved. It noted that "the fact of confinement and the needs of the penal institution impose limitations on constitutional rights," and some of the most obvious limitations are on associational rights. The Court then found that First Amendment rights were not greatly interfered with by the rules. Correspondence concerning the union was not prohibited, only bulk mailings. Although the restriction prevented use of cheaper mailing rates, it did not censor the content of the correspondence.

The prohibition on inmate-to-inmate membership solicitation was justifiable in light of the corrections officials' determination of the potential dangers to institutional order and security. In addition, the inmates had no right to form a labor union; thus, solicitation of that prohibited activity could be constitutionally prohibited.

The ban on group meetings was similarly justified by the

threat to prison order and security discussed above. The Court gave great deference to the officials' sincere belief that the union presented serious dangers to running a prison. When coupled with the recognition that "prison life. . . contain[s] the ever-present potential for violent confrontation and conflagration," the Court concluded that prison officials must be left with sufficient discretion to meet and prevent such threats "before the time when they can compile a dossier on the eve of a riot."

The regulation in question was constitutionally proper; the Court found that it met all the tests of *Procunier v. Martinez*. First, control of prisons is unquestionably within the state's power; second, the regulation in question was directly related to furthering an important or substantial governmental interest in the order and security of penal institutions. Third, the restriction of First Amendment activity is only incidental to furthering the other interests. Finally, the Court concluded that the intrusion on speech and associational rights was no greater than essential to the furtherance of the security interests, because "the perceived threat. . . stems directly from group meetings and group organizational activities of the Union."

Two aspects of the decision must be kept in mind in applying this opinion to future questions. The regulation at issue did not restrict individual activity, only group activity. It correctly viewed membership as a mental or political commitment on the part of an individual prisoner; a belief that does not necessarily entail concerted action. This "belief" aspect was distinguished from "group practice," much like the dichotomy presented in questions of religion as discussed in Chapter Three. Thus, the prison administration permitted individual membership/belief and individual expression of ideas through conversation and letters. There was no prohibition on belonging to or discussing the union, only on solicitation and group activities. The rule then was not overbroad; it targeted the activities deemed to be threatening and allowed the others to continue.

The other determining factor in the case, one repeated several times in the opinion, was that there was no evidence that the officials' fears were unreasonable. Perhaps if there had been "union" solicitation in another state, which had not resulted in the dangers feared by the North Carolina prison administrators, the decision would have been different. Lower court decisions that will be discussed in future chapters regarding religion and search and seizure have attempted to evaluate the likelihood of the potential danger in balancing the government's interests against the prisoners'. Where the possibility of a threat exists, but is shown to be very remote, practices and regulations that restrict constitutional rights may be struck down as not being the least restrictive means to achieve the desired result.

PROBLEMS

1. May the department prohibit residents from visiting with former residents? On what basis? Even if the former resident is a member of the immediate family?
2. May the department prohibit contact visits? Under what circumstances?
3. Men's hair length is limited to no longer than the collar or three inches out from the head. Does not this regulation interfere with the prisoner's personal freedom? What is the rationale for the regulation? Is it the least restrictive means to achieve that purpose? Do not the same arguments apply to women?
4. Is the prohibition on "clothing of the opposite sex" related to security? Give arguments for and against such a rule.

RECOMMENDED CASES

Mail

Procunier v. Martinez, 416 US 396 (1974) (full text in Appendix)
Wolff v. McDonnell, 418 US 539 (1974) (full text in Appendix)

Publications

Bell v. Wolfish, 441 US, 99 S.Ct 1861 (1979) (full text in Appendix)
Guajardo v. Estelle, 580 F.2d 748 (5th Cir. 1978) (personal mail and publications)
Thibodeaux v. South Dakota, 553 F.2d 558 (8th Cir. 1977) (sexually explicit

publication)
Carpenter v. South Dakota, 536 F.2d 759 (8th Cir. 1976) (sexually explicit
   publication)
Aikens v. Jenkins, 534 F.2d 751 (8th Cir. 1976)
Mukmuk v. Commissioner, 529 F.2d 272 (2d Cir. 1976) (religious literature)
Jackson v. Ward, 458 F.Supp 546 (WDNY 1978)

Equal Protection

People *ex rel.* Rockey v. Krueger, 306 NYS2d 359, 62 Misc.2d 135 (1969)

Association

Jones v. North Carolina, 433 US 119 (1977)
Butler v. Preiser, 380 F.Supp 612 (SDNY 1974)

Media

Pell v. Procunier, 417 US 817 (1974)
Saxbe v. Washington Post, 417 US 843 (1974)
Branzburg v. Hayes, 408 US 665 (1972)
Houchins v. KQED, Inc., 438 US 1 (1978)

Public Employee Speech

Givhan v. Western Line Consolidated School District, 439 US 410 (1979)

Chapter Three

RELIGION IN PRISON

GENERAL PRINCIPLES

WHEN we examine the wording of the First Amendment (quoted at the beginning of Chapter Two), we see that there are two clauses concerning freedom of religion: "Congress shall make no law [1] respecting an establishment of religion, or [2] prohibiting the free exercise thereof."

The former or "establishment" clause refers to one's freedom of belief, that government cannot dictate an official religion or punish a citizen for religious beliefs. This is generally viewed as an absolute right from governmental interference. As a practical matter, it is impossible to regulate what another believes in; it is only when those beliefs are expressed or put into practice that they become subject to restriction.

This brings us to the second, or "free exercise," clause. This protects the *practice* of religion. In the free society in this country, the practice as well as establishment of religion is largely ignored by government. The aspects that raise legal questions in free society commonly involve questions of government financial support or tax-free status. Under some circumstances, refusal to accept medical treatment or to send one's children to school for religious reasons may trigger a governmental reaction. The freedom to worship as one pleases, attend services, wear religious symbols, or read religious literature exists outside of government and goes on without governmental intervention, except in rare instances. Religion and places of worship freely exist without government's permission.

In this respect, prisons are clearly different. In prison, religion may be practiced, at least in a group sense, only if the authorities allow it. Outside, the Constitution prohibits government from interfering with the existence of religion, with the establishment of particular churches, or sects; it precludes government from monitoring the religious practices of citizens and from making decisions (e.g. employment, governmental benefits) about a citizen on the basis of that person's religious beliefs or practices.

But because prisons and jails are "total institutions," religious services, special diets, etc. cannot exist without prison authority. Unlike the issues in the speech area, with religion it is generally not a question of whether specific restrictions on the exercise of a right are legitimate, but rather, whether officials have an affirmative duty to provide the opportunity and means allowing prisoners to practice their religions.

ESTABLISHMENT

If all a prisoner wishes to do is believe in a particular faith, no problem is presented, since what goes on in a person's mind cannot be effectively regulated. But, of course, most people also wish to practice their religions, attend services, follow prayer rituals, visit with clergy, receive religious literature and articles, and follow grooming or dietary laws. To freely exercise one's faith within a prison frequently brings one in conflict with regular prison routine, as well as regulations affecting institutional security and order. For example, group meetings of prisoners are generally prohibited for security reasons; exceptions are made for religious services so long as the proper authorization and supervision is obtained. The other elements of practice listed above, though taken for granted in free society, represent significant privileges in a penal institution.

Some prisoners have tried to take advantage of this either by falsely professing to adhere to a religion or by inventing sham religions. The former situation is difficult to detect and is only at issue when the prisoner abuses the privileges by smuggling contraband, arranging a sexual rendezvous, disrupting prison routine, or the like. The possibility of sham religions is a real one; there are some "religions" that were started in prison or exist only in prison, *The Church of the New Song* being the most prominent example.

In free society, the government generally has no interest in whether a citizen calls his or her beliefs a "religion," but in prison, officials must take notice. This is because equal protection comes into play again here as it did under the *Personal Appearance* discussion in Chapter Two. The Constitution guarantees that the followers of unorthodox religions must be given the same opportunity to exercise their beliefs as is given to established or "recognized" religions. Thus, if religious services are permitted for Catholics, funding provided to Baptists, or beard restrictions lifted for Jews, the adherents of other religions must be treated equally.

Consequently, permitting a given practice often necessarily follows from a determination that the practice is a bona fide religious one. In some cases it may be appropriate for an administrator to question whether the claimed religion is in itself bona fide. In others, the religion may be recognized, but the sincerity of the particular prisoner's beliefs may be questioned. This is, obviously, a very touchy subject, and it is extremely difficult for an official to be successful in denying "religion status" to an asserted belief without concrete documentation of the prisoner's insincerity.

Unorthodox Religions

Since the Constitution protects only religion, there is the possibility of demonstrating that the claimed religion is invalid. However, any case in which an administrator attempts to do this is likely to end up in court, and judges are very loathe to rule on the question of religion. The main reason is that questioning the sincerity of a citizen's religious beliefs has always been outside the scope of the judiciary. This issue is not presented in free society; it is unique to prisons. Judges have no experience with this determination, no precedents to draw upon. Freedom of religion has a very preferred status under our Constitution, and courts, understandably, are extremely reluctant to rule that a person who swears that he believes in a particular religion does not do so sincerely, or that a particular system of beliefs is not a religion when its believers say that it is.

This uncertainty of religious criteria and judicial reluctance is illustrated by two cases concerning the *Church of the New Song*, a religion founded by a federal prisoner who made himself the head of the Eclatarian faith and sought to hold religious services and engage in other religious practices. The prisoner was placed in punitive segregation for these efforts and sued the prison officials for violation of his civil rights. The initial decision held that the Church of the New Song was a religion which should be permitted to hold religious services (*Theriault v. Carlson*); however, this was overturned on appeal, and the case returned to the trial court for a hearing. Since the prisoner had been transferred from a federal prison in Georgia to one in Texas, the hearing was held in a federal court in Texas.

This time, the court found that (1) the First Amendment does not protect "so-called religions which tend to mock established institutions and are obvious shams and absurdities and whose members are patently devoid of religious sincerity," and (2) the Church of the New Song was not a religion. The court found that the sole purpose was to cause or encourage disruption of established prison discipline for the sake of disruption; that it was a "masquerade" designed to provide protection for acts that otherwise would have been unlawful or not permitted (*Theriault v. Silber*).

That ruling was overturned on appeal and another hearing ordered; appeal to the United States Supreme Court was denied. As the case goes back and forth, the administrator is left in limbo, not knowing whether previously unknown religions must be accorded equal recognition with orthodox faiths or how to determine the validity of a claimed religion. This confusion is increased by the saga of the other case involving the Church of the New Song.

One of the followers of the Eclatarian faith sued for the right to practice his religion and won a ruling that entitled it to First Amendment protection (*Remmers v. Brewer*). The court held that a showing of legitimacy of the religion was not required before a group alleging to be a religion was entitled to First Amendment protection, but that the only appropriate inquiry was whether the followers possessed a sincere and good faith belief in that creed. The court further noted that the prison authorities did not show that the beliefs were insincere or fraudulent. This decision was upheld on appeal, and the United States Supreme Court declined to review it.

Some organizations claiming to be religions may really be political groups or have psychological counseling as their primary purpose. Challenge on these grounds would be difficult, but would have the greatest chance of success if the "religion" sought followers primarily from specific interest groups or segments of society, e.g. gays, women.

Insincere Beliefs

The administrator may also be presented with a prisoner who claims to believe in a recognized religion and demands the right to engage in practices that are disruptive of prison routine. In *Ron v. Lennane,* a prisoner claimed to be an Orthodox Yemenite Jew, whose religion required prayers thrice daily. The morning prayers continued for more than an hour and must be spoken aloud without interruption. The prisoner arose before dawn and said his prayers in the television room in order not to wake the others sleeping in the dormitory. Because the morning head count often took place during these prayers, officials on at least one occasion prevented the prisoner from completing his prayers. He sued for violation of his First Amendment rights.

The court held that he must prove two things in order to establish that his First Amendment rights were violated: That the conduct prohibited by prison authorities (1) is "deeply rooted in religious doctrine," and (2) is "the product of a sincere, personal religious belief." The prayers at issue were unquestionably a traditional and legitimate religious practice. The prisoner testified at a hearing in the case, and the judge found his testimony unbelievable. The court said that both his speech and demeanor lacked credibility; this, coupled with a past record of defrauding Jews, convinced the court that the prisoner's prayer activity was not due to "a sincere, personal religious belief." Therefore, his First Amendment rights were not involved, and officials could require him to be present at head count.

Summary

The message from these cases is somewhat garbled, but it is there: Freedom of religion is a preferred right, a very fundamental one that is rarely questioned in the free society. Because of this, our courts really have no experience in, or criteria for, determining what is a bona fide religion. It is not a task of deciding what is the one, true religion, but whether there is a "religious" belief and whether it is sincerely held. Certainly, that covers a broad scope. These two criteria remain, however, (1) whether the belief is religious, and (2) whether the belief is sincere.

Some of the decisions regarding The Church of the New Song cases involved only the latter issue, sincerity. Those courts found it to be a valid religion, because there apparently was no evidence of insincere or fraudulent beliefs or other kind of impropriety that would raise questions about their validity, such as using worship services for smuggling-in contraband or engaging in sexual activities. Conversely, if officials were able to document that the religion was a sham, as through letters of prisoners discussing their real motives or activities, or by observing illegal behavior at services, then the chances would be excellent of a court ruling that there was no religion and, therefore, no entitlement to constitutional protection. The officials involved in these cases were not able to make that showing, hence, a simple claim not backed up with evidence will not suffice.

The other task is to challenge the beliefs involved, albeit sincere, as not being religious. This was attempted unsuccessfully in some of the Black Muslim cases. Still, it is a viable alternative, although again it would require considerable documentation to substantiate.

In either case, the onus is on the officials to establish that the beliefs are not valid; the presumption is that a claimed religion is a genuine one and that an apparent follower is sincere.

FREE EXERCISE

The cases involving challenges to restrictions on religious

practices are generally from lower courts and were decided in the 1960s prior to the United States Supreme Court decisions concerning mail and the other First Amendment rights. They involved a variety of fact situations and regulations. Sometimes a consistent pattern is difficult to discern, as some emphasize discretion, others the cost involved, and still others impose very strict First Amendment standards, e.g. services would only be prohibited if they presented a "clear and present" danger to institutional security.

Since these cases preceded the Supreme Court's formulation of mail censorship standards in *Procunier v. Martinez* (*see* Chapter Two), they were decided without the benefit of an underlying principle or referent against which to measure their particular factual circumstances. But analysis of religion cases in light of *Martinez* reveals that the Supreme Court's standards regarding mail are equally applicable in this First Amendment area as well.

In *Martinez*, the Court held that any censorship or withholding of a prisoner's mail must (1) further a substantial governmental interest in security, order, or rehabilitation, and (2) be no more intrusive than necessary to protect that governmental interest. The second prong is also referred to as the "least restrictive alternative test."

These principles are appropriate for testing the restriction of any First Amendment right in prison, not just mail. When the religious exercise cases are measured against the *Martinez* standards, common threads appear, and the decisions appear more consistent and understandable. By this approach we are able to discern distinguishing characteristics between, and patterns in, the cases. This will aid predicting the course of future decisions and provide an informed basis for making administrative decisions.

The "free exercise" cases often present problems that shift from the prohibition against interfering with a religious practice to a request imposing an affirmative duty on a corrections official. Whichever type of relief is asked for, a decision — in court or administratively — should be based upon answers to the following questions:

1. Is a constitutional right involved?

2. If so, the administrative action affecting that right must be appropriately justified in accord with *Martinez*.
3. If no constitutional right is involved, then administrative action can be taken to restrict the practice so long as it is not arbitrary or capricious.

Prohibitions

Examples that do involve constitutional rights, and thus necessitate proper justification, include regulations against prisoners in segregation attending religious services, prohibitions against particular religious groups having collective worship services, and refusal to admit the minister of a particular faith to visit or conduct services.

If a threat to one or more of the governmental interests of security, order, or discipline can be shown, then the restriction will be upheld *if* it is the least intrusive means of preserving that governmental interest. Security problems can generally be shown in regard to allowing segregated prisoners to attend services. However, if the prisoner is to be segregated for a lengthy time or there are several prisoners in segregation who wish to attend services, complete prohibition on attending services may not be the least restrictive alternative. If the danger is in a segregated prisoner being allowed into the general population, then perhaps arrangements should be made for a religious service to be held in segregation. If the administrator consciously looks for the in-between solutions, realizing that it is not an all-or-nothing choice, it is likely that an accommodation can be found that fully protects both the institution's security interests and the inmate's rights.

The prohibition on group worship or the exclusion of a minister is more difficult to justify, though security concerns may well be present. Specific justification must be shown; speculation about potential dangers is not sufficient. The Black Muslim cases illustrate this well. A large number of the prison religion cases were brought by the Black Muslims in the 1960s. Although some administrators refused to recognize them as a religion, most acknowledged their religious nature, but refused to allow followers to practice their beliefs. The Muslims won most of these challenges, resulting in a clear enunciation of the equal protection principle of nondiscrimination. All religions must be treated alike; only if concrete evidence of security threat is presented may one religious group be denied opportunities available to others.

Prison administrators feared that disruptions threatening discipline and security would occur if Black Muslims were permitted to congregate, since a basic tenet of their beliefs at the time was hatred of the white race and encouragement of violence against whites. However, courts found that assumptions by administrators as to the problems that such gatherings *might* cause did not justify total bans on their meetings. Nevertheless, when officials could point to specific occurrences of violence and disruption due to Black Muslims, their decision to prohibit collective worship was upheld.

Affirmative Obligations

The language of the Constitution is in terms of forbidding *prohibitions* in free exercise of religion; this is usually interpreted as an assurance of noninterference, that no unreasonable barriers may be placed in the way of a person's desire to practice religion. Thus, prisons may be ordered to allow visits by clergy, even if the particular minister in question has a criminal record (the reason given by New York for excluding Malcolm X in the early 1960s); or to post weekly menus indicating pork dishes and arranging menus so that such dishes are evenly distributed throughout the week. These measures allow an inmate the choice to practice his or her religion without any real burden on the institution or the other inmates. But how far must officials go? At some point the line between removing barriers and assuming positive duties is crossed.

It is clear that the constitutional right is to not be interfered with; that is, barriers to religious practice must be removed so that outside ministers are permitted to visit or hold services, and a prisoner will not be disciplined for possession of religious literature or for declining to eat certain foods. But it is very questionable whether the constitution requires that special needs be affirmatively provided for, e.g. hiring of clergy, purchase and preparation of substitute foods. As we move from rejecting prohibitions to imposing affirmative obligations, we gradually find ourselves outside the constitutional sphere.

Where the constitutional rights are not implicated, then the *Martinez* justification is not necessary, and the administrative decision will be upheld if it is not arbitrary or capricious, that is, if it has a rational basis. Consequently, the decision whether to assume the affirmative obligation need only be a rational one and need not meet the more stringent First Amendment test. In these cases, money is a valid consideration, and the cost would justify not taking the action. Clearly, cost considerations would not justify refusal to allow any services or clergy — for the effect would be a complete prohibition on religious exercise; but where opportunities to practice religion exist and are not being interfered with, further efforts may be declined on the basis of cost.

Frequently, in-between alternatives are available and should be considered. For example, the Constitution does not require officials to provide special foods for those seeking to follow religious dietary laws so long as a prisoner who wishes to abstain from certain foods (e.g. pork) is not punished for doing so and is provided a nutritious diet from other available foods. Thus, the prison's only responsibilities are to notify prisoners of the content of the dishes being served so that they may avoid food items conflicting with their religious beliefs and to provide a sufficiently nutritious menu so that a person who does abstain from certain foods will not have a nutritionally deficient diet. In addition, of course, the administration may allow substitute food items meeting religious criteria to be sold in the commissary. In this way, special foods are available for those who wish them, and the cost is borne by the purchaser, not the institution (government).

PROBLEMS

1. A number of prisoners state they are members of the Metropolitan Community Church, whose avowed ministry is to homosexuals. Many of the prisoners who state that they are members are known homosexuals. They ask permission to hold weekly religious services with an outside minister. Will

you approve their request? Why or why not?

2. Members of the Universal Church request pizza and beer as sacraments at their monthly services. They present to you the bylaws of the church that do say that pizza and beer are the sacraments of that church. Will you allow them to have pizza and beer? Why or why not?

RECOMMENDED CASES

Beliefs

Ron v. Lennane, 445 F.Supp 98 (D Conn. 1977)

Remmers v. Brewer, 361 F.Supp 537 (SD Iowa 1973) *aff'd* 494 F.2d 1277 (8th Cir. 1974) *cert denied* 419 US 1012 (1974), *remanded* 529 F.2d 656 (8th Cir. 1976)

Theriault v. Carlson, 339 F.Supp 375 and 353 F.Supp 1061 (ND Ga. 1972), *remanded* 495 F.2d 390 (5th Cir. 1974) *cert denied* 419 US 1003 (1974), *on remand sub nom* Theriault v. Silber, 391 F.Supp 578 (WD Tex. 1975), *vacated and remanded* 547 F.2d 1279 (5th Cir. 1977)

Kennedy v. Meachum, 540 F.2d 1057 (10th Cir. 1976) (satanic religion)

Teterud v. Burns, 522 F.2d 357 (8th Cir. 1975) (American Indians)

Moskovitz v. Wilkinson, 432 F.Supp 947 (D Conn. 1977) (Orthodox Jews)

Lipp v. Procunier, 395 F.Supp 871, *consent order* 402 F.Supp 623 (ND Cal. 1975) (gay religion)

Practice

Montoya v. Tanksley, 446 F.Supp 226 (D Colo. 1978) (segregation inmates)

Burgin v. Henderson, 536 F.2d 501 (2d Cir. 1976) (Muslim beards and prayer hats)

Cooper v. Pate, 382 F.2d 518 (7th Cir. 1967) (group meetings)

Cooke v. Tramburg, 205 A.2d 889 (NJ 1964) (group meetings)

Mukmuk v. Commissioner, 529 F.2d 272 (2d Cir. 1976) (literature)

Kahane v. Carlson, 527 F.2d 492 (2d Cir. 1975) (diets)

Walker v. Blackwell, 411 F.2d 23 (5th Cir. 1969)

Brown v. McGinnis, 10 NY2d 531, 225 NYS2d 497, 180 NE2d 791 (1962) (Muslim practices)

Equal Protection

Cruz v. Beto, 405 US 319 (1972) (unorthodox beliefs)

People *ex rel.* Rockey v. Krueger, 306 NYS2d 359, 62 Misc.2d 135 (1969) (Muslims and Jews)

Chapter Four

SEARCH AND SEIZURE

GENERAL PRINCIPLES

THE Fourth Amendment to the United States Constitution reads: "The right of the people to be secure in their persons, houses, papers and effects against unreasonable searches and seizures shall not be violated, and no warrants shall issue, but upon probable cause, supported by oath or affirmation, and particularly describing the place to be searched, and the persons or things to be seized."

Reasonableness

The starting point for analyzing a prisoner's Fourth Amendment rights is the wording of the amendment; the language is all-important. Notice that, by its very terms, the Fourth Amendment does not protect a person against all searches, but only *unreasonable* ones. This indicates that there must be some searches that would be considered reasonable and, therefore, not violative of the Constitution. The key question, then, in examining a particular search situation is whether the search is an "unreasonable" one.

Since the 1967 United States Supreme Court case of *Katz v. United States* (389 US 347), the applicable principle for deciding this question is to determine whether the person searched had "a reasonable expectation of privacy" in the place searched. This emphasizes that the Fourth Amendment protects privacy, not property, and people, not places.

Again, notice the wording; the test is both subjective and objective. The person must first have, in fact, expected that the place involved was private *and* that expectation must be deemed reasonable by society. This second aspect is crucial in prison cases, as we shall soon see. The *Katz* case well illustrates the principle of "reasonable expectation of privacy." The search in question involved the wiretapping of the defendant's telephone conversation in a public telephone booth.

In response to the argument that there was no Fourth Amendment violation because the defendant was in a public place, the Supreme Court stated that it is not the nature of the place that determines the Fourth Amendment's applicability, but the nature of the defendant's privacy interest. It pointed out that one could not reasonably expect to be hidden from public view in a phone booth, but it was reasonable to expect that one's conversation would be private. Consequently, the eavesdropping in this case did constitute an unreasonable search and seizure.

Warrant Requirement

The second clause of the Fourth Amendment sets forth the warrant requirement. Where an activity is an "unreasonable search" within the meaning of the Constitution, then it can only be conducted after a search warrant is obtained. A search warrant can be issued only by a judicial officer, and there must first be "probable cause" to believe that evidence of a crime will be found in a specific place. There is a great deal of case law pertaining to the constitutionality of warrantless police searches in a wide variety of factual circumstances. This is the main source of litigation concerning searches in the "free society;" whether there was probable cause and whether a warrant was required. Volumes have been written concerning the interpretation and implementation of the warrant requirement.

Remember, however, that the warrant requirement comes into play only when the answer to the first question is "yes," i.e. only when the search is an unreasonable one. For reasons that will be discussed shortly, the answer to this question in a prison situation is almost always "no." Thus, the warrant requirement is not relevant to our purposes here, and its elaboration will be left to criminal procedure and other specialized texts.

Consent

It is a general constitutional principle, both within and

without prison, that if a person consents to the interference with his or her rights, then what would otherwise be a constitutional violation is not. In the search area this means that if a person consents to a warrantless search, then the search does not violate the Fourth Amendment warrant requirement.

To be effective, a consent may be given only by the person having a protected privacy interest in the place to be searched and must be knowingly and voluntarily given. Since a consent is really a waiver of one's constitutional rights, only the person who has the right can waive it. Many questions arise in terms of "third-party consent" to warrantless searches where a relative, roommate, or landlord "consents" to the police searching another person's belongings or room. Only if the person consenting has a privacy interest in the particular place or things searched will that search be constitutional. If not, the "consent" is meaningless, and the warrant requirement, with its precondition of probable cause, must be complied with.

The problem of third-party consents is presented in free society, but rarely in prison. The other essential, though, that the consent be understandingly and freely given, is presented in both realms. This standard applies to the waiver of any right. It means that the person must understand what he or she is agreeing to and must do so of his or her own free will. At times, courts have found that the presence of the police or other circumstances surrounding the "consent" were so coercive that it could not be considered a voluntary waiver of rights.

This "voluntariness" question arises when a prisoner, parolee, or probationer consents to search. The consent will likely be upheld if it is to a particular search at a particular time and there is no indication of coercion other than that arguably present in the status of the person as a prisoner or parolee. However, courts do not look kindly upon "blanket" consents or waivers. These contain broad language stating that the person is subject to search at any time or any place and often must be signed as a condition of living in a particular housing unit or being granted parole or probation. Although such a "condition" may be considered to be notice of the rules, it will likely be held invalid as a consent to all kind and manner of search.

To require a person, even a prisoner, to surrender *all* rights against unreasonable search and seizure is repugnant to our Constitution. Even where a blanket consent has been signed, the search in question will still be measured by the constitutional standard of reasonableness.

Exclusionary Rule

The importance of these considerations of probable cause, reasonableness, and consent is clear in criminal trials where the "exclusionary rule" applies. This is a rule imposed by the United States Supreme Court as a sanction against unconstitutional police conduct. It provides that objects seized in an illegal search may not be admitted in evidence in a criminal prosecution. Since the illegally seized evidence is often the only evidence against the defendant, its suppression frequently results in the case being dismissed. The purpose is to deter police misconduct by hitting them where it hurts: loss of the conviction.

The wisdom and effectiveness of the exclusionary rule have been debated at length. However, at the present time it is a fact of life, and its sanction must be considered when examining search and seizure issues. As a general matter, though, courts have held that the exclusionary rule applies only in criminal trials, not in parole or probation revocation proceedings or prison administrative hearings. Thus, even evidence seized in an unconstitutional search can generally be used in a revocation or disciplinary hearing.

THE PRISON ENVIRONMENT

The administrators of prison facilities are charged with responsibility for the control, security, and discipline of their institutions and the prisoners in their custody. Surveillance, inspections, and searches are necessary to fulfill this responsibility. Under these conditions, an inmate in a penal institution cannot *reasonably* expect that his or her person and belongings are private. The courts agree that, as a general matter, there is no "reasonable expectation of privacy" in prisons. As a matter of fact this applies to employees and visitors, as well as prisoners. Thus, an employee, a visitor, or prisoner can be required to submit to search upon entering or leaving a penal institution. All are on notice that while within the prison gates they are subject to the degree of scrutiny necessary to maintain the security, control, and discipline of the facility.

Even if people believe or expect that they have privacy, society does not consider that expectation a reasonable one. This being so, prison searches generally do not violate Fourth Amendment protections. Exceptions to the position that, generally, searches within prison facilities are not constitutionally unreasonable will be covered in succeeding subsections.

Practice Tip

To safe guard searches against Fourth Amendment challenges, especially those of visitors and employees, prison administrators can take a few simple steps to ensure that any expectation of privacy one might have before entering the facility is effectively destroyed. This merely entails putting people on notice that they are subject to search if they enter the facility. Signs should be posted at all gates and entrances warning that all persons and packages are subject to search. Similar statements should be included in employee handbooks, prisoner rule books, and informational slips sent by new prisoners to their families and friends. No expectation of privacy can be reasonable after such well-publicized notice. These steps should serve to uphold a search against challenge (subject to problems with the *Degree or Manner of Search* discussed later) and deter potential smugglers of contraband as well.

Framework for Analyzing
Challenges to Prison Searches

Claims that Fourth Amendment rights have been violated may involve a challenge to a specific search with assertions that the fact that the person was searched at all under the circumstances, or the manner in which the search was conducted, was unconstitutional. Or the lawsuit may claim that a departmental or institutional rule governing search procedures violates the prisoners' rights by failing to adhere to constitutional standards in authorizing searches.

In either case, the court will analyze the issues in terms of the principles covered in Chapter One. First, it will determine whether a constitutional right was involved; if there was any kind of search, Fourth Amendment rights are implicated, but are triggered only if the search is unreasonable. From our earlier discussions, we know that a prisoner's Fourth Amendment rights are not being interfered with unless the search is unreasonable. If the officials show that the prisoner had no "reasonable expectation of privacy" in the situation under challenge, then the court will find that no constitutional right was interfered with and dismiss the case, *unless* the prisoner also claims that the search was conducted for an unlawful purpose or in a constitutionally unreasonable manner.

If the court determines that the search interfered with a prisoner's Fourth Amendment rights, it will examine the specific facts of the particular case to find whether there was proper reason for restricting the exercise of the right. Recall the Chapter One admonition that a prisoner's constitutional rights may not be interfered with without a showing of proper justification specifically related to the facts of the particular case. Reasons must be given why that search was conducted.

The reasons for the search may be an explanation of the specific observations or facts that created a suspicion that the person searched possessed contraband. Perhaps the inmate had been seen in an unauthorized area, appeared very nervous, or had been seen passing items to another inmate. The specific activities observed should be described objectively, not in conclusory language. Or, perhaps, it was simply a routine cell search and evidence is submitted that the prisoner had no reasonable expectation of privacy because the rule book made clear that such searches would be regularly conducted.

Unlawful Purpose

Even though a prison search does not invade a reasonable expectation of privacy, it may still be unconstitutional if conducted for an unlawful purpose. Some courts have held prison searches invalid where they were not conducted for the purpose of maintaining prison security, control, or discipline, but instead, prison officials acted as agents of the police in searching for evidence to connect the prisoner to a crime of which he was suspected.

The reasoning here is that because prison officials have the duty to maintain their institutions, searches conducted in furtherance of that responsibility are not unreasonable. However, searches unrelated to these overriding governmental interests of security, order, and discipline must be judged by the usual Fourth Amendment standards. Since the police are not relieved of the warrant requirement when they wish to search a suspect who happens to be a prisoner, they cannot avoid the Constitutional strictures by having prison officials conduct the search for them; the warrant and probable cause requirements still apply. Any evidence seized in such a search will be excluded from the criminal trial.

Another ground for finding a search unreasonable is if it is conducted for the purpose of harassment or humiliation. Like the law enforcement searches just discussed, these searches are not conducted for the legitimate purposes of security, order, or discipline. These illegal purposes may be difficult for a prisoner to prove, but the lack of legitimate security concerns will certainly bolster the allegation. These issues will be discussed more thoroughly in a later subsection on *Manner of Search.*

TYPE AND DEGREE OF SEARCH

A variety of prison security activities implicate Fourth Amendment rights; these range from seizure and inspection of mail, to eavesdropping on conversations, blood and other tests for drugs and alcohol, cell searches, and searches of the person, from frisk to body cavity.

Mail

The opening and refusal to deliver mail is a search and seizure. However, cases challenging mail regulations have almost always been brought under the First Amendment; these were discussed in Chapter Two. The courts have not had to define the extent of Fourth Amendment protections in this area because application of the First Amendment guarantees uncensored correspondence.

Since it is freedom of expression that is protected by the First Amendment, opening envelopes or packages to merely inspect for contraband and not read the contents or examining them (e.g. by means of x-ray) does not interfere with First Amendment rights. It does call search and seizure questions into play, nonetheless. In the civilian context, where postal inspectors or police agencies have conducted similar inspections on personal mail while in post offices en route to delivery, courts have strictly adhered to the warrant and probable cause requirements.

This conclusion is to be expected, for there is every reason for individuals to have a "reasonable expectation of privacy" in their sealed mail. In the prison environment, however, where the security considerations are so immediate, it is likely the courts would find the kind of inspection and examination referred to above as reasonable in light of the governmental interests.

Eavesdropping

The Fourth Amendment protects private conversations as well as private places and belongings. In nonprison situations, law enforcement agents may not constitutionally record or eavesdrop on another's private conversation without having probable cause and obtaining a warrant. There are frequently additional statutory requirements as well.

Again prisons are different, and prisoners have generally been unsuccessful in challenging the monitoring of their conversations. It is not reasonable for a prisoner to expect that conversations with visitors or other prisoners are private in such a controlled environment, unless, of course, the visit or conversation carries additional constitutional protections against interference. Visits and conversations with one's minister should reasonably be expected to be private, due to freedom of religion guarantees; conferences with one's attorney must be private to safeguard the Sixth Amendment right to counsel. Moreover, prison policies or representations in a particular case may give rise to a reasonable expectation of privacy in other situations.

Alcohol and Drug Testing

Use of alcohol and drugs is a common problem in prisons. A prisoner who is under the influence, or in possession of an intoxicating substance, is subject to discipline and may also be in need of medical attention. A prisoner who is "acting strange" in the cell block or upon return from a furlough may be "high" or may have some other problem. For both the security of the institution and the welfare of the prisoner, the officials want to be able to establish what the problem is, if any.

Officials may, for example, request the prisoner to take a tongue test with specially treated papers, which identify marijuana in saliva, or produce urine for testing. If the prisoner consents, there is no problem. If he or she refuses, however, officials must decide whether the interest in determining the use of alcohol or drugs is sufficiently important to warrant the use of force. If the prisoner is determined to be uncooperative, then much more serious problems may be created by forcing compliance. In some cases, blood samples may be taken by qualified medical personnel with little or no force.

A prisoner's refusal to comply may not be of assistance in a disciplinary hearing where the prisoner's denial of using drugs would be unsupported by hard evidence and would be contradicted by detailed descriptions of his or her appearance and behavior indicating intoxication.

Things-Inventory Searches

Whenever a person is arrested and taken to the police lockup or jail, his or her belongings are inventoried. That is, before being locked in a cell, part of the processing entails emptying pockets, purses, etc., and turning all of these effects over to the jailer. The jailer lists, or inventories, all of the items, which will be returned upon release. Although this is a search, it is a reasonable one and may be conducted without a warrant. Its primary purpose is to provide an accurate accounting of all the items each inmate arrives with so that all will be returned.

Similar reasons for inventorying a prisoner's effects apply in prison whenever a prisoner's property must be packed up to move to another cell or institution. While packing the property, an officer may discover contraband. If so, it may be seized and used as evidence against the prisoner. The search is legitimate and reasonable.

Places

Cell Searches

RATIONALE. Prisons severely restrict the numbers and kinds of items that an inmate may possess. Obvious items of contraband are drugs, alcohol, and weapons. Another important item that is taboo in prison is money. From the administration's point of view, money very nearly is the "root of all evil." Among other ills, it provides an object of theft and extortion, a means of exercising control over other inmates, and the wherewithal to purchase drugs and other contraband. Of course, without real money, other items take on value, but their potential is minimal compared to that of currency.

Other seemingly innocent objects are also frequently classified as contraband. In fact, the definition of contraband is essentially "anything that is not authorized." Consequently, items of clothing that do not meet authorized styles or colors or are not colorfast or exceed the authorized value or number are also contraband. So are books obtained from unauthorized sources or without prior approval. Certainly any item found in a prisoner's cell or room with another prisoner's name or number on it is contraband.

Administrators justify these restrictions on the basis of security, control, and discipline: clothing restrictions promote the ready identification of prisoners; restrictions on accumulation of goods prevent health and fire hazards, as well as undermine inmate power building; restrictions on sources are aimed at preventing contraband from entering the institution; limits on the number and value of clothing items decrease the likelihood of theft and fights over property.

BASES FOR SEARCH. Employees are constantly on the lookout for contraband. Sometimes searches are random, sometimes on a tip. Since there is no reasonable expectation of privacy in one's prison cell, these searches may be conducted without a warrant and without probable cause. Anything seized as a result, including evidence of a crime, should be admissible in either an administrative disciplinary proceeding or in a criminal prosecution.

Increasingly, recommendations are being made that routine or random searches be greatly curtailed and that an officer have some articulable suspicion that contraband exists in a prisoner's cell before searching it. Some would also require an administrative search warrant or at least authorization from a supervisory level employee before a search could be conducted. Although such restraints are not now constitutionally required, their adoption could help avoid future constitutional problems.

At this writing, very few courts have decided prison search cases. Thus far, the only decisions finding search practices unconstitutional pertained to strip and body cavity searches (*see* following subsections). Important in these decisions was the manner in which the searches were conducted and the lack of justification for their intrusiveness. They went further than was necessary. It is not implausible that future courts may measure cell searches by a similar yardstick, especially if presented with a case where no contraband is found and the prisoner's personal property is damaged or missing.

It is helpful, then, to recognize that all searches are not alike. There are different degrees appropriate for different purposes. A periodic visual inspection of the room or cell should be sufficient to determine whether fire or health hazards are present and whether the institution's housekeeping standards have been complied with. A thorough search of a prisoner's room is then appropriate when an officer has reason to believe that evidence of illegal activity or contraband will be found. For those who wish to pursue this analysis and examine specific regulations tuned to the differing degrees of search, the thorough study presented in *Model Rules and Regulations on Prisoner's Rights and Responsibilities* (West 1973) by Krantz and others is recommended.

PROCEDURE. A great number of complaints handled by prison grievance systems relate to loss of personal property. Many that complain of cell theft by other prisoners may be unavoidable, but those that allege that property was lost or stolen in the course of search or movement by officials could likely be prevented or quickly resolved if the search procedures included elements designed to meet these problems.

Procedures could provide that cells would be searched only in the prisoner's presence, unless special circumstances warranted otherwise. Receipts could be issued for all property seized as contraband or all property inventoried prior to transfer to another location. The prisoner could be asked to sign the property receipt when the property is returned. Later complaints that a radio, etc., was missing can be efficiently disposed of if the prisoner signed in receipt of the "missing item." Whether or not requiring authorization prior to a search is adopted, recommended procedures include a written report afterwards describing, at least, the reason for the search, items seized, if any, and persons present. None of these procedures is constitutionally required, as the Supreme Court made clear in *Bell v. Wolfish* (*see* Appendix), and they may not be feasible in many institutions. However, where security problems are not presented, these procedures may be worthwhile trade-offs to reduce grievances and lost property claims.

Community Corrections Centers

A community corrections center is a residence that is halfway out of prison. It houses prisoners who work or go to school in the community but who are not yet on parole. Thus, a community center resident is still a prisoner and in the custody of the corrections department. The department's responsibility to maintain control, security, and discipline over all those committed to its jurisdiction applies as fully in the community as in a maximum security institution. The person's status remains that of prisoner.

If the resident were housed in an institution, it is clear there would be no reasonable expectation of privacy. Legally, the only difference in being housed in a community center is one of geography; the status of the resident is still that of a prisoner, and the department's obligation is still to maintain control, security, and discipline. Thus, it is not reasonable for a community corrections center resident to expect privacy in his or her room unless representations to that effect are made by those who run the center. Nevertheless, it is advisable to include in the center's rules that the residents, their rooms, and belongings are subject to search.

PERSONS

Like cell searches, searches of persons can be of different degrees. The least intrusive is a frisk or pat down of the prisoner's outer clothing for the purpose of finding weapons. The next level would be a thorough search of a prisoner who remains clothed. Although this may be irritating to an inmate, it is not humiliating, embarrassing, or degrading. Thus, unless conducted in an unreasonable manner, or for an unlawful purpose, this frisk and search present no constitutional problems. Further, it is reasonable to expect that they would be conducted frequently within a prison.

The strip search and body cavity inspection raise new issues, however. In a strip search, a prisoner is required to remove all clothing and both the clothing and the prisoner are closely searched. This may include inspecting the prisoner's hair, mouth, feet, and genital and anal areas. Further inspection of the body cavities may be conducted by trained medical personnel.

In some states these detailed strip searches with body cavity inspections are required on every prisoner leaving a visit, leaving or entering an institution, or leaving or entering the segregation unit, regardless of any suspicion that the prisoner may be concealing contraband.

Analysis of Constitutionality

Although some courts have upheld even the routine application of these procedures, other decisions have held that the body cavity inspection must be limited to circumstances in which there was cause to believe that contraband was being smuggled into the institution.

One court described the procedure as follows: "The whole challenged procedure appalls. Inmates are required to open their mouths, wag their tongues, turn and show the bottoms of their feet and spread their toes — a procedure akin to displaying slaves for auction, cattle for market, and animals for sale. The ultimate degradation is the required lifting of the testicles and the bending over to spread the buttocks." *Hurley v. Ward*, 448 F.Supp 1227, 1230 (SDNY 1978).

This court and others found the body cavity inspection procedures to be degrading and dehumanizing. Unquestionably, they constitute a severe and drastic invasion of privacy. However, finding that the prisoners' rights were infringed upon, as we know, does not end the inquiry. It next must be determined whether there are legitimate interests justifying this invasion.

The officials justify the procedures on the basis of the need to control contraband. However, when questioned regarding the most degrading aspects, the officials in some of the cases were unable to show that any weapon was ever found concealed in the buttocks. In *Hurley*, an officer with eight years, seven months experience testified that he found marijuana only once and money only once during the testicle inspection.

The officials in each case asserted that the possibility of contraband was very real. However, some courts found that, based upon what experience had shown, the likelihood of the harm (concealed contraband) was very low. This was balanced against the very high degree of intrusion and resulted in banning the anal and genital inspection search procedures unless specific cause existed in a particular case.

An evaluation of the likelihood of the harm also led some courts to consider alternative methods of preventing the harm. For example, metal detectors appeared to adequately safeguard against the concealment of weapons in the anal cavity, and their use was much less intrusive of the prisoner's privacy.

The United States Supreme Court, however, was not so quick to restrict these procedures when it was presented with the issue. In *Bell v. Wolfish,* the Court examined a practice at the federal Metropolitan Corrections Center in New York City requiring all inmates to submit to strip search including body cavity inspections after every contact visit.

At the lower court hearing, "corrections officials testified that visual cavity searches were necessary not only to discover, but also to deter, the smuggling of weapons, drugs, and other contraband into the institution." Although these inspections revealed contraband on only one inmate during the three years this facility had been open, there was documentation presented from other institutions.

The Court stated that to determine the constitutionality of the search procedure "requires a balancing of the need for the particular search against the invasion of personal rights that the search entails. Courts must consider the scope of the particular intrusion, the manner in which it is conducted, the justification for initiating it and the place in which it is conducted." Considering all of these factors and recognizing the "serious security dangers" present in detention facilities, the Court held that, in this case, the body cavity inspection requirement was not unreasonable and was constitutional, even where there was not probable cause to believe that the inmate was concealing contraband.

The strip search cases are cited at the conclusion of this chapter. Each deals with slightly different procedures and applications. A reading of these opinions illustrates the truth of our earlier statement that "the facts make the difference and the facts are always different." In these cases, the facts must be considered in the most minute detail to properly reach a conclusion regarding the challenged procedures.

MANNER OF SEARCH

The Supreme Court in *Wolfish* warned that ". . . abuse cannot be condoned. The searches must be conducted in a reasonable manner." A search that is conducted under circumstances where there is no reasonable expectation of privacy may still be unconstitutional if it is conducted for a nonlegitimate purpose, such as harrassment, or done in an unreasonable manner. This is true when the search is conducted in such a way as to unnecessarily humiliate, degrade, or injure the prisoner. The term "unnecessarily" here recognizes, for example, that the effect of a strip search may always be humiliating, no matter how carefully conducted; or that some injury may result to a prisoner who forcibly resists a demanded search. This is distinct from cases in which humiliation may be intended; for example, where a strip search is justified (e.g. segregation prisoner leaving a contact visit) but it is conducted in the midst of twelve to fourteen officers who interject sexual comments as the prisoner is inspected. Such behavior by the officers renders an otherwise legitimate search unconstitutional.

Even in the most secure areas of the most secure prisons, some privacy interests remain. The more extensive the search, and thus the invasion of these interests, the greater is the burden to justify both the purpose and the manner of the search. The officials must demonstrate that the kind of search conducted was necessary to protect the security of the institution. This claim may not be convincing when the circumstances indicate that it was almost impossible for the prisoner to have access to contraband since being strip-searched earlier. This evaluation of likelihood of risk was instrumental in decisions holding unconstitutional routine body cavity searches of inmates who were *leaving* a segregation unit. Since they had been thoroughly searched upon entry, were housed in sterile cells that were frequently searched, had no contact with general population prisoners, and only very small objects could be concealed in the rectum, there was no legitimate justification for this humiliating type of search except in specific cases where reasonable grounds existed to believe that the particular prisoner was concealing contraband in the rectal area.

The fact that the institution's rules require that the search be done routinely is not sufficient; there must be specific justification in terms of real life situations. The likelihood and seriousness of the particular potential harm must be balanced against the degree and manner of intrusion on the prisoner's right of privacy. If less intrusive alternatives can adequately protect the security interests, then they will be preferred.

DISCUSSION PROBLEMS

1. If a prisoner refuses to cooperate in a search, may the employee use force to accomplish the search? Under what circumstances should force be used?
2. If no contraband is found during a search, did the search violate the prisoner's rights?
3. May strip searches be randomly conducted on female visitors to a men's prison?

RECOMMENDED CASES

Prison Search Generally

United States v. Hitchcock, 467 F.2d 1107 (9th Cir. 1972)

Visitors/Strip Search

Black v. Amico, 387 F.Supp 88 (WDNY 1974)
State v. Martinez, 580 P.2d 1282 (Haw. 1978)
People v. Thompson, 523 P.2d 128 (Colo. 1974)

Employees/Warning Signs

Gettleman v. Werner, 377 F.Supp 445 (WD Pa. 1974)
United States v. Kelley, 393 F.Supp 755 (WD Okla. 1975)
United States v. Sihler, 562 F.2d 349 (5th Cir. 1977)

Prisoner/Strip Search

Bell v. Wolfish, 441 US, 99 S.Ct 1861 (1979) (See Appendix C)
Frazier v. Ward, 426 F.Supp 1354 (NDNY 1977)
Hurley v. Ward, 584 F.2d 609 (2d Cir. 1978)
Hodges v. Klein, 412 F.Supp 896 (DNJ 1976)

Prisoner/Cell Search

United States v. Ready, 574 F.2d 1009 (10th Cir. 1978)

Prisoner/Halfway House

United States v. Lewis, 400 F.Supp 1046 (SDNY 1975).

Eavesdropping

United States v. Hearst, 563 F.2d 1331 (9th Cir. 1977)
Matter of Kozak, 256 NW2d 717 (S.D. 1977) (prisoner-attorney conversations)
Christman v. Skinner, 468 F.2d 723 (2d Cir. 1972)
North v. Superior Court, 8 Cal. 3d 301, 502 P.2d 1305, 104 Cal. Rptr. 833
        (1972) (prisoner-spouse visit)

Prisoner/Blood Samples

Ferguson v. Cardwell, 392 F.Supp 750 (D. Ariz. 1975)

Blanket Consent

United States v. Baumgarten, 517 F.2d 1020, 1028 n7 (8th Cir.) *cert den* 423 US
        878 (1975)
State v. Ellefson, 266 SC 494, 224 SE2d 666 (1976)

Packages

United States v. Van Leeuwen, 397 US 249 (1970)

Chapter Five

CRUEL AND UNUSUAL PUNISHMENT

GENERAL PRINCIPLES

THE Eighth Amendment to the United States Constitution provides: "Excessive bail shall not be required, nor excessive fines imposed, nor cruel and unusual punishment inflicted." The last phrase is the guarantee we are concerned with in this chapter. Its wording alone does not provide a clue to what actions are prohibited under this amendment. There are many who say that prison itself is cruel, if not unusual; while others assert that any punishment imposed upon a convicted criminal is justifiable and hardly unconstitutional. Perhaps even more than other constitutional protections, the meaning of the Eighth Amendment cannot be gleaned from dictionary definitions of its component words.

Again, unlike the other constitutional guarantees, the cruel and unusual punishment provision centers on the person convicted of a crime. It applies to governmental sanctions that have either the purpose or effect of inflicting punishment. This clearly includes determinations whether particular sentences violate the Eighth Amendment, e.g. banishment (yes), and the death penalty (to be discussed later). It also has been applied to strike down penalties that are imposed because of a person's status (registration of narcotics addicts). In addition, conditions of confinement in penal institutions generally, and segregation units in particular, have been measured against the cruel and unusual punishment standard and frequently have been found wanting. The lack of medical care in prisons has also been singled out and challenged as cruel and unusual punishment.

Each of the topics will be discussed in detail; but first, the principles. The courts have held that the cruel and unusual punishment provision does not have a single, limited definition clearly classifying punishments as constitutional and unconstitutional. At the time the Constitution was adopted, torture and other types of physical barbarity had been common punishments in England. It was these types of physical cruelty that the framers of the Constitution doubtless had in mind. But even though sentences of branding, maiming, and whipping are no longer imposed, the Eighth Amendment is still viable and still provides protection against extreme forms of punishment.

In interpreting the cruel and unusual punishment provision, the Supreme Court and other federal courts have formulated a variety of standards to express its meaning. It is said that —

> the scope of the Amendment is not "static." It "must draw its meaning from the evolving standards of decency that mark the progress of a maturing society." . . . The Eighth Amendment's basic concept "is nothing less than the dignity of man" and assures that a state's punishment power "be exercised within the limits of civilized standards." . . . And the emphasis is on man's basic dignity, on civilized precepts, and on flexibility and improvement in standards of decency as society progresses and matures. (*Jackson v. Bishop*, 404 F.2d 571, 579 (8th Cir 1968) quoting from *Trop v. Dulles*, 356 US 86 (1958)).

In examining a challenged punishment, a court will apply the following tests. Is the punishment in question

(1) so barbarous as to shock the conscience?
(2) grossly disproportionate to the offense?
(3) the unnecessary and wanton infliction of pain?

USE OF FORCE

Privilege v. Punishment

A peace officer on the "outside" or a corrections officer in prison has the privilege to use force in certain prescribed circumstances. In extending a privilege to these authorized agents, the law permits them to commit what would otherwise be assaults. The fact situations in which the privilege is generally recognized are self-defense; defense of third persons; maintainence of order and control; and prevention of a felony, including escape.

The officer may use only the amount of force that is reasonably necessary to defend or control the situation.

Guidelines

Although challenges to use of force are commonly thought of in terms of criminal prosecution for assault, the excessive use of force also violates the victim's civil rights, thus providing grounds for a §1983 Civil Rights Action. A method for analyzing these cases will be suggested here that applies equally to the two different kinds of liability.

First, it is suggested that the use of force will violate a prisoner's civil rights only if it was used in a nonprivileged situation. Therefore, the first question is to determine whether the force was used in one of the four privileged circumstances. If it was not, then it should be presumed to have been used for the purpose of punishment, and the three cruel and unusual punishment tests should be applied to determine whether the Eighth Amendment was violated.

If the force was used in an apparently privileged circumstance, then it was not "punishment" within the meaning of the Constitution. But the analysis does not stop there. Two more questions follow: (1) Was the force necessary at all? (2) Was the amount used reasonable under the circumstances? In determining whether the amount of force actually used by the employee was reasonable, the following factors should be weighed: (a) the amount of force threatened or actually used by the prisoner, including whether the prisoner had a deadly weapon; (b) the employee's reasonable perception of the danger; note this is not the actual, subjective perception, it must be deemed a reasonable one; and (c) the reasonable availability of nonforceful alternatives to handling the situation.

In addition, deadly force, that which is likely to cause death or serious injury, may be used only as a last resort.

All of the facts should be taken into account in making the decision whether the force was reasonable. Factors such as the kind of weapon used by the employee (fists, club, gun, gas), the area of the prisoner's body that was struck (legs, head), or the extent of the injury inflicted may indicate that the action taken was either appropriate or inappropriate.

Excessive force is that which goes beyond what is reasonably necessary to control the situation or defend oneself or another. As a general rule, *responsive* force is legitimate force. The officer who is not the initiator, but responds to the force used by the prisoner, only to the extent necessary to control that prisoner, will run little risk of exceeding the reasonable force standard.

In summary, the following method of analysis is appropriate for determining whether excessive force was used for either criminal or civil liability:

1. Was the force used in privileged (authorized) circumstances?
2. If some force was authorized under the circumstances, was the amount actually used reasonable?
   a. amount of force responding to?
   b. reasonable perception of danger?
   c. nonforceful alternatives?
3. If the force was not privileged, but was used as punishment, did it violate the Eighth Amendment?
   a. shock the conscience?
   b. grossly disproportionate?
   c. unnecessary and wanton infliction of pain?

As usual, as the facts change, what force is reasonable also may change. The amount of force reasonably necessary to enforce institutional rules is certainly less than that necessary to defend oneself from being attacked. Nonforceful methods of dealing with rule violators are generally readily available through the disciplinary process. Of course, an enforcement of rules situation can escalate into one of self-defense if the prisoner actively and physically resists. Even if the prisoner is assaultive, calling in backup assistance may be sufficient to gain control of the situation. The next step short of force may be use of tear gas. In most circumstances a number of alternatives are available, short of direct physical force. Corrections officials should be aware of the alternatives, if for no other reason than that the courts will look for them.

Examples

EXCESSIVE FORCE IN PRIVILEGED CIRCUMSTANCES. A prisoner passively resisted being placed in solitary confinement by bracing himself in the doorway, holding onto both sides with his hands. To force him into the cell, the jailers repeatedly struck the prisoner's hands with handcuffs, keys, and other objects, severely breaking a finger. The court noted there were other "defensive" alternatives, such as prying his hands from the door frame and pushing him through. "Defensive" alternatives were deemed reasonable under these circumstances where there was no imminent threat to persons or property or to the general prison discipline. Since they were not utilized, the prisoner was awarded damages for his injured hand. *Jackson v. Allen* (case cited in full at end of chapter).

In *Suits v. Lynch*, another prisoner refused to re-enter his cell and was forced to do so by several officers. They did so in a "defensive" way by pushing him to the floor and sliding him through the door, during the course of which he received several bruises and swellings. The court found it proper to use force under the circumstances and that the amount of force used was reasonable. It also noted the potentially dangerous situation because a number of cells were open for inspection at the time.

FORCE AS PUNISHMENT. The court in *Inmates of Attica* held that if the prisoners' allegations were true, their Eighth Amendment rights were violated. It thus, ordered a hearing on the claims that after the state had regained control of the facility,

> guards, State Troopers, and correctional personnel had engaged in cruel and inhuman abuse of numerous inmates. Injured prisoners, some on stretchers, were struck, prodded, or beaten with sticks, belts, bats, or other weapons. Others were forced to strip and run naked through gauntlets of guards armed with clubs which they used to strike the bodies of the inmates as they passed. Some were dragged on the ground, some marked with an "X" on their backs, some spat upon or burned with matches, and others poked in the genitals or arms with sticks.

In *Jackson v. Bishop*, the court outlawed whipping as a punishment for prison rule violations. Whipping was the primary disciplinary measure in the Arkansas penal system until restricted by court order in 1965, then abolished in 1968. The court found that the use of the strap "offends contemporary concepts of decency and human dignity and precepts of civilization which we profess to possess. . . ."

The possible fact situations are infinite, and each must be examined closely to determine whether the force used was excessive in light of all the circumstances of the particular case. It is clear that not every "offensive touching" is an assault or cruel and unusual punishment. Frequently quoted is the following statement from a case concerning jail inmates at the Manhattan House of Detention:

> not every push or shove by a prison guard violates a prisoner's constitutional rights; in determining whether the constitutional line has been crossed, a court must look to such factors as the need for the application of force, the relationship between the need and the amount of force used, the extent of injury inflicted, and whether force was applied in a good faith effort to maintain or restore discipline or maliciously and sadistically for the very purpose of causing harm. *Johnson v. Glick*, 481 F.2d 1028 (2d Cir. 1973), US *cert denied* 414 US 1033.

DUTY TO PROTECT

Excessive use of force may be characterized as a sin of commission; its obverse, the sin of omission, is "failure to protect." Penal authorities, having total control over those committed to their facilities, have the legal responsibility to protect prisoners from mistreatment by themselves or others. This includes the duty to take precautions to prevent an inmate from committing suicide and from being assaulted by other prisoners. The failure to fulfill this duty, resulting in injury or death to a prisoner, may amount to cruel and unusual punishment.

Assault among prisoners, particularly sexual assault, is a very real problem. There are also very real problems in protecting every inmate at every moment. Not infrequently, the physical layout of an institution, or lack of space for separating prisoners, compounds the difficulties. It is unreasonable to hold corrections officials liable for every injury to a prisoner regardless of the circumstances; this strict liability rarely applies in the free world either. Under our system of law, people are only liable for injuries that they caused or which their negligence permitted to occur.

Similarly, the law recognizes the jailer's duty to protect those in his or her care. But the jailer will not be held responsible for injuries occurring despite the jailer's exercise of reasonable care. Liability will be imposed where the jailer had actual knowledge of the danger, or reason to believe that it existed, *and* was negligent in failing to protect the prisoner against the injury. "Notice" of the danger is present when threats have been made; there were prior incidents of violence between the attacker and victim; there was some other reasonable cause to fear physical harm; known hostile inmates were brought within access of each other; or the prisoner has a history of suicidal attempts. Prior incidents of assault also may put the jailer on notice of the dangerous nature of the facility and need for additional precautions.

In sum, once the corrections official has knowledge of danger, or reason to believe that a threatening situation exists, there is the duty to take reasonable steps to protect the prisoners, and failure to do so will subject the official to liability for any injuries occurring as a result of that failure.

DISCUSSION PROBLEMS

1. A prisoner refuses to move to another cell as ordered. His resistance is limited to refusing to get up and walk. How should he be moved? He is striking at the block officer with his fist. How should he be moved this time? A female prisoner resists in the same way; is there any difference in the response?
2. An armed tower officer sees two prisoners in the yard striking a third prisoner with their fists. Approximately twenty other inmates are gathered nearby. What should the officer do? Does the racial mix of the prisoners make any difference in the recommended course of action?

3. Resident Smith asks to be locked up for his own protection; he states that "they" are after him, but will not give names or any other information. There are no cells left in segregation. Two days later, resident Smith is beaten in his own room by two unknown residents. Are the employees liable for failing to protect Mr. Smith? What factors should be considered?

CONDITIONS OF CONFINEMENT

Generally

Prisoners frequently bring suits challenging one or more of their living conditions as cruel and unusual punishment. In these cases, the courts will examine the conditions to determine if the living situation presents a threat to the prisoners' physical or mental well-being. This comes close to finding a constitutional guarantee for a "decent living environment."

Many times each condition by itself would not amount to cruel and unusual punishment, but the "totality" of the conditions taken as a whole does violate the Eighth Amendment. For example, overcrowding of an institution in itself is not unconstitutional, but it may be a factor that, when combined with others, renders an institution violative of protections against cruel and unusual punishment. Overcrowding has also been challenged as a violation of due process. In the recent Supreme Court decision concerning some of the conditions in a modern federal jail, *Bell v. Wolfish* (*see* Appendix), it was alleged that housing two prisoners in a room designed for one was unconstitutional. In this particular jail, each room contained approximately seventy-five square feet of floor space. Inmates were locked-in only from 11 PM to 6:30 AM and "during the rest of the day, they may move freely between their rooms and the common areas."

The Court noted that the conditions of traditional jails were "markedly different" from those in this case and that "confining a given number of people in a given amount of space in such a manner as to cause them to endure genuine privations and hardships over an extended period of time might cause serious questions under the Due Process Clause. . . ." However, the Court concluded that the conditions of this case did not approach such hardship. Under the facts of this particular case, double bunking was not unconstitutional.

The basic living conditions that are examined are cell size, adequacy of lighting, heat, and ventilation, diet, opportunity for exercise, hygiene, and sanitation. These are all weighed and evaluated in terms of any threat to the prisoners' physical and mental well-being. In the abstract, this may sound like an easy test to meet; many conditions pose some health threat. However, that is not so in practice. It is generally only the very extreme living conditions that are found to be unconstitutional. Recall the discussion in Chapter One concerning *The Role of the Courts*; constitutional guarantees set *minimum* standards. Conditions can be very unpleasant, but still not unconstitutional. Only when they are "so barbarous as to shock the conscience" or present the "unnecessary and wanton infliction of pain" do they impose cruel and unusual punishment.

There are cases where entire prison systems or jails have been held unconstitutional because of the "totality of the conditions of confinement" found therein. The conditions in many of the early cases can readily be described as brutal and dehumanizing, such as the electric shock "Tucker telephones" in Arkansas. The decisions present lengthy lists of objectionable conditions, commonly including prevalence of sexual assaults, extreme unsanitariness, lack of medical care, lack of any educational or training programs, and overcrowding.

More recent cases have included challenges to noise level, exercise opportunity, telephone and visit restrictions, and many other aspects of the prison environment. Many complaints do not raise constitutional questions. It has been held that lack of educational programming, furloughs, etc. does not impose cruel and unusual punishment. There is no constitutional right to rehabilitation.

These cases are very complex and time-consuming to bring, and the ability of a court to fashion and enforce an appropriate remedy is limited. When the conditions of an institution are held unconstitutional, the usual remedy is not damages, but an injunction to prohibit continuation of the unconstitutional conditions and a plan to correct them to bring the institution up to Eighth Amendment standards. Sometimes the corrections officials are unwilling to comply with the court's order. In others, they are willing, but financially unable to fulfill the legal mandates. In either case, the court has very real enforcement problems. The powers the court has are negative and are very drastic: to hold the offending officials in contempt and sentence them to jail (probably their own unconstitutional jail!) or to close the facility down. Courts have rarely resorted to these methods, preferring instead to work out plans cooperatively among the parties involved. Frequently, this process takes years and even then may not be successful.

An example is the lengthy Arkansas saga. The first court decision regarding the Arkansas prison system was handed down in 1965. Few changes were made, and additional cases were brought during the following years. The "totality of the conditions" of the prison system were declared unconstitutional in 1969, and the court ordered the department to improve them; the details were not imposed by the court, but left to the department. Progress was erratic, and additional hearings and appeals were held. Considerable improvements were found in 1973, but a hearing in 1976 revealed that conditions had worsened.

In 1976, after concluding that the constitutional violations had not been remedied, the court kept an earlier promise to impose sanctions on the state for failure to comply with the court's orders. It made an express finding that the state had acted in bad faith; it then ordered the state to pay $20,000 in counsel fees to the inmates' attorneys. The state appealed. The court of appeals affirmed the order and added another $2,500 counsel fees for the appeal. The state then appealed to the United States Supreme Court.

In *Hutto v. Finney*, the Supreme Court upheld the finding of bad faith and the award of attorney fees. In doing so, it discussed the difficulties courts have in enforcing orders in these kinds of cases,

> federal courts are not reduced to issuing the injunctions against state officers and hoping for compliance. Once issued, an injunction may be enforced. . . . If a state agency refuses to

adhere to a court order, a financial penalty may be the most effective means of insuring compliance. . . .

In this case, the award of attorney's fees for bad faith served the same purpose as a remedial fine imposed for civil contempt.

The $20,000 award did not begin to compensate the attorneys for the time they actually spent on the case, but was clearly intended as a penalty on the state.

Segregation

Conditions in segregation involve much more severe deprivations than those in the general prison population. Segregation cells are used to punish prisoners for disciplinary violations and to isolate those believed to be violent or disruptive, or those seeking protection. Commonly, segregation cells have only a bed, toilet facilities, and water (some do not even have these); the prisoner is not allowed any personal property, does not participate in any institutional activities, and must stay locked in the cell, except to exercise and shower.

Segregation itself is not unconstitutional. The courts agree that segregation areas serve a legitimate penological purpose; just as a community needs a jail to hold its violent and law-breaking citizens, a prison needs a segregation area for much the same function. Thus, the question becomes one of the specific conditions present and the length of time a prisoner is subjected to them. The tests for measuring the constitutionality of the conditions and their duration are the same as those set forth at the beginning of this chapter:

1. Are they so barbarous as to shock the conscience?
2. Are they grossly disproportionate to the offense or to the reason for the prisoner's assignment to segregation?
3. Do they unnecessarily and wantonly inflict pain? This is also sometimes stated, is it an unnecessarily cruel means to accomplish a legitimate penological purpose?

In the cases concerning segregation conditions, there has been no dispute as to the facts. In the typical "strip cell," used for solitary confinement of a prisoner being disciplined, the prisoner was kept naked in a 6′ × 8′ cell having no light, heat, or ventilation; a hole in the floor served as a toilet and could only be flushed from outside the cell; the only place to sleep was the bare concrete floor with no blanket; there was no water or any other means for maintaining personal hygiene.

Corrections officials in these cases did not deny the descriptions of conditions in segregation. Instead, they asserted that such deprivations were necessary to prevent access to weapons, to remove "incorrigible" inmates to protect the rest of the population from them, or to prevent suicidal inmates from harming themselves. These explanations did not satisfy the courts. Confinement under conditions such as those described above was repeatedly held to be cruel and unusual punishment. The courts held that the "elemental concepts of human decency" were not met; that these conditions were "shocking to the conscience," degrading, and unnecessarily cruel.

In response to the officials' claims of necessity, the courts found that the legitimate purposes of protection and safety could be met by alternative methods that were less severe and degrading. The uncleanliness of the cells and living conditions was particularly offensive to the courts and found to be life threatening.

Clearly, the courts were correct in their judgments. Certainly the filth in which the prisoners were forced to live serves no legitimate purpose. Many of the unconstitutional aspects of these cells could be (and have been) corrected without presenting any greater likelihood of access to weapons.

The conditions of total deprivation described above are unconstitutional no matter how brief the prisoner's stay. The typical segregation cell should be minimally equipped with the basic means of maintaining personal hygiene, mattress and blanket, adequate heat, light and ventilation, clothing, and normal meals. Generally, opportunities for visits, mail, practice of religion, access to courts, and legal materials can safely be provided without endangering the security or discipline of the facility. There are occasionally individual circumstances that justify their deprivations, such as a particularly assaultive or destructive incident giving rise to placement in segregation, or destructive behavior (e.g. burning mattress, tearing out plumbing) while in segregation. These increased deprivations will likely be countenanced for very short time periods, but once it stretches into weeks and months, the officials will be required to demonstrate that there is continued necessity.

The *Hutto v. Finney* case, discussed above in terms of bad faith and attorneys fees, also involved an order prohibiting the Department of Corrections from placing inmates in punitive isolation (segregation) for more than thirty days. This, too, was appealed to the United States Supreme Court. Holding that placement in punitive isolation for indefinite periods of time is not always unconstitutional, the court upheld the thirty-day limitation ordered in this case.

The court had considered "the inmates' diet, the continued overcrowding, the rampant violence, the vandalized cells, and the 'lack of professionalism and good judgment on the part of maximum security personnel.'" In addition, "The Commissioner of Correction himself stated that prisoners should not ordinarily be held in punitive isolation for more than 14 days."

The length of time in isolation may not be considered in a vacuum, but must be evaluated in light of the conditions. "A filthy, overcrowded cell and a diet of 'grue' might be tolerable for a few days and intolerably cruel for weeks or months." Conversely, if conditions in segregation "are not materially different" from those in the general prison population, then a prisoner could be kept there for his or her entire sentence without violating the cruel and unusual punishment provisions. As the conditions improve, the permissible duration of confinement may lengthen.

As segregation areas have become physically less barbarous, questions have been raised of whether the conditions are dangerous to the prisoner's sanity. Although the potential threat to a prisoner's mental well-being after being isolated for lengthy periods has not in itself been found to be cruel and unusual punishment, courts are increasingly considering the conditions' cumulative effect on a prisoner's mental and physical well-being.

DISCUSSION PROBLEMS

1. There was a disturbance three weeks ago in the yard and since then all outdoor recreation has been stopped. The

general population residents are suing, stating that the deprivation of their right to fresh air and exercise is cruel and unusual punishment. Is it? What factors should be considered in reaching a decision?

2. The conditions in the segregation block are being challenged because (a) rats and roaches are frequently in the cells, and (b) the windows are frequently broken by inmates; during the winter, this brings constant cold air into the cells near the windows, causing those inmates housed near the windows to have persistent colds. Do these conditions violate the Eighth Amendment? Does it make a difference if the department has periodically brought in exterminators and tries to keep the windows repaired (although unsuccessfully)?

3. Resident Smith is in segregation; he set fire to his mattress, burned his clothes, and broke the plumbing in his cell. He did the same thing last month when he was in detention for five days. The deputy ordered that the destroyed items not be replaced for Smith. Is this subjecting Mr. Smith to cruel and unusual punishment? Can these items be denied no matter how long Smith stays in segregation?

MEDICAL CARE

Eighth Amendment issues concerning medical care fall into three categories: (1) allegations that the general level of medical treatment in an institution is inadequate; (2) claims that medical treatment for a specific medical problem has been denied; and (3) charges that a person has been involuntarily subjected to medical treatment. It may appear surprising that there is a constitutional right to any level of medical care. But, this is a necessary result of the total control the government must exercise over those it imprisons. The responsibility that this relationship imposes upon the state was explained by the United States Supreme Court in *Estelle v. Gamble*:

> [The Eighth Amendment] principles establish the government's obligation to provide medical care for those whom it is punishing by incarceration. An inmate must rely on prison authorities to treat his medical needs; if the authorities fail to

do so, those needs will not be met. In the worst cases, such a failure may actually produce physical "torture or a lingering death". . . . In less serious cases, denial of medical care may result in pain and suffering which no one suggests would serve any penological purpose. . . . The infliction of such unnecessary suffering is inconsistent with contemporary standards of decency as manifested in modern legislation codifying the common-law view that "It is but just that the public be required to care for the prisoner, who cannot, by reason of the deprivation of his liberty, care for himself."

The prisoner's ability to obtain medical assistance is at the mercy of his or her keepers; access to medical care is totally within the hands of the officials. Thus, they have the duty to provide sufficient care to meet constitutional standards.

General Level of Care

Attacks on the general level of medical care in a facility or, more accurately, the *absence* of medical care are commonly combined with challenges to other conditions of confinement. To provide adequate medical care, a facility would need medical personnel on staff or have prompt access to nearby medical treatment sufficient to properly respond to the prisoners' continuing medical needs. Cases that have been successful have been able to show that there really was no medical care available to prisoners within a reasonable time. Of course, what is reasonable depends generally upon the size of the inmate population and, in specific cases, the nature of the medical ailment. Three days may be a reasonable wait to have a back problem examined, but excessively long for a person running a temperature and vomiting blood.

Clearly, the institution must meet emergency needs as well as handle routine sick calls. Interminable delays and outright denial of treatment to suffering prisoners results in unnecessary suffering and infliction of pain in violation of the Eighth Amendment.

Individual Cases: Denial v. Inadequacy

Claims of denial of treatment or inadequate care in individual cases rarely establish a constitutional violation. If it can be shown that the prisoner had a (1) known medical ailment or other acute physical condition, (2) which officials deliberately ignored or refused to treat, (3) causing the prisoner pain or injury, then a constitutional violation is established. But anything short of meeting all three of those conditions will likely be found not to amount to cruel and unusual punishment.

It is almost impossible for a prisoner to succeed on an Eighth Amendment ground if *some* treatment, no matter how inappropriate or inadequate, was provided. For, to violate the Constitution, the medical care must "shock the conscience," not be "mere negligence." A difference of opinion between the patient and doctor over the relative effectiveness of a particular mode of treatment does not establish a constitutional claim.

This is as it should be. No court is in the position to second-guess the prescription or diagnosis of a medical expert. Even in more serious cases where the treatment given is so inadequate as to be grossly negligent, the constitutional standard may not be met. Remember once again that the Constitution prohibits only the most extreme deprivations; it establishes minimums, a floor. Everything that is wrong is not unconstitutional. Similarly, every erroneous medical treatment, even if it amounts to malpractice, is not a constitutional violation. Only inadequate treatment under circumstances that would produce the "unnecessary and wanton infliction of pain" amounts to cruel and unusual punishment.

This standard was clearly set forth by the United States Supreme Court in *Estelle v. Gamble.* There a prisoner suffered from severe back pain after being injured while on his work assignment. He was seen by medical staff as soon as he requested it, but his back pain persisted. After three months of medical attention, but persistent pain, during which he was disciplined and segregated for refusal to work, the prisoner sued. The treatment he was provided consisted almost entirely of prescriptive pain relievers and muscle relaxants; none of which appeared to relieve his pain.

The Supreme Court recognized "that deliberate indifference to serious medical needs of prisoners constitutes the 'unnecessary and wanton infliction of pain'. . . proscribed by the Eighth

Amendment." However, the Court found that this standard was not met in Mr. Gamble's case. It held that —

> an inadvertent failure to provide adequate medical care cannot be said to constitute a "wanton and unnecessary infliction of pain" or to be "repugnant to the conscience of mankind." Thus, a complaint that a physician has been negligent in diagnosing or treating a medical condition does not state a valid claim of medical mistreatment under the Eighth Amendment. Medical malpractice does not become a constitutional violation merely because the victim is a prisoner.

The result, then, is that the denial of medical treatment violates the Constitution, but provision of the wrong treatment does not, unless it is so grossly erroneous that it can be seen as "deliberate indifference" to serious medical needs. This was so when the doctor injected a prisoner with penicillin, knowing the prisoner to be allergic to the drug, then refusing to treat the allergic reaction (*Thomas v. Pate*). It should be noted that denial of medical treatment may be at the hands of medical staff who refuse to administer treatment, or at the hands of nonmedical staff. For example, an officer who refuses to forward a request for medical assistance or to provide an ordered prescription may be sued for cruel and unusual punishment.

The finding that inadequate care is not cruel and unusual punishment in no way indicates a stamp of approval. A low level of treatment does not necessarily qualify as a reasonable standard of care; it is simply not so extremely horrendous as to fall below the constitutional floor. A prisoner who has received inadequate medical care is not completely without remedy either. Although a Civil Rights Action under §1983 may fail, a lawsuit in state court for malpractice may be successful.

Involuntary Treatment

By far, most cases involve efforts of inmates to obtain requested medical treatment. However, others involve the difficult issue of when medical assistance can be forced on an unwilling patient. Suits have been brought by mental patients, as well as prisoners, who have been involuntarily subjected to medication or other medical treatment. The few courts that have examined these issues have prohibited involuntary medical treatment, finding that compulsory medical treatment against the patient's will (a) amounts to assault and battery, and (b) violates the patient's right to bodily privacy. The patient's First Amendment rights may also be interfered with if his or her religious beliefs forbid medication or operations or if the drugs affect the patient's mental processes.

This is a problem that is presented in the "outside" world in occasional, dramatic, life-or-death situations. Periodically, governmental agencies seek court permission to appoint the agency as a guardian for a child for purposes of consenting to an operation that the child needs, but that the parent, usually for religious reasons, refuses to allow. Government intervention over parental objections raises very troublesome questions regarding individual rights. When it is truly a question of life or death, however, we opt for life, even if the recipient is unwilling.

The same principles that apply outside should apply as well in prison. Short of life or death circumstances, the will of the prisoner-patient should be determinative of whether medication or other medical treatment is administered. Thus, courts have held that, unless the informed consent of the prisoner is obtained, he or she may not be subjected to "adverse therapy" (e.g. administering drugs that cause the patient to vomit) or medication that affects one's mental process, including drugs administered for the purpose of subduing violent or disruptive behavior. If the prisoner does not choose to consent, then other constitutional means may be used to isolate or control. But the spectre of compulsory governmental tampering with an individual's mind or body is too threatening to our concept of individual rights to be permitted without emergency life-threatening circumstances.

Discussion Problems

1. Resident Jones was on sick call twenty-eight times in two months, each time complaining of headache, dizziness, and "eye trouble." The medical staff gives him aspirin each time and, after ten visits, also puts eyedrops in his eyes. His com-

plaints persist. After several months, an eye doctor finally examines him and diagnoses glaucoma. It can be arrested, but he has already lost 90 percent of his vision in one and eye and 40 percent in the other. He sues, claiming that the inadequate medical treatment amounted to "deliberate indifference" to his serious medical needs, violating the Eighth Amendment. Is the medical staff liable? Explain why or why not.

2. Resident Brown is in administrative segregation. He complains to the block officer that his head hurts, and he needs to see a doctor. The officer ignores Brown's complaints, since he is always complaining about something. Brown sues the officer for cruel and unusual punishment by denial of medical care. How would you decide the case? Would your decision be different if the last time the officer conveyed Brown's request to the clinic the doctor told him, "I don't want to hear anything more about Brown; he just wants an excuse to get out of his cell?"

3. Resident White was just involved in a fight and is placed in segregation. He immediately tears up his cell, throws objects at the officers, and is yelling profanities at the top of his lungs. The officers try to ignore him, but the yelling and throwing objects continue. After about forty-five minutes of this the other prisoners in segregation, each of whom is securely locked in his own cell, are also yelling. Many of them are calling to the officers to shut White up. After an hour, the officers call the doctor to see if he can give White something to put him to sleep. When the doctor arrives, White refuses to agree to the medication. Should the doctor administer it?

CAPITAL PUNISHMENT

The final area in which cruel and unusual punishment questions have arisen is the death penalty. Many people assert that capital punishment is unconstitutional, that the government's taking a life as punishment for crime can never be justified. It was not until 1972 that the United States Supreme Court was faced with this issue in the case of *Furman v. Georgia*. In the decision, the court struck down that particular death penalty statute, because the procedures by which the death penalty was imposed created a substantial risk that it would be inflicted in an arbitrary and capricious manner, in the Court's words, "wantonly and freakishly." The Court found that, although it was authorized in many cases, the death penalty was actually imposed in very few. Studies showed that capital punishment was disproportionately carried out on the poor, blacks, and other unpopular groups. In light of this evidence, the Court ruled that, to be constitutional, a statute providing for the death penalty must direct and limit the discretion of the sentencing body to minimize the risk of its arbitrary and capricious imposition.

Excessiveness

In response to the Court's invalidation of the Georgia statute in *Furman*, thirty-five states redrafted or enacted new capital punishment laws. Soon, more cases were before the Supreme Court challenging the constitutionality of the new statutes. In 1976, the Court decided cases from several states, upholding some laws and striking down others. The constitutional standards were fully discussed and clearly set forth.

The 1976 cases all involved convictions for murder, and the Court held that capital punishment was not excessive for that crime since it involved neither the unnecessary and wanton infliction of pain nor was it grossly out of proportion to the severity of the crime. Thus, the decisions found that death was not *per se* an unconstitutional punishment for murder.

Before proceeding, it is important to note once again the limited role of the Court and the Constitution. It is not within their province to determine what is the most appropriate punishment, nor does the Constitution require the least severe penalty. Their only power is to prohibit inhumane or disproportionate punishments. Only these are unconstitutional. The question of constitutionality is unrelated to issues of deterrence, rehabilitation, etc. These are policy questions for the legislatures to decide within the parameters of the Constitution.

In 1977, the Court finally decided a nonmurder case, *Coker v. Georgia*, in which capital punishment was imposed for the rape of an adult woman. The excessiveness question was examined thoroughly, resulting in expanded definitions. A punishment is excessive within the meaning of the Eighth Amendment, "if it (1) makes no measurable contribution to acceptable goals of punishment and hence is nothing more than the purposeless and needless imposition of pain and suffering; or (2) is grossly out of proportion to the severity of the crime."

To assist in determining whether a sentence was excessive, the Court found important indicators in current public judgment. First, although thirty-five states had capital punishment laws, only Georgia authorized death for the rape of an adult, and only two more authorized it for the rape of a child. Secondly, in Georgia, nine-out-of-ten defendants convicted of rape were not given the death penalty. Thus, death was an extreme punishment, only rarely imposed. The Court concluded that capital punishment is an unconstitutionally excessive punishment for the crime of raping an adult woman.

Procedures

In upholding the death penalty against challenges that it was unconstitutional *per se*, the Supreme Court further held that the decision to impose capital punishment must be individualized. It may not be imposed in an arbitrary or capricious manner; there must be standards set forth to properly guide the discretion of the sentencing body, whether judge or jury.

Although it did not mandate detailed procedures, the Supreme Court identified four essential elements:

1. accurate sentencing information; this requires information about the defendant, as well as the crime, most of which is inadmissible at trial; therefore, a separate sentencing hearing is recommended after the criminal trial;
2. clear and objective legislative standards concerning the factors to be considered in imposing the death penalty;
3. specification by the sentencing body of the particular fac-

tors relied upon in each decision;
4. meaningful appellate review of cases in which capital punishment is imposed to ensure that the death sentence in that case is consistent with sentences imposed in similar cases.

These elements are clearly intended to ensure that when the death penalty is imposed, it is done on the basis of adequate information within rational, consistent guidelines, and the sentence is appropriate to the circumstances of the individual case. The Supreme Court has held that these purposes are not achieved when statutes require that the death penalty be mandatory for specified crimes. A mandatory scheme is a standardless one. Forbidding the jury or judge to consider facts particular to the defendant before it does not rationalize the sentencing process; it merely encourages a jury to act lawlessly through acquitting the defendant to avoid imposition of death.

In examining the history of mandatory death penalties, the court found clear evidence that the jury's response to the mandatoriness of the sentence was to refuse to convict. Even when death was mandatory for only a narrow range of crimes, juries still avoided it. Consequently, all states eventually removed mandatory requirements and gave juries sentencing discretion. In this light, the abolition of mandatory death penalties can be seen as an indication of the evolving standards of decency.

Further, experience with discretionary death penalty revealed that it was infrequently imposed, even for first-degree murder. Thus, the new mandatory capital punishment laws did not reflect a change in societal values, but a misinterpretation of the meaning of the Supreme Court's earlier decision in *Furman v. Georgia*. As such a marked departure from contemporary standards, they amounted to cruel and unusual punishment.

RECOMMENDED CASES

General Principles

Weems v. United States, 217 US 349 (1910)
Trop v. Dulles, 356 US 86 (1958)

Status

Robinson v. California, 370 US 660 (1962)

Use of Force —
Authorized Circumstances

Jackson v. Allen, 376 F.Supp 1393 (ED Ark. 1974)
Suits v. Lynch, 437 F.Supp 38 (D Kan. 1977)

Punishment

Inmates of Attica Correctional Facility v. Rockefeller, 453 F.2d 12 (2d Cir.
　　1971)
Jackson v. Bishop, 404 F.2d 517 (8th Cir. 1968)

Duty to Protect

Holt v. Sarver, 309 F.Supp 362 (ED Ark. 1970)
Barnard v. State, 265 NW2d 620 (Iowa 1978)
Stevens v. County of Dutchess, NY, 445 F.Supp 89 (SDNY 1977)
West v. Rowe, 448 F.Supp 58 (ND Ill. 1978)

General Conditions

Holt v. Sarver, 309 F.Supp 362 (ED Ark. 1970), *aff'd*, 442 F.2d 304 (8th Cir.
　　1971)
Gates v. Collier, 349 F.Supp 881 (D Miss. 1972) *aff'd*, 501 F.2d 291 (5th Cir.
　　1974)
Battle v. Anderson, 564 F.2d 388 (10th Cir. 1977) (Mental and physical well-
　　being); *compliance hearing and new order*, 457 F.Supp 719 (ED Okla.
　　1978)
Palmigiano v. Garrahy, 443 F.Supp 956 (DRI 1977)
Newman v. Alabama, 559 F.2d 283 (5th Cir 1977), *remanded on other grounds
　　sub nom*
Alabama v. Pugh, 438 US 781 (1978)

Segregation

Hutto v. Finney, 437 US 678 (1978)
Finney v. Arkansas Board of Corrections, 505 F.2d 194 (8th Cir. 1974)
Sostre v. McGinnis, 442 F.2d 178 (2d Cir. 1971)
Wright v. McMann, 387 F.2d 519 (2d Cir. 1967)

Landman v. Royster, 333 F.Supp 621 (ED Va. 1971)
Hancock v. Avery, 301 F.Supp 786 (MD Tenn. 1969)
Jordan v. Fitzharris, 257 F.Supp 674 (ND Cal. 1966)

Medical Care

Estelle v. Gamble, 429 US 97 (1976) (individual)
Todaro v. Ward, 565 F.2d 48 (2d Cir. 1977) (general)
Bishop v. Stoneman, 508 F.2d 1224 (2d Cir. 1974) (general)
Thomas v. Pate, 493 F.2d 151 (7th Cir. 1974)

Involuntary Treatment

Scott v. Plante, 532 F.2d 939 (3d Cir. 1976)
Runnels v. Rosendale, 499 F.2d 733 (9th Cir. 1974)
Knect v. Gillman, 488 F.2d 1136 (8th Cir. 1973)
Winters v. Miller, 446 F.2d 65 (2d Cir.), *cert denied* 404 US 985 (1971)

Death Penalty

Furman v. Georgia, 408 US 238 (1972)
Gregg v. Georgia, 428 US 153 (1976)
Coker v. Georgia, 433 US 584 (1977)

Equal Protection

Glover v. Johnson, 478 F.Supp 1075 (ED Mich 1979) (conditions in women's
institutions)

Chapter Six

ACCESS TO THE COURTS

GENERAL PRINCIPLES

THE right of access to the courts is implicit in the Due Process Clause of the Fourteenth Amendment to the United States Constitution. In many contexts, both civil and criminal, in prison and out, the courts have repeatedly asserted that all persons in American society have the right to reasonable and meaningful access to the courts.

Our judicial system is open and public, available to all who have legal controversies to be resolved. There are no governmental rules prohibiting certain classes of persons from bringing suits, limiting the number of cases a person can file, or requiring the lawsuit to be screened and approved before being accepted by the courts. In free society, the only real barrier between an individual and the courts is money: the cost of bringing an issue to the attention of the judicial system.

The right of access to the courts, however, means more than the doors are open if you can get there. The opportunity to resort to the courts must be real and meaningful and must be available to all equally. When the government imposes a price on utilizing the courts, as through a filing fee or transcript charge, the Constitutional guarantees of both Equal Protection and Due Process are brought in. For example, in *Griffin v. Illinois*, the state, although not constitutionally required to do so, granted defendants the right to appeal their criminal convictions. A transcript of the trial court proceedings is essential to properly prepare an appeal; however, transcripts are expensive. Thus, a poor person would be unable to exercise the right of appeal because without a transcript the opportunity to appeal would be without meaning.

The Supreme Court found that if a state provided appellate review, it must be "adequate and effective." It could not achieve this without providing full access to all persons; consequently, indigents were entitled to free transcripts: "In criminal trials a state can no more discriminate on account of poverty than on account of religion, race or color. Plainly, the ability to pay costs in advance bears no rational relationship to a defendant's guilt or innocence and could not be used as an excuse to deprive a defendant of a fair trial."

To prevent the right of access from becoming illusory, the Supreme Court has also invalidated filing fees for poor persons in habeas actions, criminal appeals, and divorce cases.

PRISONS

Perspective

Since on the "outside," lack of money is the only potential obstacle to exercising the right of access, it is logical that rulings dealing with this economic factor rely upon equal protection analysis. However, much more than finances are at stake in the prison environment. Security and control issues, which permeate every facet of institutional life, are also inextricably intertwined with a prisoner's right of meaningful access to the courts.

The fact of total control in a penal institution expands the financial and constitutional dimensions of the problem. Although the economics of implementing the right of access in free society may burden the budgets of governmental units, there are no other obstacles to reaching the courts. Implementation in prison, however, presents many of the same problems we faced in discussing religion in Chapter Three. There is a similar shifting of concern from issues of noninterference to those of affirmative obligation.

However, the fundamental dichotomy that we saw between the two issues in regard to exercise of religion is not found in the access sphere. In discussing religion, we suggested that the line can legally be drawn between noninterference and affirmative obligation, that the administrators' constitutional duty does not extend to the latter. This position is supported by the wording of the First Amendment, which forbids "prohibiting the free exercise" of religious beliefs. "Access to the courts" is an implied right with no explicit language to guide us.

This linguistic difference is not significant in explaining the Supreme Court's unusual decision imposing a duty on prison authorities, not simply to cease interference with inmates' efforts to reach the courts, but to *assist* them in achieving meaningful access. The real distinction lies in the nature of the rights involved and the differing ability to exercise them personally without the necessity of outside resources or experts.

An individual's right to practice religion can be ensured by permitting contact with clergy or attendance at group services. Holy books and other religious articles considered essential are few and can be obtained without great compromise to either a prisoner's religious principles or administrators' security concerns. Meaningful access to the courts, however, involves more than simply mailing papers to a judge. Proper and adequate preparation of those papers may depend upon using law books and consulting with an attorney, a paralegal, or another inmate.

Prisoners, not unlike free persons, are typically untrained in the law, and many are functionally illiterate. The law is a field totally dependent upon the written word. Effective use of the right of access requires familiarity with procedural rules and knowledge of legal concepts, principles, and prior case decisions so that the issues presented to the court can be properly framed and argued.

Where there is the absolute right to appeal a conviction, the Constitution also guarantees the right to counsel. But in most kinds of suits that a prisoner is likely to bring, e.g. writ of habeas corpus, §1983 Civil Rights Action or other civil suit for divorce, contract rights, personal injury, etc., there is no right to an assigned attorney. A nonprisoner who wished to bring one of these lawsuits would have the mobility to go to the local law library and do some research, consult attorneys in hopes of finding someone willing to take the case on a contingent or installment fee basis, or visit a legal services office. A prisoner does not have these options.

Since an inmate has no mobility, even if prison officials never interfered with a prisoner's communications with attorneys and courts, meaningful access would still be an illusion. A great deal of research and knowledge is necessary to make an adequate and effective presentation of any kind of case; this cannot be acquired simply through letter writing. Simply put, if Mr. Jones cannot go to the law, the law must come to Mr. Jones.

MEANINGFUL ACCESS

Noninterference

CORRESPONDENCE. The first "access" case regarding prisoners reached the United States Supreme Court in 1941, *Ex parte Hull*. That decision invalidated a Michigan prison rule that required all papers an inmate intended to file with the courts to first be submitted to a prison official for approval. The Supreme Court held that the state "may not abridge or impair petitioner's right to apply to a federal court for a writ of habeas corpus," and struck down the regulation. The approval process pertained, in part, to examining the legal papers for proper form. In this regard, the Court noted "The considerations that prompted its formulation are not without merit, but . . . . Whether a petition for a writ of habeas corpus addressed to a federal court is properly drawn and what allegations it must contain are questions for that court alone to determine."

In essence, the Court held that what a prisoner seeks from a court is none of the administrators' business. It is a matter strictly between the court and the petitioner (person seeking access) and is not to be approved, reviewed, or evaluated in any way by other parties. A natural extension of this holding is that all mail between prisoners and courts is confidential and not to be interfered with by prison officials.

INMATE MUTUAL LEGAL ASSISTANCE. It was twenty-eight years before another prisoner "access to courts" case reached the high court. In 1969, the Supreme Court decided *Johnson v. Avery*, in which inmates challenged a Tennessee prison regulation that prohibited any inmates from assisting other inmates with writs of habeas corpus or in other legal matters. The prisoners claimed that the effect of the regulation was to deny illiterate inmates access to the courts because they were incapable of preparing their own papers and had no alternative means of assistance. The Court agreed with the prisoners and struck down the regulation.

The officials argued that the regulation was necessary for the "disciplinary administration of the prisons." The rule was really aimed at abolishing prison "writ writers" or "jailhouse lawyers" who set themselves up as legal experts and charge considerable fees for aiding other prisoners with their cases. Jailhouse lawyers present a threat to prison security and order, not because they assist others in asserting their rights, but because they wield a great deal of power and influence with the general prison population. They sometimes practice extortion more than law in demanding high fees from fellow prisoners who have no other alternative. And, although some jailhouse lawyers have developed considerable expertise in writs or criminal appeals, etc., many are not very skilled and do not provide worthwhile assistance to their "clients."

Although the Court recognized that jailhouse lawyers can be "a menace to prison discipline," it found the administrative concerns to be insufficient justification for a regulation obstructing prisoners' access to the courts: "There can be no doubt that Tennessee could not constitutionally adopt and enforce a rule forbidding illiterate or poorly educated prisoners to file habeas corpus petitions. Here Tennessee has adopted a rule which, *in the absence of any other source of assistance* for such prisoners, effectively does just that." (Emphasis added).

The key to the decision is the *italicized* portion, the lack of alternative assistance. As in other areas, the Court balanced the administration's interest in the rule against the prisoners' right. Here it found that the effect of the rule was not only to restrict or regulate access to the courts, but it actually worked to completely prevent access in a large number of cases. This was not the administrators' purpose, of course; they were simply interested in the orderly administration of their institution. But the clear result was that a majority of the prison population was deprived of the only source of assistance available to them and, thus, was denied meaningful access to the courts.

Since the rule prohibited, not just restricted, the exercise of an important constitutional right, it must be invalidated unless justified by very important reasons. The interest in disciplinary administration, although valid and important, did not rise to the significance necessary to support the rule.

The Court reemphasized, however, the role of alternatives. It noted that in some states public defenders, law students, or volunteer attorneys were regularly available to assist prisoners in preparation of writs. The message was made even clearer: "We express no judgment concerning these plans, but their existence indicates that techniques are available to provide alternatives if the State elects to prohibit mutual assistance among inmates."

It was not the prohibition of mutual assistance that was unconstitutional, but the prohibition on access to the courts. When the only source of assistance available to an illiterate inmate was from other inmates, barring that assistance resulted in denial of access. But a state could provide other means of assistance so that jailhouse lawyers could be prohibited without interfering with the right of access.

The Court closed with a specific recognition that even if jailhouse lawyers were the only source of legal assistance in a prison, "reasonable restrictions and restraints" could be imposed upon their activities. Examples offered were regulating the time and location of providing mutual assistance and punishment for giving or accepting a fee for the assistance. Thus, jailhouse lawyers could be regulated, but not prohibited, unless a reasonable substitute was made available by the state.

As one would expect, subsequent cases followed the two paths the Supreme Court had barely marked and tested (1) the validity of restrictions on jailhouse lawyers, and (2) the adequacy of alternative legal assistance programs.

RESTRICTIONS. California revised its prison regulations following *Johnson v. Avery* and removed the ban on mutual inmate assistance. Instead, while allowing such assistance, it prohibited the "jailhouse lawyer" from (a) accepting compensation for the assistance; (b) possessing the legal papers of another inmate; (c) filing papers in Court on behalf of his "clients;" (d) corresponding with "clients" at other institutions; (e) interviewing inmates confined in segregation; (f) having access to "clients'" disciplinary records; (g) using the law library for more than the limited number of hours scheduled per week; (h) keeping more than a limited number of personally owned lawbooks; and (i) acquiring lawbooks from any source other than an institution-approved vendor.

The California Supreme Court ruled on all of these restrictions in the case of *In re Harrell.* Its analysis of each provides a helpful guide to evaluating the legitimacy of other similar regulations.

In looking at each aspect of the regulations, the *Harrell* court scrupulously followed *Johnson v. Avery* and other constitutional decisions. This involved a two-step process. First, if the regulation was one that *prevented* mutual prisoner assistance rather than reasonably restricting it, and there were no suitable alternatives, then the regulation was unconstitutional.

However, if the effect was not to prohibit access, but simply to place restrictions on the manner of providing assistance, then the validity of the rule could be determined only after balancing the extent of the interference with the right against the need for the restriction, i.e. the administration's interests. In determining whether a particular restriction is constitutional, the Court noted that the following questions must be answered first:

(1) To what extent does the application of the particular rule have the actual effect of impeding or discouraging mutual prisoner assistance?

(2) From the standpoint of legitimate custodial objectives, how undesirable is the conduct sought to be avoided by the particular rule?

(3) Are there reasonable alternative means of dealing with the undesirable conduct which do not entail so significant a restriction upon mutual prisoner assistance? (This is the same as the "least restrictive alternative" test discussed in Chapter Two.)

One further point must be made before proceeding to apply this analysis to each of the restrictions: whose right is involved, the "client's" or the jailhouse lawyer's? It is clear from *Johnson v. Avery* that the Constitution is protecting the rights of the inmates seeking assistance and seeking access to the courts. There is no right of a prisoner to "practice law" or represent other inmates. Since cases challenging these restrictions typically were brought by jailhouse lawyers, they sought to invalidate rules that interfered with their ability to provide assistance. The answers to the above questions might be different if that were the issue, but the constitutional question is whether the inmate *seeking* assistance is prevented from obtaining it.

In reviewing each of the restrictions listed above, the court first noted that the prohibition on compensation was specifically authorized by *Johnson v. Avery*. The prohibition on possession of another inmate's legal papers was a different story, however. The court answered the first question by finding that this restriction "has a severe effect upon the ability of an illiterate or uneducated prisoner to gain assistance from a more gifted one." This was because the type of assistance that is usually sought is the actual drafting of the papers to be filed with the court. This would be impossible without access to the papers, such as transcripts, briefs, and prior applications of the inmate seeking assistance. Under the rule, either the assistance would have to be provided without reference to the essential documents, or all drafting would have to be done in the presence of the other inmate. This result the court found to be "wholly impractical and adverse to the purpose to be served by permitting mutual assistance."

The second inquiry concerns the undesirability of the restricted conduct from the point of view of "legitimate custodial objectives." The court accepted the officials' statements that abuses by jailhouse lawyers included withholding legal papers for purposes of extortion and that disputes over these matters were very conducive to violence.

Thus far we have determined that the rule has the effect of preventing inmates from obtaining mutual assistance, but that the reasons behind the rule are substantial and legitimate concerns. Now, the third question comes in to tip the balance. Is the regulation at issue the least restrictive means of achieving the administration's purpose of preventing abuses by jailhouse lawyers? The court said no, that the problem of abuse could be attacked directly through disciplinary action for abusive conduct. The withholding, destruction, or damage of another's legal papers can be punished directly without infringing upon the right of access, thus, the restriction must fall.

The next four restrictions must be examined while keeping in mind that it is the "client" inmate, not the "jailhouse lawyer," whose rights are protected. It is only when a restriction on the jailhouse lawyer also "has the additional effect of preventing or tending to prevent disadvantaged inmates from receiving aid" does it offend the principle set forth in *Johnson v. Avery.*

When evaluated from this perspective, the restrictions do not offend the right of access. The jailhouse lawyer has no right to "practice law;" an illiterate inmate has a constitutional right to assistance, but no right to assistance from a particular inmate. The court found that the right to mutual assistance can be effectively safeguarded despite rules against correspondence, interviews in segregation, and access to disciplinary records and upheld these provisions. The court determined that the prohibition on filing papers on behalf of another inmate did not prevent access to the courts, either. But, as in *Ex parte Hull*, the rule was invalidated because it is the role of the courts, not prison officials, to review the sufficiency of court documents.

The final three restrictions on use of the law library and possession of personal law books were also upheld because they involved reasonable regulations that did not have the effect of cutting off access to the courts. A law library was available during regularly scheduled hours each week; the number of visits per inmate each week must necessarily be limited to provide equal availability to the entire prison population. The court found that the rules were reasonable and that Mr. Harrell had not been treated in a discriminatory manner.

Nor was an inmate completely prohibited from possessing personal law books. However, no more than sixteen could be kept in a cell at a time because of space limitations and fire hazards. A prisoner with more books, however, could rotate his personal library by sending some home and receiving others within the sixteen-volume limit, or the excess could be readily available by donating them to the prison law library. Under these circumstances, the court found no constitutional violation.

The vendor-only rule is a common one in prisons where

books provide great potential for smuggling drugs, money, and other contraband. The rule applies to nonlaw books as well and prohibits acquiring books from unapproved sources. The court found this rule reasonable and proper because it allowed access to the books, but limited only the source. There was no indication that law books could not be obtained from authorized sources. The Supreme Court in *Bell v. Wolfish* (*see* Appendix) recently upheld a similar "publisher-only" rule followed in federal prisons. The Court found that the rule was a "limited restriction . . . a rational response by prison officials to an obvious security problem."

All restrictions reviewed by courts will be subjected to the tests as applied in *Harrell*: (1) Is the effect of the rule to prevent access to the courts? If so, the rule is unconstitutional, (2) If the effect is not to prevent but to restrict access, then (a) the interests of the administration in restriction will be balanced against the extent of the interference with the prisoners' right of access, and (b) a less restrictive means of promoting the administration's interests will be sought.

ALTERNATIVES. What must a state provide to enable it to prohibit jailhouse lawyers? You can see that the officials are now beginning to back into assuming a positive duty to provide the tools of meaningful access to the courts. With the incentive of abolishing writ writers, prison administrators cast about for volunteer bar association programs, law students, and public defenders. None of these would come out of the corrections department's budget; so, even though some officials may not have been eager to have these outsiders around, it appeared a worthwhile trade to get rid of jailhouse lawyers.

It was not that simple, however. Texas, for instance, prohibited any form of legal assistance by one inmate to another. They insisted they had provided a reasonable alternative by hiring one attorney to provide legal assistance in a system of more than 13,000 prisoners!

In *Novak v. Beto*, the United States Court of Appeals reversed a lower court decision that Texas had sufficiently complied with the requirement of *Johnson v. Avery*. Instead, the court of appeals held that when a state decides to prohibit mutual inmate assistance, it has a very heavy burden to carry to establish that it has provided a reasonable alternative. In order to justify its rule, the state must produce "evidence that establishes *in specific terms* what the need is for legal assistance . . . and by demonstrating that it is reasonably satisfying that need." In describing the need for legal assistance, officials must "give special consideration to the high illiteracy rate of the inmates," the number who do not speak English, and the geographical dispersion of the state's penal facilities.

Simply pointing to the availability of some legally trained personnel is not sufficient; the prison officials must show that they have ensured the systematic availability of sufficient legal assistance to meet the needs of the prison population.

Affirmative Obligations

Instead of providing legally trained personnel for inmates to consult, a state may choose another alternative, law libraries. An adequate law library is considered a suitable alternative to mutual inmate assistance so that jailhouse lawyers may be prohibited. It is the alternative chosen by many departments, even though law books obviously cost money. The establishment of real law libraries where only a few volumes previously existed was definitely a response to *Johnson v. Avery*. They appeared in the guise of a substitute for writ writers and were often paid for by federal grants.

But somewhere we crossed the line from noninterference to affirmative obligation. What began as a prohibition on obstruction of an illiterate inmate's only source of legal assistance, other inmates, became the duty to provide either adequate law libraries or legally trained personnel! It is tempting to conclude that none of this would be required if officials had only left jailhouse lawyers alone.

It is unlikely that the state of the law would be much different, though. The right of meaningful access to the courts would still be there; and a prisoner was bound to question whether that right was not denied when the only avenues to its exercise were jailhouse lawyers and a sprinkling of law books. The cases would not be cast in the language of evaluating a substitute for mutual legal assistance, but instead would stem directly from a definition of "meaningful access." The Supreme Court's most recent pronouncement, *Bounds v. Smith,* does just that.

Before discussing *Bounds,* however, we should review its predecessor, *Younger v. Gilmore.* In a one sentence opinion, the United States Supreme Court affirmed a California federal district court's decision regarding prison law libraries. Since the Supreme Court simply adopted the lower court's holding the analysis by the district court is important.

The case was decided one year after *Johnson v. Avery* and concerned a prison regulation itemizing, and consequently limiting, the law books to be available in California prison libraries. Unlike restrictions covered earlier pertaining to the manner or procedures for obtaining legal assistance and materials, this regulation narrowly restricted the *kinds* of available legal materials.

The state justified the regulation on the basis of the government's interests in economy and standardizing the libraries in numerous institutions. Besides, the officials said a law library was a privilege, not a right, so it could be restricted as the state pleased. The court rejected this reasoning, finding that, by whatever name, "the basic test remains the same: the asserted interest of the State in enforcing its rule is balanced against the claimed right of the prisoner and the degree to which it has been infringed by the challenged rule."

The court found the law library list in question totally inadequate; it contained some state but no federal statutes, no case reporters, and no rules for the federal district court in which writs of habeas corpus are filed. The state's position that a prisoner need not know anything about the law, but need only file a brief statement of facts of his or her situation ignored reality and was found untenable." 'Access to the courts,' then, is a larger concept. . . . It encompasses all the means a defendant or petitioner might require to get a fair hearing from the judiciary on all charges brought against him or grievances alleged by him. . . . Johnson v. Avery . . . makes clear that some provision must be made to ensure that prisoners have the assistance necessary to file petitions and complaints which will in fact be fully considered by the courts."

After finding that the prisoners' right of access was severely impeded by the highly restricted book list, and that the state's rationale was not sufficient to justify the extensive infringement, the court still did not order a specific book list. Instead, it invalidated the rule in question and left to the state the decision whether to expand the law libraries or find a different substitute for mutual legal assistance. The Constitution requires an alternative, sufficiently adequate to ensure meaningful access, but the choice of that alternative is within the state's discretion.

Since the reason given in *Johnson v. Avery* for the necessity of writ writers was that illiterate inmates were unable to effectively assert their rights and needed assistance to utilize the courts, subsequent cases followed this concern for those who could not help themselves. As we have seen, the validity of restrictions on jailhouse lawyers was determined with reference to the effect of those restrictions on the "client" inmate.

Prisoners, however, continually pushed for the greater availability of the "tools" of access, i.e. legal research facilities and assistance from legally trained personnel. A state with only one or two prisons may more readily accede to demands for law libraries, but a state with numerous small facilities faces enormous expenditures if required to provide a full library at each prison.

Probably because of these financial considerations, the State of North Carolina chose to read *Johnson v. Avery* literally. Accordingly, it decided to allow jailhouse lawyers to function, believing that this relieved it of any "further obligation to expend state funds to implement affirmatively the right of access." This position was squarely rejected by the United States Supreme Court in *Bounds v. Smith*. Although the case was presented in the context of reviewing North Carolina's plan for prison law libraries, its decision went much farther than the "reasonable alternative" formulations of earlier cases.

The Court stated that the holding in *Johnson v. Avery* "did not attempt to set forth the full breadth of the right of access;" it dealt with only one aspect of it. Subsequent cases invalidated interference with other aspects even though some access was available. For example, in *Procunier v. Martinez*, while California had law libraries and allowed mutual inmate assistance, the Court still struck down a regulation prohibiting paralegals working for attorneys who represented inmates from visiting their clients. Similarly, the Court noted that in *Wolff v. McDonnell*, the sufficiency of a single inmate legal advisor could be challenged despite the existence of an adequate law library.

In *Bounds* the Court declared that " 'meaningful access' to the courts is the touchstone." In so deciding, it found, as had the *Gilmore v. Lynch* court discussed above, that legal research was essential to the adequate preparation of legal papers. Thus, untrained writ writers are not enough. Law libraries or other forms of legal assistance are necessary to assure meaningful access.

Prisoners, like nonprisoners, have the right to bring writs of habeas corpus and civil rights actions in federal courts. State law may guarantee other rights, such as appeal from conviction and state writs of habeas corpus. As stated at the outset of this chapter, the existence of the right is illusory if it cannot be meaningfully exercised. The state may not place obstructions in the way of the right of access. One of the obvious purposes of imprisonment is to immobilize those incarcerated, to restrict their movement and contacts with others. A natural effect, then, is that meaningful access to the courts is also rendered virtually impossible without outside assistance or the availability of the legal tools for self-help. The decision in *Bounds*, then, was automatic: "We, hold, therefore, that the fundamental constitutional right of access to the courts requires prison authorities to assist inmates in the preparation and filing of meaningful legal papers by providing prisoners with adequate law libraries or adequate assistance from persons trained in the law."

Practice Tips

Having laid down that rule, the Court left the choice of method up to each individual state or department. The constitutional line has been drawn; the method of implementation is left to the discretion of the administrators. Although there is still room to quibble about what year case reporters should begin, whether legal encyclopedias must be included, how many law students are adequate, etc., an administrator who chooses a plan that provides reasonable access to inmates in the areas in which there is a clear right of access to the courts will likely overcome any challenge. It is the official who tries to get away with the least possible who is apt to run into problems, as did Texas with one attorney for 13,000 prisoners.

It is worth noting that the library plan proposed by North Carolina, which was affirmed by the Supreme Court, did *not* provide for a law library at every single facility. At the time of this litigation, the state housed 13,000 inmates "in 77 prison units located in 67 counties. Sixty-five of these units hold fewer than 200 inmates." The plan called for seven libraries in men's prisons across the state, a smaller one in the segregation unit of the Central Prison, and a library in the Women's Prison. Arrangements would be made to transport inmates to a law library for a day's work; appointments must be made, and it was anticipated that a three to four week wait would not be unusual for those without immediate deadlines.

The Court has repeatedly said that the choices are the state's; that there is much flexibility allowed in meeting the constitutional standard. An administrator should determine the demand for law libraries or other legal assistance. That demand may well be greater in institutions holding prisoners with longer sentences or those with fewer privileges; the more unpleasant the environment and the longer one will be subjected to it, the more likely one is to complain.

Once the demand is determined, a plan must be designed that will accommodate that need, taking into consideration reasonable restrictions on the time, place, and manner of the availability of the legal research.

PROBLEMS

1. Can the prison officials take a survey to determine the population's interest in the law library and then not provide a library if it finds that less than 5 percent of the prisoners are interested in using one?
2. Must mail between jailhouse lawyers and their "clients" be treated as legal mail?

3. Can the institution so restrict the hours of a law library operation that it would be available only five hours per day?

RECOMMENDED CASES

Equal Protection

Griffin v. Illinois, 351 US 12 (1956) (transcripts)
Smith v. Bennett, 365 US 708 (1961) (filing fee for writs)
Douglas v. California, 372 US 353 (1963) (right to counsel on appeal)
Boddie v. Connecticut, 401 US 371 (1971) (filing fee for divorce)

Prisoner Access to Courts

Ex parte Hull, 312 US 546 (1941) (correspondence with courts)
Johnson v. Avery, 393 US 483 (1969) (jailhouse lawyers)
Younger v. Gilmore, 404 US 15 (1971) (per curiam *aff'g.* 319 F.Supp 105 (ND Cal. 1970) (law libraries)
Wolff v. McDonnell, 418 US 539 (1974) (legal mail and expanded right of access to civil rights actions)
Bounds v. Smith, 430 US 817 (1977)
Procunier v. Martinez, 416 US 396 (1974) (visits with law students and paralegals)
In re Harrell, 3 Cal. 3d 683 (1970)
Novak v. Beto 453 F.2d 661 (5th Cir. 1971)

Alternative Means

Bryan v. Werner, 516 F.2d 233 (3d Cir. 1975) (restrictions on inmate law clinic)
Williams v. Leeke, 584 F.2d 1336 (4th Cir. 1978) (jail law library)
Hohman v. Hogan, 458 F.Supp 669 (D Vt. 1978) (alternatives)
Fluhr v. Roberts, 460 F.Supp 536 (WD Ky. 1978) (library availability)

Chapter Seven

DUE PROCESS IN PRISON DISCIPLINE

DEVELOPMENT OF DUE PROCESS

THE Fourteenth Amendment to the United States Constitution provides in part: " . . . nor shall any state deprive any person of life, liberty, or property, without due process of law. . . . " This is the well-known "Due Process Clause;" it is frequently referred to, both in prison and out. Its entry into the corrections realm is quite recent, however, and can best be understood by reference to its development in the nonprison context.

The purpose of the Due Process Clause is to protect citizens against arbitrary or erroneous governmental action. It is a restraint on governmental interference with an individual's life and property. The government's power to take life, liberty, and property from its citizenry is checked by the due process guarantees.

There are always two questions involved in due process issues: First, does due process apply in the particular situation? Second, if it does, what process is due, i.e. how extensive are the required procedures?

Does Due Process Apply?

For many years, the Due Process Clause was viewed as applying only under circumstances where the citizen had a *right* to the liberty or property that the government sought to take away. When the government interfered with someone's rights, that person had the right to due process protections. The rights guaranteed in criminal trials are an example of due process requirements necessary before depriving a person of life or liberty.

However, it was believed that if a citizen had no right to the liberty or property that the government desired to take, then the government could take action summarily without having to adhere to any citizen safeguards. For this reason due process was deemed not to apply to a vast multitude of administrative actions where the government terminated or revoked a benefit or privilege, which the state voluntarily had provided through its generosity. Thus, since a person had no constitutional right to welfare benefits, or a driver's license, for example, the government could deprive the recipient of the privilege without a hearing or other attributes of due process.

By 1970, the United States Supreme Court had clearly rejected the privilege-right distinction as the determinant for the applicability of due process. In that year, the Court decided *Goldberg v. Kelley*, a case involving the termination of welfare benefits. Agreeing that there is no constitutional right to these benefits, the Court found that due process still applied to their termination to safeguard against arbitrary or erroneous decision-making.

Although not required to do so by the Constitution, legislatures had created welfare benefits establishing eligibility and termination criteria. Thus, benefits were a "statutory entitlement;" once a person met the statutory eligibility criteria, she was entitled to the benefits. They could not be taken away at the government's whim, but only if the recipient no longer met the statutory criteria. Thus, the recipient had a state-created property interest that warranted the protection of the Due Process Clause. The necessity of such protection was further emphasized by an appreciation of the consequences of erroneous termination. By definition, a person eligible for welfare benefits needs that assistance to survive at the minimum standard of living; there is no "cushion." Thus, erroneous termination of the benefits of a person who was still, in fact, eligible for assistance could have disasterous consequences, or, as the Court termed it, result in a "grievous loss." Consequently, due process applied.

The "grievous loss" language appeared in subsequent court decisions, especially in lower courts. But as cases reached the United States Supreme Court asserting that due process applied to other aspects of administrative decision-making, the Court emphasized that the factor triggering due process protections is not whether the governmental action will result in a "grievous loss," but whether a recognized "liberty or property interest" is involved.

Revocation of a driver's license may not work a grievous loss, but due process still applies because the statutes providing for licensing and revocation entitle a driver to keep his or her license unless certain defined events take place (number of accidents, points, etc.). Therefore, as the Court later said in *Wolff v. McDonnell,* "the determination of whether such behavior has occurred becomes critical, and the minimum requirements of procedural due process . . . must be observed."

Conversely, loss of employment almost certainly works a "grievous loss," but a university professor deprived of his job was not entitled to due process protections because he had no property interest in his position (*Board of Regents v. Roth*).

After several cases involving protected property interest were decided by the United States Supreme Court, the first case concerning a liberty interest reached it. The case was *Morrissey v. Brewer* and raised the question whether due process applied to revocation of parole. The Court examined what it called, "the function of parole in the correctional process." After discussing the history and purpose of parole, the Court observed that "the essence of parole is release from prison, before the completion of sentence, on the condition that the prisoner abide by certain rules during the balance of the sentence." Thus, the Court concluded, "Implicit in the system's concern with parole violations is the notion that the parolee is entitled to retain his liberty as long as he substantially abides by the conditions of his parole."

The state, then, has created a liberty interest. The Court then examined the nature of that liberty interest to determine whether it came within the protection of the Fourteenth Amendment. The Court noted that although a parolee may be subjected to many restrictions, he or she lives a relatively normal life. The life of a parolee is almost that of a free citizen and is worlds apart from that of a prisoner.

The Court again rejected the labels "right" and "privilege" and held that "By whatever name the liberty is valuable and must be seen as within the protection of the Fourteenth Amendment. Its termination calls for some orderly process, however informal." The answer then: this state-created liberty interest was entitled to due process protection just as were state-created property interests.

Morrissey was followed in short order by *Gagnon v. Scarpelli*, applying due process to probation revocation, *Wolff v. McDonnell* inserting due process into prisoner discipline (discussed below), and *Meachum v. Fano*, holding that due process does *not* apply to transfers between prisons (discussed in Chapter Eight).

What Process is Due?

Determining that the Due Process Clause applies to a particular action is just half the battle. There is not a uniform set of procedures that automatically applies in every case. As in so many other areas of constitutional law, which we have already discussed, now is the time for the balancing act. Due process is a flexible concept, and the procedures required depend upon weighing the state's interests against the individual's.

At the very minimum, due process in any context requires *notice* of the government's proposed action and an *opportunity to be heard* in regard to the planned deprivation before someone other than the original decision-maker. On this spare foundation, additional specific procedures are built to fit the particular circumstances of the type of action. The essence of due process, however, is notice and the opportunity to be heard. Any additional procedures simply provide further detail and refinement to the implementation of these two fundamental guarantees. For example, due process in a particular type of case may require that the notice be in writing, personally served, and received no less than three days before the proposed governmental action. In other cases, written notice twenty-four hours in advance may be sufficient, or perhaps even verbal notice.

The "opportunity to be heard" could range all the way from an informal interview setting to a formal, adversary trial-type procedure. Depending upon the balance of interests, the opportunity to be heard may not be accorded until after the governmental action, instead of before.

The specific procedural protections applicable to a particular type of governmental action or deprivation depend upon weighing the particular state interest involved in the case against the nature of the individual's liberty or property interest.

PRISON DISCIPLINE

Background

A prison, like any other society, has rules that govern it. Since a prison is a total institution in which every aspect of a prisoner's life is regulated, there are innumerable rules, written and unwritten, governing prisoner behavior. A prisoner who does not conform to the rules is subject to discipline. Depending upon the seriousness of the misconduct or violation, the disciplinary action could range from a simple verbal warning to loss of institutional privileges, twenty-four hour lockup in the prisoner's own cell, placement in segregation, or loss of earned good time credits.

All but the most minor disciplinary violations generally go on a prisoner's institutional record and are referred to in decision-making concerning what prison to house the inmate in, what programs he or she will be allowed to participate in, and when parole should be granted.

When a prisoner loses privileges, is locked up, or is denied program participation because of alleged disciplinary violations, that prisoner is being punished. Whatever name may be applied to those deprivations, be it penalty, sanction, or "adjustment," it is obviously punishment: the prisoner is suffering some loss, albeit minor, because of failure to comply with the rules. Changing the name does not change the effect.

These labels will not serve to camouflage the disciplinary process from judicial scrutiny. As illustrated above, the courts look behind the labels of "right" and "privilege" to the nature of the interests themselves in determining whether due process applies. They follow the same course when presented with other labels. The issue is whether protected liberty or property interests are affected by government action. Whether the process of deprivation is called "discipline" or "adjustment" is of no legal consequence.

As we shall see, not all prison discipline is subject to the Due Process Clause. Only where the disciplinary action results in the deprivation of a liberty or property interest, which is protected by the Fourteenth Amendment, will the constitutional protections come into play. *Wolff v. McDonnell* (reprinted in full in Appendix) was the landmark Supreme Court decision holding that due process does apply in appropriate circumstances in the prison context. In the Court's words, "There is no iron curtain drawn between the Constitution and the prisons of this country."

Good Time and Due Process

The *Wolff v. McDonnell* case challenged the procedures used by the Nebraska prison system in handling serious disciplinary violations. The penalty for serious misconduct under Nebraska law was forfeiture or withholding of good time credits or confinement in a disciplinary (segregation) cell. The Court made clear that its decision applied only to those two penalties and not to lesser penalties, such as loss of privileges.

The good time credits referred to are created by state statute. Every state has some statutory provision reducing a prisoner's sentence by a specified proportion or designated number of days for maintaining a clean disciplinary record while incarcerated. These "good time" credits are often earned on a monthly basis and may be deducted from the maximum and/or minimum sentence, depending upon the statute. The good time credits, once earned, shorten an inmate's stay in prison. Their forfeiture would result in lengthening the time of confinement or, in other words, deprive the prisoner of liberty. The usual good time statute further provides that the earned good time credits may be taken away only if the prisoner commits a serious misconduct.

Presented with such a statute, the Supreme Court was faced with the prisoner's assertion that due process applied to the disciplinary procedures that could result in loss of good time, and the administrators' claim that disciplinary procedure was "a matter of policy raising no constitutional issue."

The Court rejected the administrators' position without hesitation. Then, analyzing the statute and its effect, it found that prisoners have a protected liberty interest in their earned good time credits and that this interest was entitled to be safeguarded against state infringement by the Due Process Clause. The state had created a statutory right to good time and provided that it could be forfeited only for serious misconduct. Forfeiture clearly affected the prisoner's liberty, and the liberty was entitled to constitutional protection.

Since the good time could be forfeited only if the prisoner committed serious misconduct, it was essential that the determination of guilt or innocence be fair and accurate. It is that determination of guilt or innocence which must be safeguarded against arbitrariness. Guilt cannot be assumed; it must be established before sanctions may be imposed. The purpose of due process protections is to ensure that the determination of guilt or innocence is done fairly, based upon both sides of the incident. The danger to avoid is presuming guilt from the fact that charges are made; those charges must be substantiated to establish guilt. Questions of proof and other aspects of decision-making in disciplinary hearings will be discussed shortly.

Notice again that in deciding whether due process applied in prison discipline, the Court did not look at the charges or the kinds of acts that were defined as misconduct. It looked instead as the possible deprivation, at what could be lost as the end result of the disciplinary process. Since liberty could be lost through forfeiture of good time credits, the due process safeguards were triggered.

Balancing: The *Wolff* Decision

Once the Court determined that due process applied to serious prison misconduct, it balanced the state's interests against the prisoner's. The Court viewed the state as being interested in accurate, but swift determinations and imposition of sanctions.

The Court also gave great weight to the prison environment, which it described as a "closed, tightly controlled environment" where "tension . . . is unremitting. Frustration, resentment, and despair are commonplace." Against this backdrop, the Court felt that adversary-type proceedings would jeopardize the personal safety of guards and inmates by increasing confrontations, promoting retaliation, and escalating personal antagonisms.

All of this was balanced against an inmate's interest in protecting the liberty represented by good time credits. The Court recognized that the loss of good time was "a matter of obvious great moment" to the prisoner. But it was viewed as being qualitatively different from the loss of parole involved in the Court's earlier *Morrissey* decision. The Court found that the loss of good time "is not the same immediate disaster" as parole revocation; that its effect on conditions of imprisonment and parole eligibility was speculative.

Thus, in striking the balance between the competing interests, the Court found that due process required fewer protections in prison discipline hearings than it did in parole revocation or any other due process cases that had gone before. The *Wolff v. McDonnell* decision guarantees a prisoner the fundamentals we spoke of earlier: notice and an opportunity to be heard. It further elaborated on these elements by requiring that the prison provide a prisoner accused of serious misconduct the opportunity for a hearing *prior* to the determination of guilt or innocence or imposition of sanction. Specifically, the accused prisoner has the right to —

1. Written notice of the charges at least twenty-four hours prior to the hearing.
2. Be present at the hearing and to speak and present written documents on his or her own behalf.
3. A qualified right to present defense witnesses, if doing so "will not be unduly hazardous to institutional safety or correctional goals."
4. Staff or inmate assistance in preparing for the hearing when the issue is very complex or the accused prisoner is illiterate.
5. A written statement of the decision with the evidence re-

lied on and reasons for the decision.

In addition, the Court specifically held that a prisoner had no constitutional right to confront or cross-examine adverse witnesses at the hearing, or retained or appointed counsel in discipline proceedings. A later case, *Baxter v. Palmigiano,* reemphasized this decision and further held that there is no right to counsel at a disciplinary hearing even when there are criminal charges pending based on the same alleged misconduct. There is the right to counsel in the criminal proceeding.

THE IDEA OF DUE PROCESS AND ITS IMPLEMENTATION

An administrator who closely follows the *Wolff* decision in adopting policy will still have many unanswered questions when seeking to implement the Supreme Court's mandate. *Wolff* lays a bare foundation only; to properly design the appropriate structure calls for familiarity with legal principles and standards that permeate judicial decision-making. The *Wolff* decision is the enunciation of several legal requirements, but these must be implemented in context, not in a vacuum. Traditionally, prison discipline was imposed simply on the basis of an officer's word. There were not two sides to the story; no thought that the officer might be mistaken.

Under a "due process" system, discipline must be approached differently. The matter does not begin and end with the officer's report. That is an accusation, not a decision, and it must be supported by reliable evidence. The prisoner has a right to know the nature of the accusation and to answer that accusation. Even if the prisoner committed the acts complained of, that conduct must be measured against the written rules to determine if the behavior is, in fact, a violation. The existence of defenses must also be recognized; a prisoner is not guilty of the misbehavior no matter what the reason for committing it. There are times when those reasons must be looked into and a finding made whether the prisoner was acting in self-defense, was coerced by someone else, or was justified due to misunderstanding, e.g. led by an officer to believe that no violation existed under the particular circumstances.

A prisoner is no longer automatically guilty. Implementing a "due process" disciplinary system that complies with constitutional requirements necessitates new attitudes as well as new procedures. And it is difficult. There are real security issues to be recognized and accommodated. There are also very tough hearing decisions to be made. It is much easier to decide a problem when there is only one point of view to be considered. But now that there are two to be taken into account, the determination of guilt or innocence is much more difficult, time-consuming, and subject to criticism by staff and inmates alike.

A "due process" disciplinary system needs the strong and visible support of the department and institution heads to work effectively. Employees must realize that hearing officers have the duty to hear both sides of a case and make their decisions based on all of the evidence, not just on the officer's report. Hearing officers must be insulated against pressure from co-workers and supervisors so that they will be able to meet the responsibility of making independent decisions.

Effective discipline is a necessity in a penal institution. There is no good reason, however, why effective discipline cannot also be fair discipline. "Due Process" is more than changing a few forms and procedures; the system must be fair in practice, not just look good on paper. The *Wolff* requirements are not incompatible with security, but to properly implement them one must understand both the legal context from which they are drawn and the prison environment in which they are inserted.

Perhaps more than any other case decided by the courts, *Wolff* impinges upon the relationships and issues which are fundamental to running a prison. Because of its importance and the unfamiliarity of many of its concepts, the remainder of this chapter will concentrate on discussing *Wolff* in terms of its practical application. The emphasis will be on the hearing and its decision-making process, because genuine implementation of even the limited due process requirements of *Wolff* will necessarily have a ripple effect on the way misconduct reports are written, investigated, and considered. Thus, it is essential that everyone, not just those holding hearings, have a real appreciation for the due process dynamics.

PREREQUISITES TO *WOLFF*

A Disciplinary Process

Wolff was concerned only with the hearing procedures; the point at which guilt or innocence is determined. However, major misconduct proceedings involve much more than the hearing itself; the hearing is really one of the last stages in the process. Before a hearing officer becomes involved in a case, misconduct usually has been (1) charged by the reporting officer, (2) screened by a supervisory reviewing officer, and often (3) investigated by a hearing investigator. After the hearing, most departments also have appeal provisions.

Each of these people has functions to perform, which are essential to the proper outcome of the hearing process. The hearing officer can base his or her decision only on the evidence presented at the hearing. No matter if the reporting officer caught the accused prisoner "red-handed," if the violation is mischarged, carelessly reviewed, or poorly investigated, the hearing officer may have no choice but to find the inmate not guilty. The disciplinary process will be effective only if the personnel at each stage view themselves as part of a process and not in isolation from the others.

Written Rules

Before examining the disciplinary process in detail, it is important to recognize an often overlooked element of due process. Due process is commonly referred to as "basic fairness." Long before the hearing stage, due process comes into play in any system where individuals are subject to punishment (by whatever name) for violating standards or norms of behavior. In these circumstances, due process guarantees that people have the right to know what behavior is expected of them, and, conversely, what behavior will be punished. This necessitates written rules.

The rules for prisoner conduct, or a school's rules for student conduct, serve the same function as the penal code does in society at large. It defines the norms of behavior and sets forth punishments for violating those norms. Due process guarantees that a person cannot be convicted of a "crime" that does not exist in the penal code, because it is unfair to punish someone for behavior that is not listed as improper. Similarly, a prisoner or student should not be punished for behavior that is not prohibited by written rule.

This does not mean that the person writing the rules has to think of every possible way of disobeying an order or being out of place, for example; the penal code does not try to enumerate every method of committing assault or robbery. It is not humanly possible to foresee every possible fact situation. Further, rules that are too detailed are difficult to administer and defeat the purpose of providing notice of what is expected. It is possible, however, to identify the categories of conduct that are unacceptable and define them with sufficient specificity to provide adequate notice of what will be punished. A model misconduct code that was developed by the author for the Michigan Department of Corrections can be found in Appendix D.

Carefully worded written rules not only provide prisoners with notice of what is expected, but they greatly assist staff as well. The existence of a uniform list of misconduct charges helps ensure consistency in identifying violations and equal treatment of all prisoners. It also encourages the formulation of appropriate charges likely to withstand the many review stages of the disciplinary process.

Procedures at the Hearing

Written Notice

The purpose of giving the inmate written notice of the charges prior to the hearing is to inform him or her of the accusation and enable him or her to prepare a defense. A prisoner can waive or give up the twenty-four-hour period and any other right, so long as the waiver is made willingly and with understanding of the consequences (e.g. the consequence of waiving the twenty-four hours is that the hearing may be held immediately; the consequence of waiving the right to appear at the hearing is that a guilty finding may be made on the basis of the misconduct report).

But what does this "notice" consist of? Since the purpose is to allow the accused prisoner to defend against the charges, the notice must be sufficiently specific to inform the prisoner of what the accusation is. This is the same function served by a prosecutor's information or complaint in a criminal proceeding. The "notice" or report should identify the rule that was violated and describe the actions of the prisoner, which allegedly amounted to misconduct. The time, date, and location of the incident should be specified, as well as the names of anyone else involved.

Also, the report should be based upon first-hand observation; the officer who witnessed the alleged misconduct should write the report. In cases where the incident was not witnessed by an employee, but was reported by another inmate, as is common with assaults and sexual abuse, the officer who received the report should try to corroborate it before charging the accused inmate with misconduct. The identity of the informant need not be revealed to the accused prisoner because of the danger of retaliation. However, the informant should appear before the hearing officer, unless even this confidential testimony would place the informant in danger.

The report should recite exactly what the officer observed, without making assumptions or conclusions. For example, that the inmate threatened an officer is a conclusion; the officer must describe the behavior that constituted the threat, such as, "Resident *A* threatened me by saying, 'I'm going to get you,' and approaching me with his fists clenched." Similarly, "I then gave him a direct order" is a conclusion; instead, the exact words of the order should be quoted.

The content of the report directly affects the decision that will be made at the hearing. The conclusions are for the hearing officer to make, not the officer writing the report. The hearing officer must have evidence, i.e. direct observations, on which to base a decision of guilt or innocence.

Witnesses

Defense

A prisoner has a qualified right to present witnesses in his or her own behalf. There is no right to confront or cross-examine adverse witnesses. As discussed earlier, the Supreme Court in *Wolff* was very concerned about the potential for disruption in a prison; therefore, it carefully limited a prisoner's right to call witnesses.

Wolff authorizes a refusal to call a witness on the following grounds: (a) irrelevance, (b) lack of necessity, or (c) hazardous to institutional safety or correctional goals. Thus, a person who actually witnessed the event in question and has something to say relevant to the issues, and is not simply being repetitious of other witnesses, should be allowed to appear before the hearing officer unless doing so presents a hazard to security or safety.

When the hearing officer determines that the proposed witness will not be physically present at the hearing, the hearing officer should either personally question the witness or ensure that the witness is interviewed and his or her statement is available at the hearing.

Cross-examination

The Supreme Court's ruling that a prisoner charged in a disciplinary hearing does not have the right of cross-examination is an exceptional one. This right is a very fundamental one in the American system of justice. Cross-examination is the primary method of testing the reliability of evidence in our adversary system. That is, in most trials and hearings, the decision-maker does not make an independent investigation of the case and is forbidden to do so. All evidence is presented by the parties in the case, the adversaries. Each presents evidence favorable to his or her point of view, but also subject to questioning by the opponent to point up errors, inconsistencies, or possible bias. It is believed that the truth will best emerge through this adversarial testing.

The purpose of the prisoner disciplinary system is the same:

find the truth so that guilt or innocence can be determined. However, what is viewed as the most effective tool for achieving this, cross-examination, is not available. Therefore, reasonably adequate substitutes must be found. The use of an investigator or the appearance of witnesses before the hearing officer, with the prisoner excluded if necessary, are recommended.

Whether the investigator or the hearing officer sees and questions the witnesses, the purpose of cross-examination should be kept in mind. The questioner should be attuned to the potential problems affecting the reliability of a witness's statement. The questioner will want to "test" for the witness's (1) perceptive abilities (sight, hearing), (2) quality of memory (how long ago; remember the events immediately preceding and following in as great a detail as the alleged misconduct?), (3) ability to communicate what perceived (may have to ask numerous questions to "fill in the blanks"), and (4) sincerity and integrity (is there any specific reason the witness would be biased for or against either the officer or the prisoner; or the reporting officer biased against the accused prisoner?).

It is clear that the prisoner does not have the constitutional right to confront and cross-examine accusing witnesses. However, this is due to the potential for harm caused by the confrontation. The information these witnesses have concerning the incident is still necessary to making the decision and must be presented to the hearing officer. The report of the charging officer will always be available, but the hearing officer should go beyond that. Preferably, the officer who wrote the report and other accusing witnesses should appear before the hearing officer. If this is not feasible, the hearing officer should be able to call upon a staff investigator to personally interview the witnesses.

Whether the witnesses appear before the hearing officer or, instead, are interviewed by an investigator, the quantity and quality of the evidence available is determined by the effectiveness of the questioner. The hearing officer or investigator must be an active interviewer, not a passive recipient of information. The investigator must analyze the misconduct report and the accused prisoner's statement, then ask witnesses specific questions regarding any discrepancies. General questions such as "do you have anything to add?" or "is this true?" are likely to get a brief "no" or "yes" and add nothing to the evidence-gathering effort.

Investigator

If the hearing officer uses an investigator instead of personally interviewing the witnesses, the investigator's role is critical. Since the hearing officer will be making the decision based on second-hand information, it is essential that the investigator carefully test the witnesses' statements.

Although the credibility and possible bias of witnesses are always at issue, these are generally best left to the determination of the hearing officer. The area to which most of the investigator's efforts will likely be directed is the reporting officer's powers of observation. The investigator must learn how much of the incident the officer saw (maybe the fight reported was in response to an earlier attack not seen by the officer), how fully the incident was reported, whether the officer correctly identified the inmates involved, whether the officer actually saw a fight or instead heard arguing and jumped to a conclusion, and other similar factual issues that the inmate disputes.

To most effectively accomplish this, the investigator should interview the accused prisoner before talking to witnesses. Thus, armed with the misconduct report and the inmate's version, the investigator can zero-in on any discrepancies. To the extent possible, the investigator should resolve any factual questions that can be answered by checking-out the accused prisoner's claim of alibi, permission by another officer, etc., and include these findings in the report to the hearing officer.

The reporting officer or other witness should not take the investigator or hearing officer's questioning as an insult or an implication that he or she is lying, but see it as an opportunity to fill in the details that could not be included in the limited space available on the misconduct report.

The resident's version of the incident frequently does not deny the officer's, but instead presents an alternative, plausible explanation. It is rarely a case of one must be lying, but more often is a situation where the questions raised by the resident's version are unanswered in the report. It is the investigator's job to gather all the specific information available to present to the hearing officer, especially where there are discrepancies between the two versions. Where the officer will not appear at the hearing, cooperation with the investigator is the only way to ensure that complete information is available to the hearing officer.

The investigator is just that: an impartial evidence-gatherer, not an advocate for either the resident or the reporting officer. Consequently, all known, relevant witnesses should be interviewed, not just those who are requested. The evidence should be reported as it is found, i.e. relevant witness statements should be reported verbatim, not summarized. Generally, the evidence should be allowed to speak for itself, without conclusions or interpretations made by the investigator. In cases where the investigator determines that it is necessary to add his or her opinion, this may be done so long as it is clearly indicated as such, e.g. a paragraph headed "Investigator's Evaluation."

Assistance

Wolff held that although a prisoner does not have the right to an attorney, "Where an illiterate inmate is involved, however, or where the complexity of the issue makes it unlikely that the inmate will be able to collect and present the evidence necessary for an adequate comprehension of the case, he should be free to seek the aid of a fellow inmate, or if that is forbidden, to have adequate substitute aid in the form of help from the staff or from a sufficiently competent inmate designated by the staff." The Supreme Court did not elaborate upon this right since it was not at issue in that case.

Most prisons do not allow one inmate to assist another; instead, they opt for providing employees to fill this role. The investigators, discussed above, could also provide assistance to inmates in gathering needed documents, interviewing witnesses, etc. Some argue that the inmate must be provided with an "advocate," not an "investigator;" someone to speak on his or her behalf, or present only favorable evidence.

However, it is submitted that advocacy is not the type of assistance the Supreme Court had in mind. The Court sought to make the disciplinary process as nonadversary as possible, which was the primary reason for rejecting the insertion of attorneys. It is further submitted that, as a practical matter, an accused prisoner needs an evidence-gatherer much more than he or she needs an orator. Consequently, it is recommended that the position of an independent, full-time hearing investigator be created, and the services of that investigator be available when needed by an accused inmate or by the hearing officer.

Written Statement

One of the basic rights guaranteed by *Wolff* is that "there must be a written statement by the fact finders [hearing officers] as to the evidence relied on and reasons for the disciplinary action." The Supreme Court found that written reasons were essential to protect the prisoner against adverse collateral consequences, e.g. transfer, denial of community programming or parole, based on a misunderstanding of the nature of the misconduct violation. Further, the Court said, written decisions help ensure that the department will act fairly in conducting and reviewing disciplinary hearings.

The written summary safeguards against several kinds of arbitrary action. Since the evidence relied upon in making the decision must be put in writing, it is assumed that only proper evidence will be used, that is, the hearing officer must reach a decision on only the evidence presented at the hearing and only that evidence related to the specific misconduct charged.

To achieve these purposes, the statement of reasons must be meaningful. It must be complete enough that someone who was not at the hearing can tell what the conflicting evidence was and why the resident was found guilty.

It must also always be kept in mind that it is the *prisoner's right* to have written reasons for the decision. Therefore, the statement must be clear and complete enough for the prisoner to understand what was decided and why. (Of course, the reasons should also be explained verbally to the inmate at the hearing).

Conclusory Phrases Taboo

The statement of reasons must not be general conclusions, such as "the report is clear" or "the facts are clear." If the prisoner contradicted the report, it is not clear at all; the facts are in dispute, and the hearing officer must make a decision. The "reasons" must set forth the specific facts the hearing officer is finding in making the decision. The old song "accentuate the positive and eliminate the negative," provides a good lead: indicate the evidence that is being relied on to make the finding of guilty or not guilty. It should be stated directly and matter-of-factly, because the hearing officer is finding that that is the way the incident happened.

To state that the resident is "guilty by a preponderance of the evidence" or that "the report clearly indicates guilt" is totally meaningless. It gives no explanation to anyone as to what the hearing officer found the facts to be. Similarly, phrases such as, "it is more likely than not that the violation was committed as charged" and "the report does (or does not) substantiate the charge" are completely inadequate. These are not magic phrases; they are superficial conclusions. What is the specific evidence they are based upon?

Suggested Approaches

There are some phrases that can be helpful in writing reasons for decisions so long as they are used in conjunction with the specific evidence in the case. For example, the prisoner may not "plead guilty," but will often admit the conduct described in the body of the report.

The resident may disagree that those acts amount to the charged misconduct (admits saying particular words to the officer, but argues that it does not amount to a threat). However, the hearing officer, in knowing the definition of the rule violation and required elements, applies these to the prisoner's admitted conduct to decide whether the prisoner is guilty of the charged violation. In these cases, the reason for the finding is that the "prisoner admitted . . . (state specifics).

There are other cases where the prisoner does not admit the behavior, but also does not really contradict the information in the report. He or she may offer some explanation or talk about other irrelevant issues. In these situations, the reasons for decision may properly be that "the officer's statement that . . . (give specifics) is uncontested."

Of course, the evidence relied on may be specific statements or observations made in the misconduct report, which are not discredited by other evidence. Conversely, where the allegations of the misconduct are refuted by the charged prisoner or another witness, then the inmate will be found not guilty based upon a statement of what the hearing officer has found the facts to be.

A great many cases will fit into these two categories when close attention is paid to precisely what the prisoner is saying about the charges. Of course, there will always be some cases where the two versions are in direct contradiction. In these, the hearing officer must make a decision. The reasons should be stated affirmatively and need not recite the evidence disbelieved. As, "the officer directly observed R . . . " (give specifics). The Hearing and Appellate Officer Checklist (included in Appendix) may be helpful in this regard. The reasons may be positive statements of the evidence fulfilling the required elements.

CONFIDENTIALITY. Some of the evidence relied upon may be from confidential sources. In giving the reasons for the decision, the identity of the informant may be excluded "when personal or institutional safety" is endangered (*Wolff*). Normally, safety necessitates keeping only the identity of the source confidential, not the substance of the information. Therefore, the specifics of the evidence, e.g. dates, places, kinds of contraband, relied upon must still be given. In rare cases, personal or institutional safety would be threatened by revealing the information as well as the informant. Under these circumstances, this evidence may be excluded from the report so long as the fact of its omission is indicated.

DENIALS OF REQUESTS. When a resident requests documents,

witnesses, a hearing investigator, or a postponement, and is denied, the hearing officer should include the reasons for denial in the hearing report. This is essential for purposes of review for two reasons: (1) If the prisoner raises a denial of rights on appeal, the record will show whether it was requested and dealt with at the hearing stage. If there is no discussion of it in the hearing report, the appellate officer should be able to conclude that the inmate did not make the claimed request. (2) If the matter was requested and denied, the reasons given are the basis to determine whether the denial was proper.

Standard of Review

An administrative hearing decision is in the same relationship to its reviewing officials as a trial court is to appellate courts. A court will uphold the decision of a disciplinary hearing (1) if the procedural requirements are followed, and (2) if there is evidence in the record to support the decision. That is, a court will examine the case to see if all the rights were given, but will not second-guess the credibility of the witnesses nor the wisdom of the decision; if arrived at properly, it will be upheld. If a prisoner's rights guaranteed by *Wolff* were denied, however, the decision will be reversed and a new hearing may be ordered, depending upon the circumstances.

Since the reviewers may not substitute their judgment for that of the trier of fact (hearing officer), determinations of fact and credibility may not be second-guessed. The decision will not be reversed unless the evidence fails to support the finding of guilty. Consequently, it will be reversed when the hearing officer merely states the finding of guilt in conclusory language and does not make any findings on the questions raised by the conflicting evidence.

The Hearing Officer:
Considerations in Decision-making

Right to a Hearing

It is the "opportunity to be heard in person" that is the

prisoner's right. The prisoner may waive this and any other right, so long as he or she understands what the waiver means and chooses to do so voluntarily. There is no reason to force an inmate to have a hearing or make a statement who does not wish to do so; it is the inmate's choice. The purpose of the hearing is to decide whether the charged misconduct occurred. It is clear, then, that if the prisoner does not contest the charges, either through admitting the misconduct or by refusing to appear, a full hearing is unnecessary to make a finding of guilt and disposition.

Appropriate Charging

LESSER INCLUDED CHARGES. Many rule violations necessarily include other less serious violations. This is where the violations are similar and have common facts or elements. For example, the "lesser included" violations of escape are: attempted escape, out of place, missing count, and late furlough return. Being insolent to an officer is a lesser included violation of threatening an officer; fighting may be a "lesser included" of assault. When a prisoner is charged with misconduct and the evidence does not support the particular violation charged, but does establish a lesser included violation, the hearing officer or committee has the authority to find the prisoner guilty of the lesser included violation. The prisoner's consent is not needed to do this, since the lesser charge is necessarily part of committing the more serious one, of which notice was given in the misconduct report.

DUPLICATIVE CHARGES. At the hearing, any duplicative charges should be combined, i.e. the prisoner may not have two separate findings of guilty for a single act of misconduct. For example, "insubordination" and "disobeyed a direct order" should be combined: disobeying the order is the kind of insubordination that occurred.

SEPARATION OF EVIDENCE AND CHARGES. The hearing officer must make a finding of guilty or not guilty on each charge separately. The evidence in the report supporting each charge should be identified, the prisoner asked to respond to each, and a finding made on each. Maintaining these distinctions will make the hearing and report more understandable and identify duplicate charges.

Evidentiary Aspects

RELEVANT EVIDENCE. As stated at the beginning of this section, the hearing officer's responsibility is to determine guilt or innocence on the specific violations charged. The only evidence that can be considered must be presented *at* the hearing and be related only to the present charges, not to any past bad conduct of the prisoner. The inmate's disciplinary record may not be examined until after a finding of guilt or innocence is made. If guilty, the past record can be examined in determining the appropriate disposition.

Further, decisions on the misconduct must be separated from issues of questionable institutional or staff practices. Unless these circumstances amount to a defense to the charges, they must not interfere with the determination of whether the misconduct was committed. They cannot be ignored, however; it is the hearing officer's responsibility to bring questionable and inconsistent staff actions regarding the disciplinary process to the attention of the appropriate supervisor.

AMOUNT OF EVIDENCE. The standard used to determine *how much* evidence is sufficient to establish guilt in administrative hearings is "proof by a preponderance of the evidence." This is much less than the "proof beyond a reasonable doubt" needed in a criminal trial.

The "preponderance of the evidence" is the standard or yardstick a hearing officer uses to determine whether guilt has been established on a particular charge. It is *not a reason* for finding someone guilty. The reason is the specific evidence presented in the case. When the evidence for guilt is more than the evidence against guilt, a preponderance of evidence is established.

Defenses

To be found guilty of misconduct, a prisoner must have acted voluntarily *and* either intentionally, recklessly, or negligently. At least three kinds of defenses may be presented.

MENTAL ILLNESS. If a prisoner is not responsible for his or her actions because of mental illness, the charges should be dismissed. If a hearing officer suspects that a prisoner may not have been acting rationally, referral should be made for psychiatric evaluation before making a finding of guilty or not guilty. Such cases should be treated as medical, not disciplinary, problems.

SELF-DEFENSE. There are certain narrow circumstances under which a prisoner is entitled to act in self-defense. The conditions that must be met are set forth on page three of the Hearing and Appellate Officer Major Misconduct Checklist (*see* Appendix).

The issue will generally arise in charges of fighting or assault. In applying the standards for self-defense, keep in mind that the force used in self-defense must always be proportionate to the force initially used. If excessive force is used, it is no longer self-defense. Further, evidence of former quarrels and prior threats and provocations may also be used in deciding whether self-defense is established in the particular case. If self-defense is proven, the prisoner must be found not guilty.

DURESS (ESCAPE). If a prisoner is coerced into committing a misconduct through threats or physical force, the defense of duress may be established. This does not apply, however, if the prisoner put himself or herself in a situation or relationship likely to be coercive. The defense of duress is most likely to apply in escape cases.

In some cases, a prisoner may admit the escape, but claim that it was justifiable because he or she feared homosexual attack. Under certain circumstances, the fear of such attack is a valid defense to a criminal prosecution for escape. The courts have set forth standards for determining when this defense of duress is established. Hearing officers should follow the same standards in deciding whether the misconduct of escape is proven.

A prisoner who admits escape but claims that he or she did it under duress to avoid homosexual attack has the onus of proving that he or she really was "under duress." The prisoner's defense is established where the evidence shows —

1. The threatening conduct was sufficient to create in the mind of a reasonable person the fear of death or serious bodily injury
2. The threatening conduct in fact caused such fear in the mind of the prisoner
3. That fear or duress was operating on the mind of the prisoner at the time of the escape.
4. The prisoner escaped for the purpose of avoiding the threatened harm.

A hearing officer should look for the following kinds of evidence in deciding whether the above factors were present:

1. A specific threat of death, forcible sexual attack, or substantial bodily injury in the immediate future.
2. No time for complaint to the authorities or opportunity to resort to the courts.
3. No force or violence used towards prison personnel or other innocent persons in the escape.
4. The prisoner immediately reported to proper authorities when he or she attained a position of safety. (Whether the prisoner immediately reported to authorities has a bearing on both (3) and (4) above, regarding whether the escape was really prompted by fear and for the purpose of avoiding attack.)

In deciding whether a prisoner has a valid defense of duress, the hearing officer or committee must examine all the evidence to determine whether the facts show that the prisoner was threatened, was so fearful of harm that his or her free will was overcome, and escaped because of that fear. Certainly the absence of one or more of the above items would discredit a claim that an escape was justified by a fear of attack.

If a prisoner presents the defense of duress and is found guilty of escape, the hearing officer must specifically respond to the defense in the "reasons" portion of the hearing report. For example, the defense may not be believed if the prisoner was never threatened with injury or homosexual attack (although he or she may have been requested to engage in sex) or the prisoner did not voluntarily surrender to authorities, or delayed in doing so.

PROBLEMS

In situations 1 through 5, decide if a disciplinary report should be written on the prisoner; if so, what is the supporting evidence? If a report is written, how should the matter be handled by the hearing officer? If no report should be written, how should the officer handle the situation instead?

1. Officer Jones observes prisoner Smith walking along the gallery. He appears unsteady, is weaving back and forth, holding onto the rail for support. Officer Jones asks him some questions and notices that Smith's eyes are glazed and speech slurred. Smith tells Jones that he is on prescribed medication for a medical problem.

2. The officer hears loud arguing from up on the gallery, goes up and finds two inmates squared off at each other.

3. Resident Green is found in an area that is off limits to prisoners; he says that the officers on the other shift gave him permission to be there.

4. Temporary release rules require that a prisoner must return from furlough in the same clothes that he left in. Prisoner Smith returns on time, but in different clothes; he has no other contraband. Smith said that he was on a job interview that afternoon, which ran late, so instead of going back home for his other clothes, which would have made him late returning to the institution, he came straight back in different clothes.

5. The institution's rules state that an inmate cannot leave her work pass assignment without the permission of the supervisor. The supervisor has signed an agreement that no one will be allowed off the assignment. The prisoner is observed returning from a park across the street from the assignment with other, nonprisoner employees. The supervisor acknowledges that he allows the prisoner to go to the park with other employees during breaks.

6. Resident Allen is caught assaulting another prisoner. He has a misconduct hearing and loses three months good time. Can he still be prosecuted in criminal court for the assault?

7. At the misconduct hearing, inmate Jones demands that the officer who wrote the report be present for questioning.

What should the hearing officer do? Will any of the following factors affect your answer:

a. Jones' explanation of the incident is very plausible and raises questions not dealt with in the misconduct report.
b. This incident and hearing are in a minimum security institution.
c. The hearing officer personally believes that the officer who wrote the report is a poor officer, and it is rumored that he sets inmates up and fabricates reports.
d. Inmate Jones is a very active jailhouse lawyer.

In answering this question, do not simply rely on *Wolff's* holding that an inmate does not have the right to cross-examine adverse witnesses. The law does not prohibit cross-examination. Therefore, you should balance the interests involved in each of the above circumstances and decide what the hearing officer *ought* to do in the situation. Also, remember that the hearing officer questioning a witness in the inmate's presence is different from allowing the inmate to ask questions. Determine if this or any other in-between approaches are appropriate.

RECOMMENDED CASES

Goldberg v. Kelley, 397 US 254 (1970) (welfare benefits)
Bell v. Burson, 402 US 535 (1971) (drivers' licenses)
Board of Regents v. Roth, 408 US 564 (1972) (loss of employment)
Cafeteria Workers v. McElroy, 367 US 886 (1961) (principles of due process)
Anti-Fascist Committee v. McGrath, 341 US 123 (1951) (principles of due process)
Dent v. West Virginia, 129 US 114 (1889) (purpose of due process)
Goss v. Lopez, 419 US 565 (1975) (school discipline)
Morrissey v. Brewer, 408 US 471 (1972) (parole revocation)
Gagnon v. Scarpelli, 411 US 778 (1973) (probation revocation)
Wolff v. McDonnell, 418 US 539 (1974) (*See* Appendix for full text) (prison discipline)
Baxter v. Palmigiano, 425 US 308 (1976) (prison discipline)

Escape-Duress Defense

People v. Luther, 394 Mich. 619, 232 NW2d 184 (1975)
People v. Lovercamp, 43 Cal. App. 3d 823, 118 Cal. Rptr. 110 (1974)
People v. Unger, 362 NE2d 319 (Ill. 1977)

Chapter Eight

DUE PROCESS IN OTHER
CORRECTIONAL DECISION-MAKING

INTRODUCTION

T HE 1974 *Wolff v. McDonnell* decision was seen by many as bringing due process into the prison as a whole, not solely into disciplinary proceedings. Indeed, it was a landmark ruling clearly stating for the first time that internal decision-making in areas not involving specific constitutional rights could be held answerable to constitutional standards.

Earlier cases involving First Amendment issues placed restrictions on institutional interference with specific constitutional rights. *Wolff* did not seem to involve constitutional rights; (good time was not in the Constitution) but instead concentrated on the *way* in which decisions were made. If *Wolff* meant that no administrative decision affecting prisoners could be made without the due process guarantees enunciated in *Wolff,* then prison administrators foresaw insurmountable obstacles to running their institutions.

Prisoners quickly filed suits in lower federal courts all over the country challenging decisions that they claimed resulted in "grievous losses" or worked "serious deprivations." The "grievous loss" and "serious deprivation" language was frequently present in Supreme Court due process decisions. Now that *Wolff* had made clear that due process applied even when the interest being taken away was not a constitutional right, apparently the pivotal factor triggering due process protections was whether the prison officials' action caused a "grievous loss" or "serious deprivation" to the inmate.

Numerous courts utilized this concept and found due process applicable to a variety of correctional decisions affecting inmates, including classification, transfers, and program participation. Once these cases reached the United States Supreme

Court, however, that Court more clearly defined the process of determining when due process applies to correctional decision-making.

A second major approach to inserting due process in the corrections setting involves challenges to jail conditions for pretrail detainees. Although the general principles and their evolution will be discussed more thoroughly in Chapter Nine, two specific due process claims will be considered here: overcrowding and restrictions on receipt of packages.

TRANSFERS

Between Prisons

One of the most contested areas in the lower courts was transfers between prisons. Prisoners argued, and some courts agreed, that an administrative decision transferring an inmate to a prison having substantially less favorable conditions could not be made without first providing the notice and hearing mandated by *Wolff*. Other courts agreed with prison officials that transfers did not require due process protections. Still others found that due process did not apply to "administrative" transfers but only to "disciplinary" transfers, those ordered as result of an alleged rule violation.

Two of these transfer cases, *Meachum v. Fano* and *Montayne v. Haymes*, eventually reached the United States Supreme Court. The high court reversed the trend of the lower courts and emphasized the essence of its earlier rulings. "We reject at the outset the notion that *any* grievous loss visited upon a person by the State is sufficient to invoke the procedural protections of the Due Process Clause. . . . Similarly, we cannot agree that any change in the conditions of confinement having a substantial adverse impact on the prisoner involved is sufficient to invoke the protections of the Due Process Clause."

Transfers, like good time credits, were statutory. But unlike good time, the authority to transfer inmates from one institution to another, by the terms of the Massachusetts and New York statutes in the cases before the Supreme Court, was completely within the discretion of the prison officials. That is, an inmate was not entitled to stay at a particular institution so long as he or she had no misconduct violations. The inmate could be transferred for any reason or for no reason at all. In fact, transfers between prisons often are ordered for administrative reasons unrelated to the conduct of the particular inmate being moved, such as the prevention of overcrowding or non-availability of appropriate programming.

Thus, unlike earned good time or parole, the states in these cases had not created a right to reside in a particular prison. The statutes did not make a finding of rule violation or some other event a prerequisite to transfer. Consequently, there is no question to be decided; no reason for a hearing.

In addition, the Supreme Court considered whether the more severe deprivations found in the second prison implicated a protected "liberty" interest. It found that they did not. The Court noted that the Due Process Clause applied to the process of convicting a person of crime. "But given a valid conviction, the criminal defendant has been constitutionally deprived of his liberty to the extent that the State may confine him and to subject him to the rules of its prison system so long as the conditions of confinement do not otherwise violate the Constitution. . . . The conviction has sufficiently extinguished the defendant's liberty interest to empower the State to confine him in *any* of its prisons."

Thus, it is clear that in these cases the initial assignment to a particular prison and transfers between prisons, although perhaps resulting in grievous losses to the inmates, do not invoke due process protections. Most states have statutes like that involved in *Meachum*, granting complete discretion in transfer matters to prison authorities. In these cases, where the law attaches no conditions on the power to transfer, the inmate may be legally moved without prior notice or opportunity for a hearing. Of course, where either state law or practice creates a justifiable expectation that prisoners will only be transferred under certain circumstances, due process is triggered. A hearing is required to determine if the alleged circumstances in fact exist.

From Community to Institution

The *Meachum* ruling dealt specifically with transfers from one prison institution to another more secure prison. Its decision necessarily was dependent upon the language of the applicable state statute governing inter-institutional tranfers. Consequently, this case does not necessarily answer whether due process applies to transfer of a prisoner from a halfway house, or community corrections center, back into an institutional prison.

Certainly the person involved is still convicted, is still an inmate. We have learned, however, that those labels rarely are determinative. Instead, we must look behind the person's legal status and examine the nature of the interests involved. The Supreme Court has made clear that due process applies only when a protected liberty interest will be infringed. An inmate in a prison does not have any right to stay there as opposed to another institution; there is no liberty interest involved. Is living in a community corrections center significantly different for constitutional purposes so that a resident of a halfway house has a protected liberty interest in remaining there and not being transferred back to a prison?

Clearly, such a transfer will place the affected prisoner in a much more severe, restricted environment, resulting in a grievous loss. But, this is not determinative, either. It is the *nature* of the prisoner's interest in remaining at the halfway house that must be examined. Residence in a halfway house is much more like being on parole than being in prison. Generally, a prisoner lives at the corrections center, but goes out to work or school in the community. Frequent visits with family may also be allowed. With this in mind, the Supreme Court's language describing the nature of a parolee's interest in continued liberty (*Morrissey v. Brewer*, referred to in Chapter Seven) rings true: "The liberty of a parolee enables him to do a wide range of things open to persons who have never been convicted of any crime. The parolee has been released from prison based on an evaluation that he shows reasonable promise of being able to return to society and function as a responsible, self-reliant person." The identical words could appropriately describe a corrections center resident.

In the good time and transfer cases, the Court examined the specific statutory language involved. In one it found forfeiture of earned good time credits explicitly conditioned upon a disciplinary violation; the inmate was entitled to keep the earned good time so long as he or she maintained a clean disciplinary record. In the other, it found absolute discretion to transfer explicitly granted by the legislature to corrections officials. When parole is granted, explicit conditions are attached governing the parolee's behavior. The Court in *Morrissey* found that "The parolee has relied on at least an implicit promise that parole will be revoked only if he fails to live up to the parole conditions."

In some states, eligibility for assignment to a community corrections facility will be governed by statute, in others by department policy. In either case, the language of the applicable criteria is a starting point for examining the nature of the prisoner's liberty interest. If transfer to halfway houses is totally a discretionary action by administrators, then removal from them may be governed by *Meachum v. Fano* and not require due process safeguards. A complete absence of conditions or criteria is unlikely, however. Neither the legislature nor the corrections department will want to jeopardize the halfway-house program by inviting a public outcry against dangerous offenders being housed in the community. Thus, it is probable that eligibility requirements will be included to assist in screening out candidates likely to be unsuccessful in the program.

The rules for participation in the community corrections center program may explicitly provide that the prisoner may remain in the program *unless* he or she is arrested for a new crime, commits a serious misconduct violation, or some other specific event occurs. In these cases, removal from the program, i.e. transfer back to prison, must be accomplished in accordance with due process because a state-created right or entitlement is involved.

Where the conditions for participation and termination are not so clearly set forth, there may nevertheless be an implicit promise created by department policy or practice not to transfer except under circumstances of rule or law violation.

Several lower courts have applied this type of reasoning in finding that due process applies to removal from temporary release, a program under which approved inmates are allowed to leave their institutions for several days at a time to return home and look for work, apply to schools, renew family ties, etc. The liberty interest involved in remaining eligible for temporary release is virtually identical to that affected by transfer from a community corrections center. Thus, even though there may not yet be clear judicial direction on this particular point, it is suggested that administrators would be on "thin ice" to assume that *Meachum v. Fano* provides a firm basis for summarily ordering inmates transferred from halfway houses to institutions without any due process protections. It is further suggested that the "process which is due" in these cases is that provided by *Wolff,* rather than the more adversary procedures necessitated by *Morrissey* for parole revocation.

Comparison of a community center resident with a parolee is instructive for purposes of defining the nature of the liberty interest at stake and reaching the conclusion that due process applies. However, in then determining the appropriate procedures, that liberty interest must be balanced against the state's interests in the integrity of its community release programs, as well as in accurate and swift discipline. It is suggested that the minimal *Wolff* procedures will be sufficient to comply with the Constitution in these transfer and termination cases.

Prison to Mental Hospital

At times, a convicted prisoner becomes mentally ill while incarcerated. In order to provide proper treatment, it is generally advisable to transfer the prisoner to a mental hospital or other psychiatric facility. These facilities are usually under the jurisdiction of another department, but may be associated with the corrections agency.

Formerly, movement of a prisoner to a mental health facility was treated as just another administrative transfer. Typically, state statutes would provide for a medical determination of mental illness or need for psychiatric treatment, but not impose any further requirements. Thus, if a doctor certified a prisoner as mentally ill, he or she would be sent to a mental institution. This was so even though the prisoner may be left in the mental hospital long past the expiration of the criminal sentence.

Then, in 1966, the United States Supreme Court decided the case of *Baxstrom v. Herold.* Mr. Baxstrom had been sentenced in 1959 to a two and one-half to three-year term for assault, second-degree. In 1961 he was transferred from prison to a mental institution and remained there until released pursuant to the Supreme Court's decision. The Supreme Court found that the prisoner's equal protection and due process rights had been violated by the summary transfer and indefinite stay at the mental hospital. In fact, he had been committed to that hospital involuntarily, but without the procedural protections statutorily required for commitment of nonprisoners.

The fact of conviction, as we have seen, does not deprive a prisoner of all liberty interests. He or she is entitled to be released after service of the court-imposed sentence. This cannot be extended to a life sentence. A prisoner who has become mentally ill must be released at the termination of his or her sentence unless he or she has been civilly committed to a mental institution pursuant to procedures corresponding to those applicable to involuntary commitment of nonprisoners. Many cases were decided and statutes passed in the wake of *Baxstrom,* which now recognize the unique consequences of prison-to-mental facility transfers and ensure adherence to constitutional protections. The return trip from mental hospital back to prison does not present the same potential for loss of liberty and can be accomplished without the necessity of notice and hearing.

Due process affects these transfers at two different points in time, then. State statutes vary, but a transfer of a prisoner to a mental health facility during sentence requires at least minimal administrative due process of notice and opportunity for a hearing. Some states require a judicial hearing as well. In either case, expert medical testimony is necessary. Once a prisoner's court-imposed sentence has expired, he or she must be released, whether then in a prison or a mental institution. The regular involuntary commitment procedures must then be followed to continue the former prisoner in a mental facility.

CLASSIFICATION

Generally

Prisoners are typically administratively classified by security level (e.g. minimum, medium, maximum) and for programming. Upon reception in the prison system, a prisoner will be classified based upon his or her crime, background, skills, length of sentence, etc., as well as available space and programs within the system. This will determine the inmate's facility, as well as any job or school assignment, eligibility for temporary release, and numerous other classification-related decisions. A prisoner's classification can be changed for better or worse at any time.

The courts recognize the propriety of administrators classifying prisoners to different security levels and generally will not interfere with a particular decision unless the classification appears to be without any foundation or is discriminatory. Classification decisions take into account both characteristics of the prisoner and the needs of the system. They frequently are based upon intangible factors and require the expertise and experience of correctional staff.

Prisoners have no federally protected right to an error-free decision, nor to a particular job assignment or classification level. Since there is no constitutional dimension to these decisions, except when an equal protection claim is made, the courts' role is limited to reviewing whether prison officials followed their own regulations in making classification decisions. Certainly, authorties must adhere to any positive statutory requirements or run the risk of suit on that basis, despite the absence of constitutional standards.

Special Offender Classification

An inmate in the federal prison system who is designated a "special offender" is ineligible for furloughs, community placement, and some other rehabilitative programs. The special offender classification is based upon the prisoner's criminal history and the nature of the present offense; it may include a determination that the prisoner was involved in organized crime or is otherwise a professional criminal. Many state systems have similar designations or classifications indicating that a prisoner is, for example, a drug trafficker, professional criminal, or involved with organized crime.

Assignment to such a classification reflects a judgment that the inmate is a poor security risk in that he or she is highly unlikely to remain crime-free if permitted to have contact with the community. Because of the adverse impact these classifications have for programming, prisoners argued that the classification could not be imposed without due process. Some courts initially agreed with this position. However, later decisions rejected it, based upon the analysis presented in *Meachum*. When Congress or a state legislature gives prison officials full discretion to control classification and rehabilitation programs, due process does not apply to the classification decision.

Administrative Segregation

When segregation is due to a disciplinary violation, it usually follows a *Wolff*-type hearing. There are other times when the security and order of the facility appear to necessitate the segregation of one or more prisoners. There may have been an assault or reliable information regarding pending violence. Since officials have the duty to protect inmates from attack and self-injury (*see* Chapter Five), segregation may be the only way to achieve this in some cases. The prisoner may be segregated while a rumor or incident is investigated, or until the danger is past.

Segregation under these circumstances is based as much on prediction of the intangibles of security and order as on concrete, observable events. Still the authority to segregate prisoners is essential and is inherent in the responsibility to manage penal institutions. The wisdom of the decision is not reviewable by courts.

Application of the *Wolff-Meachum* reasoning indicates that

due process does not apply to a transfer from general population to administrative segregation since there is no protected liberty interest involved. If, however, administrative segregation appears to be used arbitrarily or for harrassment or punishment, the courts may look behind the "administrative" label to determine if security or safety is truly at issue. Any notice or hearing procedure required by statute, rule, or policy must, of course, be followed.

PRETRIAL DETAINEE CONDITIONS

The previous chapters have shown that the method of challenging conditions of confinement which do not involve a specific constitutional right (e.g. freedom of speech, freedom of religion, guarantees against unreasonable search and seizure) is through the Eighth Amendment's protection against cruel and unusual punishment. This is the appropriate standard for convicted prisoners because it assumes that punishment may be legitimately imposed, but that punishment may not be cruel and unusual. (*See* Chapter Five for complete analysis of the Eighth Amendment guarantee.)

However, a pretrial detainee is a defendant held in jail before trial only because he or she has been unable to post bail. There is no conviction, only an accusation. Consequently, a pretrial detainee may not be subjected to any punishment. Since no punishment may be imposed until after a conviction, the cruel and unusual punishment provision is inapplicable. Instead, the conditions of confinement to which a pretrial detainee is subjected must be measured against the due process clause.

The decision in *Bell v. Wolfish* (reprinted in full in Appendix) is the first United States Supreme Court ruling on the conditions of pretrial detainees. The fundamental issue of "punishment" was analyzed and then several specific restrictions were examined. Two of these conditions, double-bunking and package restrictions, were challenged on the basis of due process/punishment principles rather than separate specific constitutional rights.

As noted in Chapter Five, overcrowding by itself is not deemed to amount to cruel and unusual punishment, although when combined with other deprivations, the general conditions of a facility may violate the Eighth Amendment. The *Wolfish* holding that housing two prisoners in rooms designed for one was not unconstitutional punishment in that particular jail was also discussed. This does not mean that a jail administrator with crowded conditions never runs the risk of constitutional challenge.

A court will examine the overcrowding in context and the effects the excessive numbers have on the common facilities, on safety, on health, etc. As the court indicated in *Wolfish,* at some point "a given number of people in a given amount of space . . . might cause serious questions under the Due Process Clause." At some point the conditions amount to punishment.

Wolfish also upheld the almost complete prohibition on receipt of packages of food, clothing, and other personal items. Parcels of goods do not involve First Amendment freedom of expression issues, and possession of these items is not protected by any other constitutional guarantee. Therefore, this prohibition is invalid only if it amounts to unconstitutional punishment. The Court found that the restrictions were a reasonable response to security threats (contraband) and, consequently, were constitutional.

CONCLUSION

Despite the holdings of these cases that due process did not apply to the particular transfer or classification decision in question, or that the jail condition or restriction at issue was not "punishment" within the meaning of the Due Process Clause, it is not appropriate to conclude that these areas are safe from judicial scrutiny. All of these decisions make it clear that due process does apply to correctional decision-making as it does to that of other administrative bodies. However, just as we said of rights generally in the first chapter, due process is not an all or nothing situation. The facts and law in each case make a difference and must be weighed carefully; individualized decisions must be made. These cases provide the guidelines for determining the applicability of the due process standards. Only when they are measured against the circumstances of a particular case will a determination of what is required in that case be possible.

RECOMMENDED CASES

Meachum v. Fano, 427 US 215 (1976) (inter-prison transfers)

Montayne v. Haymes, 427 US 236 (1976) (inter-prison transfers)

Solomon v. Benson, 563 F.2d 340 (7th Cir. 1977) (special offender classification)

Baxstrom v. Herold, 383 US 107 (1966) (mentally ill prisoners)

Cruz v. Ward, 558 F.2d 658 (2d Cir. 1977) (prisoners transferred from mental hospital back to prison)

Palmigiano v. Mullin, 491 F.2d 978 (1st Cir. 1974) (classification)

Daigle v. Hall, 564 F.2d 884 (1st Cir. 1977) (placement in administrative segregation)

Chapter Nine

ADMINISTERING JAILS

THE Constitutional analysis is complicated in the jail setting; typically, the jail inmate population consists of both sentenced prisoners and pretrial detainees, those simply awaiting trial.

In the usual situation, the pretrial detainee has a right to bail and bail has been set, but the defendant cannot afford it. But for that lack of funds, the defendant would otherwise be free while awaiting trial. The detainee, like the defendant who has posted bail, is presumed innocent until proven guilty beyond a reasonable doubt.

Certainly, the constitutional principles covered in the preceding chapters apply to convicted jail inmates as well as to prison inmates. The fact that they are incarcerated in county facilities rather than state or federal institutions is of no constitutional significance. Thus, the jail administrator must be as attuned as the prison official to the balancing of interests in the areas of free speech, religion, search and seizure, cruel and unusual punishment, and due process.

The jail administrator has had two additional problems in meeting constitutional standards: first, the conditions in jails are frequently further below constitutional minimums than are those in prisons, making compliance with court decisions very difficult and expensive; second, until the recent United States Supreme Court decision in *Bell v. Wolfish,* there was a great deal of uncertainty whether pretrial detainees were entitled to a higher standard of care than convicted inmates. That is, in the balancing of detainees' rights against institutional concerns, must the detainees be given more deference because they have not been convicted of any crime?

Because they had not been found guilty through due process of law, many lower courts held that pretrial detainees could not be subjected to punishment. The courts then concluded that any "restrictions or privations," which were not either inherent in the fact of confinement or necessary to ensure the defendant's appearance at trial, were unconstitutional unless "justified by the compelling necessities of jail administration." This "compelling necessity" standard was much more difficult for officials to meet than that applicable to convicted prisoners: that the restriction simply *further* the legitimate government interest in security, order, or rehabilitation, and intrude no further than necessary to meet that interest.

Under the "compelling necessity" test, federal courts invalidated numerous jail regulations and practices that had restricted communications (telephone, visits, mail) and access to publications, or pertained to cell and body searches, clothing, and personal appearance. A security rationale was presented by administrators for many of the regulations, but the courts found no "compelling necessity."

A case that applied this standard to the conditions in the New York City Federal Metropolitan Correctional Center and found many of the conditions and practices there to be in violation finally reached the United States Supreme Court. *Bell v. Wolfish* (reprinted in full in the Appendix) is the first case in the high court concerning the status of pretrial detainees. Although it has by no means answered all the questions a jail administrator may have, it has clearly defined the basic principles involved.

The Supreme Court's view was somewhat different from that of the lower courts. Two critical points set the stage for analyzing future cases. The Supreme Court agreed that the due process clause guarantees that a pretrial detainee may not be punished while incarcerated awaiting trial. Disciplinary punishments for rule infractions were not at issue in this case; the Court was referring to general conditions of confinement as punishment. Jail administrators who adhere to the disciplinary procedures set forth in Chapter Seven should be on safe ground if challenged as unconstitutionally punishing pretrial detainees.

The question to be answered in each case is still whether the condition in question amounts to punishment. But how is that defined? At what point does a restrictive or unpleasant living situation become unlawful "punishment?" According to the lower courts, once a practice or condition worked some restriction on a detainee's constitutional rights, it was "punishment" unless justified by a "compelling necessity." Not so, ruled the Supreme Court: "Thus, if a particular condition or restriction of pretrial detention is reasonably related to a legitimate government objective, it does not, without more, amount to 'punishment.' Conversely, if a restriction or condition is not reasonably related to a legitimate goal — if it is arbitrary or purposeless — a court permissibly may infer that the purpose of the government action is punishment that may not constitutionally be inflicted upon detaines *qua* detainees."

The "legitimate goals," the Court said, not only included ensuring the detainee's presence in court, but also "effective management of the detention facility." Although rehabilitation is not one of the functions of a local jail, the maintenance of security and order are just as important in these facilities as in prisons. Restrictions that further these objectives are not "punishment" in the constitutional sense and, consequently, may be imposed on pretrial detainees.

In essence, it appears that the only conditions or restrictions that amount to punishment in the sense used here are those that either the officials intend as punishment, or those which have no other purpose than punishment, i.e. there appears to be no reasonable relationship to security, order, or presence at trial.

The Court cited several earlier prison cases and warned that determinations of whether particular restrictions are reasonably related to maintaining security and order will be left to the "professional expertise of corrections officials, and, in the absence of substantial evidence in the record to indicate that the officials have exaggerated their response to those considerations, courts should ordinarily defer to their expert judgement in such matters." Once the administrators document that the challenged restriction has a reasonable relationship to effective management of the facility (security and order), it will be upheld unless the prisoner presents substantial evidence that the restriction is an exaggerated response to the security consideration.

The Court applied these standards to areas that the lower

courts had found constitutionally deficient: (1) double-bunking in rooms designed for one person, (2) package restriction, (3) the publisher-only rule for receipt of publications, (4) procedures for room searches, and (5) body-cavity inspections following contact visits. The Court reversed the lower courts on each point and upheld each condition or restriction as not violating constitutional protections. The Court's reasoning on each issue was included at the appropriate topic in previous chapters, so will not be repeated here.

Our concern in this chapter is identifying the appropriate standards for jail administrators to apply when evaluating their operations. The result of *Wolfish* is that pretrial detainees really are not different from convicted inmates for purposes of determining the constitutionality of the conditions of their confinement. Whether convicted or unconvicted, the same principles apply, according to *Wolfish*:

1. Even "convicted prisoners do not forfeit all constitutional protections by reason of their conviction and confinement in prison." Pretrial detainees retain at least the same constitutional rights as convicted prisoners.
2. The fact of incarceration necessarily results in the restriction and limitation of rights of both pretrial detainees and convicted prisoners.
3. "Maintaining institutional security and preserving internal order and discipline are essential goals" that may justify restricting inmates' constitutional rights.
4. "Prison administrators . . . should be accorded wide-ranging deference in the adoption and execution of policies and practices that in their judgment are needed to preserve internal order and discipline and to maintain institutional security."

CAVEAT!

Jail administrators should not be too quick to breathe a sigh of relief in the wake of *Wolfish*. Although the tone and holding of the opinion unquestionably give great deference to the judgment of officials, it must be remembered that the conditions at the Metropolitan Correctional Center were atypical of most jails in the comfort and services provided. Further, the publisher-only, package, and room shakedown restrictions were indirect interferences with constitutional rights, affecting the *manner* in which rights could be exercised. Thus, *Wolfish* can be seen to be on the frontier of "prisoner's rights." Few jails are close to that frontier.

Consequently, *Wolfish* must be viewed in context. It draws a line and establishes a limit on both the interpretation of constitutional protections in the correctional setting and judicial review of administrative actions. But, it does not retract any Supreme Court decision that preceded it. There is still "no iron curtain drawn between the Constitution and the prisons [and jails] of this country."

Everything covered in this book applies to jails as much as to prisons. It is sometimes more difficult for the jail administrator to meet these constitutional standards than for the prison warden. Frequently, jail facilities are more secure and provide fewer facilities than commonly found in prisons. Since jails are intended as short-term holding facilities, they are not equipped to provide "rehabilitation" programs including opportunities for education and recreation. Most do not allow contact visits and greatly restrict visiting times, authorized visitors, and telephone contacts as well. Rooms for confidential attorney-client consultations are a recent development, and jail law libraries are generally nonexistent or extremely limited.

The duty to protect inmates from injury applies equally to jailers as to wardens. The danger of suicide appears to be higher in jails, perhaps due to the strong emotional reaction many have to initial arrest and incarceration. Classification procedures are frequently lacking in jails, and inmates may be without protection from attack by other prisoners. The *Duty to Protect* discussion in Chapter Five is particularly relevant in the jail setting.

In addition to the constitutional requirements affecting jail administration, jails are likely to have other kinds of legal requirements affecting their operation. For example, state housing laws setting living space requirements may cover jails and other local detention facilities. The same is likely to be true of health and fire codes. There may also be a state department or commission with the responsibility for overseeing jails and issuing administrative rules dealing specifically with jail operations. Thus, a jail administrator must be fully aware of all statutory and administrative requirements, as well as the Constitutional aspects discussed in this book.

RECOMMENDED CASES

Bell, V. Wolfish, 441 U.S. 000, 99 S.Ct 1861 (1979) (*See* Appendix C)
Wolfish v. Levi, 573 F.2d 118 (2d Cir 1978) (reversed by Bell v. Wolfish; applied special status approach)
Battle v. Anderson, 564 F.2d 388 (10th Cir. 1977) (minimum space requirements)
Main Road v. Aytch; 565 F.2d 54 (3d Cir. 1977)

See Chapter Four for cases re: body cavity inspections

FUTURE DIRECTIONS

THE LIMITS OF LITIGATION

EACH succeeding United States Supreme Court case has voiced stronger and stronger admonitions against judicial interference in prison administration. The lower courts have been repeatedly reminded of their limited role in reviewing challenges to prison and jail conditions (*see The Role of the Courts* discussion in Chapter One). Constitutional litigation is not a contest to arrive at the best of all possible worlds; the courts have authority to decide only whether the condition presented to the Constitution. If it does, the court may enjoin its continuation and order the department to comply with constitutional requirements. However, if the condition does not violate the Constitution, the court has no further role.

The concluding paragraph of *Wolfish* emphasized the limitations:

> But under the Constitution, the first question to be answered is not whose plan is best, but in what branch of the Government is lodged the authority to initially devise the plan. . . . the inquiry of federal courts into prison management must be limited to the issue of whether a particular system violates any prohibition of the Constitution, or in the case of a federal prison, a statute. The wide range of "judgment calls" that meet constitutional and statutory requirements are confided to officials outside of the Judicial Branch of Government.

Earlier in its opinion, the *Wolfish* court concluded that the lower courts had "simply disagreed with the judgment of . . . officials. . . . But our decisions have time and again emphasized that this sort of unguided substitution of judicial judgment for that of the expert prison administrators on matters such as this is inappropriate."

Since the Constitution sets a floor or minimum requirements, constitutional litigation necessarily is limited to the extremes or perimeters of permissible conditions and administrative actions. Once those outer limits are defined, there is no longer a role for the Constitution. In prison and jail cases that have reached the United States Supreme Court, the constitutional lines have been clearly drawn. Workable definitions have been enunciated for determining at what point the Constitution is violated in such areas as mail censorship, media interviews, associational activities, discipline, transfers, access to courts, search, and segregation conditions. The balancing test has been repeatedly described and applied.

In delineating the constitutional perimeters, the courts have also defined the realm of administrative discretion. So long as conditions or practices are on safe constitutional ground, the officials have a free hand in choosing the approach to be taken. Whether the plan be effective or not, the courts may not intervene. "A practice that may be bad from the standpoint of penology may not necessarily be forbidden by the Constitution." (*Hutto v. Finney*, 437 US 678, n12, quoting from *Holt v. Sarver II*, 309 F.Supp 362, 369 [ED Ark. 1970]).

The fact that the limits of constitutional litigation are on the horizon does not mean that prison and jail conditions will no longer be a concern of the courts. Since the facts make all the difference, challenges to administrative practices and decisions will continue. There will be disputes over which way the balance should tip in a particular case, as well as suits in areas not yet defined by the Supreme Court.

The emphasis will now shift, however, from judicial decisions to developing more specific statutes and administrative rules. Several model standards for legislation and rules have been drafted by national organizations. An administrator who does not seize the initiative in policy and rule promulgation may find detailed requirements imposed by the legislature.

Many of the rulings discussed in this text were made because the corrections officials took a hard-line, all-or-nothing position. By asserting that the Constitution had no place in prison administration, they left themselves open for adverse court decisions. Now that much of the void has been filled and there is a body of law pertaining to the Constitution in the correctional setting, the administrator should be comfortable with constitutional principles and have a feel for the balancing of interests used to measure the constitutionality of conditions and practices.

Corrections officials have complete discretion in the wide variety of daily practices and decisions which do not affect constitutional rights. In areas that do have a constitutional dimension, the choice of method for implementing the constitutional principle is left to the administrator. Effective management and agency accountability frequently call for structuring that discretion through policy, rule, and other guidelines.

Recognizing that the same legal principles apply in prison as well as out, an administrator can reflect consideration of these principles and the competing interests often involved when issuing departmental policy or rules. The adoption of rules and creation of administrative grievance procedures have long been encouraged by courts as effective alternatives to litigation.

The constitutional framework is more clearly delineated now than ever before. The foundation of legal principles is strong and firm, and the blueprints are sufficiently complete to indicate the future direction. Corrections personnel, from administrator to line employee, no longer need to grope gingerly, dodging judicial bullets. The law of the Constitution in the correctional setting is understandable. It is a way of thinking and of analyzing problems. We hope that this book will enable corrections personnel to go forth with new tools to bridge the historical gap between the world of the prisons and that of the courts.

REFERENCE MATERIALS FOR
PROPOSED STATUTES AND RULES

Corrections (1973), National Advisory Commission on Criminal Justice Standards and Goals, U.S. Government Printing Office, Washington, DC, 20402.

Manual of Standards for Adult Local Detention Facilities and Manual of Standards for Adult Correctional Institutions (1977) Commission on Accreditation for Corrections, 6110 Executive Boulevard, Suite 750, Rockville, Maryland, 20852.

Uniform Law Commissioner's Model Sentencing and Corrections Act (1979), National Conference of Commissioners on Uniform State Laws, Stock No. 027-000-00819-4, Superintendent of Documents, U.S. Gov't Printing Office, Washington, D.C., 20402.

Proposed Standards Relating to the Legal Status of Prisoners (1980), American Bar Association, 1155 East 60th Street, Chicago, Illinois, 60637.

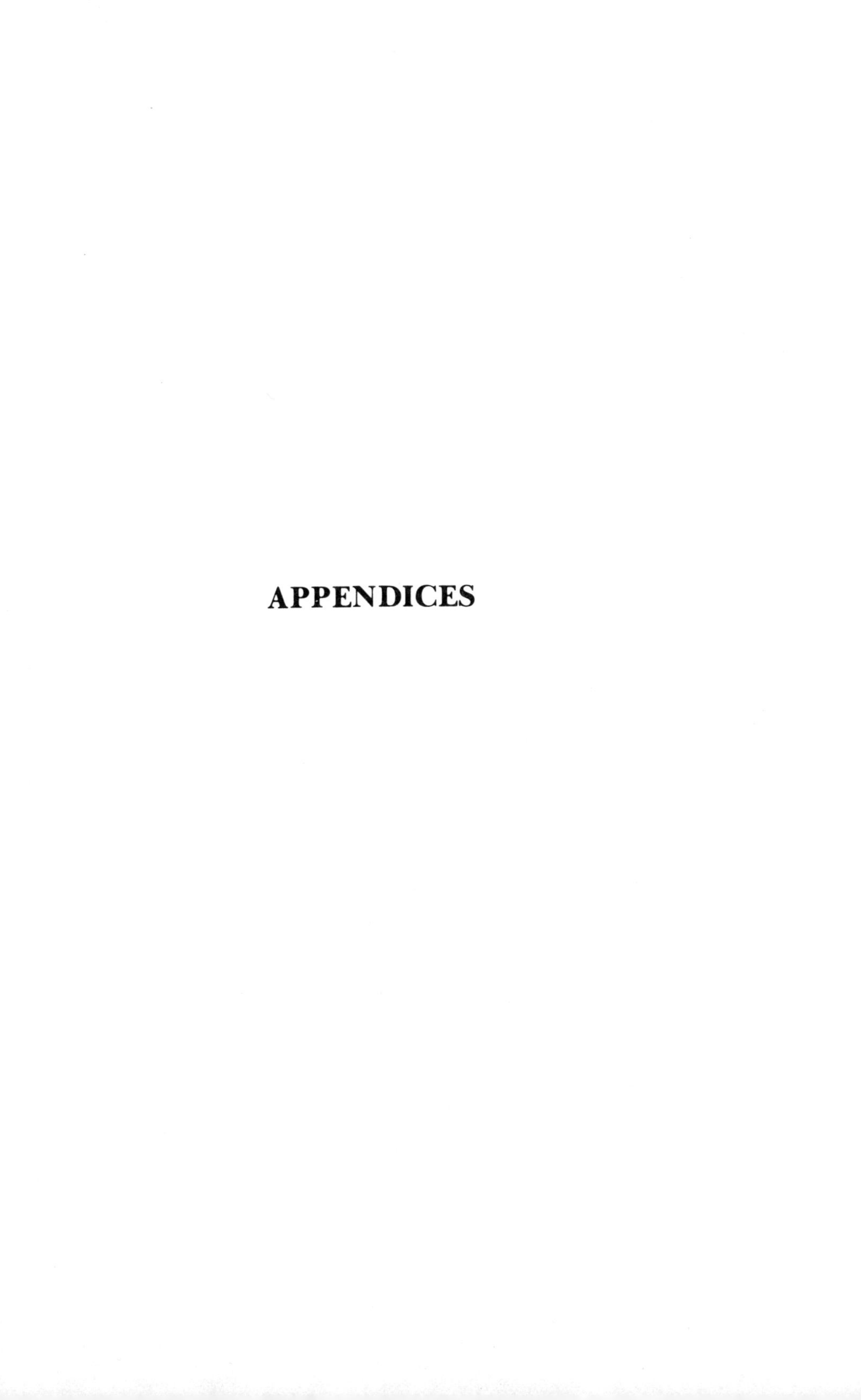

APPENDICES

RAYMOND K. PROCUNIER, Director, California Department of Corrections, et. al., Appellants,

v

ROBERT MARTINEZ et al.

416 US 396, 40 L Ed 2d 224, 94 S Ct 1800 (1974)

Opinion of the Court
[Footnotes omitted]

[416 US 398]
Mr. Justice **Powell** delivered the opinion of the Court.

This case concerns the constitutionality of certain regulations promulgated by appellant Procunier in his capacity as Director of the California Department of Corrections. Appellees brought a class action on behalf of themselves and all other inmates of penal institutions under the Department's jurisdiction to challenge the rules relating to censorship of prisoner mail and the ban against the use of law students and legal paraprofessionals to conduct attorney-client interviews with inmates. Pursuant to 28 USC § 2281 [28 USCS § 2281] a three-judge United States District Court was convened to hear appellees' request for declaratory and injunctive relief. That court entered summary judgment enjoining continued enforcement of the rules in question and ordering appellants to submit new regulations for the court's approval. 354 F Supp 1092 (ND Cal 1973). Appellants' first revisions resulted in counterproposals by appellees and a court order issued May 30, 1973, requiring further modification of the proposed rules. The second set of revised regulations was approved by the District Court on July 20, 1973, over appellees' objections. While the first proposed revisions of the Department's regulations were pending before the District Court, appellants brought this appeal to contest that court's decision holding the original regulations unconstitutional.

We noted probable jurisdiction. 412 US 948, 37 L Ed 2d 1000, 93 S Ct 3013 (1973). We affirm.

I

First we consider the constitutionality of the Director's Rules restricting the personal correspondence of prison inmates. Under these regulations, correspondence between

[416 US 399]

inmates of California penal institutions and persons other than licensed attorneys and holders of public office was censored for nonconformity to certain standards. Rule 2401 stated the Department's general premise that personal correspondence by prisoners is "a privilege, not a right. . . ." More detailed regulations implemented the Department's policy. Rule 1201 directed inmates not to write letters in which they "unduly complain" or "magnify grievances." Rule 1205(d) defined as contraband writings "expressing inflammatory political, racial, religious or other views or beliefs. . . ." Finally, Rule 2402(8) provided that inmates "may not send or receive letters that pertain to criminal activity;

[416 US 400]

are lewd, obscene, or defamatory; contain foreign matter, or are otherwise inappropriate."

Prison employees screened both incoming and outgoing personal mail for violations of these regulations. No further criteria were provided to help members of the mailroom staff decide whether a particular letter contravened any prison rule or policy. When a prison employee found a letter objectionable, he could take one or more of the following actions: (1) refuse to mail or deliver the letter and return it to the author; (2) submit a disciplinary report, which could lead to suspension of mail privileges or other sanctions; or (3) place a copy of the letter or a summary of its contents in the prisoner's file, where it might be a factor in determining the inmate's work and housing assignments and in setting a date for parole eligibility.

The District Court held that the regulations relating to prisoner mail authorized censorship of protected expression without adequate justification in violation of the First Amendment and that they were void for vagueness. The court also noted that the regulations failed to provide minimum procedural safeguards against error and arbitrariness in the censorship of inmate correspondence.

Consequently, it enjoined their enforcement.

[Abstention portion of opinion omitted.]

A

Traditionally, federal courts have adopted a broad hands-off attitude toward problems of prison administration. In part this policy is the product of various limitations on the scope of federal review of conditions in state penal institutions. More fundamentally, this attitude springs from complementary perceptions about the nature of the problems and the efficacy of judicial intervention. Prison administrators are responsible for maintaining internal order and discipline, for securing their institutions against unauthorized access or escape, and for rehabilitating, to the extent that human nature and inadequate resources allow, the inmates placed in their custody. The Herculean obstacles to effective discharge of these duties are too apparent to warrant explication. Suffice it to say that the problems of prisons

[416 US 405]

in America are complex and intractable, and, more to the point, they are not readily susceptible of resolution by decree. Most require expertise, comprehensive planning, and the commitment of resources, all of which are peculiarly within the province of the legislative and executive branches of government. For all of those reasons, courts are ill equipped to deal with the increasingly urgent problems of prison administration and reform. Judicial recognition of that fact reflects no more than a healthy sense of realism. Moreover, where state penal institutions are involved, federal courts have a further reason for deference to the appropriate prison authorities.

But a policy of judicial restraint cannot encompass any failure to take cognizance of valid constitutional claims whether arising in a federal or state institution. When a prison regulation or practice offends a fundamental constitutional guarantee, federal courts will discharge their duty to protect constitutional

[416 US 406]

rights. Johnson v Avery, 393 US 483, 486, 21 L Ed 2d 718, 89 S Ct 747 (1969). This is such a case. Although the District Court found the regulations relating to prisoner mail deficient in several respects, the first and principal basis for its decision was the constitutional command of the First Amendment, as applied to the States by the Fourteenth Amendment.

The issue before us is the appropriate standard of review for prison regulations restricting freedom of speech. This Court has not previously addressed this question, and the tension between the traditional policy of judicial restraint regarding prisoner complaints and the need to protect constitutional rights has led the federal courts to adopt a variety of widely inconsistent approaches to the problem. Some have maintained a hands-off posture in the face of constitutional challenges to censorship of prisoner mail. E.g. McCloskey v Maryland, 337 F2d 72 (CA4 1964); Lee v Tahash, 352 F2d 970 (CA8 1965) (except insofar as mail censorship rules are applied to discriminate against a particular racial or religious group); Krupnick v Crouse, 366 F2d 851 (CA10 1966); Pope v Daggett, 350 F2d 296 (CA 10 1965). Another has required

only that censorship of personal correspondence not lack support "in any rational and constitutionally acceptable concept of a prison system." Sostre v McGinnis, 442 F2d 178, 199 (CA2 1971), cert denied, sub nom Oswald v Sostre, 405 US 978, 31 L Ed 2d 254, 92 S Ct 1190 (1972). At the other extreme some courts have been willing to require demonstration of a "compelling state interest" to justify censorship of prisoner mail. E.g., Jackson v Godwin, 400 F2d 529

[416 US 407]

(CA5 1968) (decided on both equal protection and First Amendment grounds); Morales v Schmidt, 340 F Supp 544 (WD Wis 1972); Fortune Society v McGinnis, 319 F Supp 901 (SDNY 1970). Other courts phrase the standard in similarly demanding terms of "clear and present danger." Wilkinson v Skinner, 462 F2d 670, 672-673 (CA2 1972). And there are various intermediate positions, most notably the view that a "regulation or practice which restricts the right of free expression that a prisoner would have enjoyed if he had not been imprisoned must be related both reasonably and necessarily to the advancement of some justifiable purpose." Carothers v Follette, 314 F Supp 1014, 1024 (SDNY 1970) (citations omitted). See also Gates v Collier, 349 F Supp 881, 896 (ND Miss 1972); LeMon v Zelker, 358 F Supp 554 (SDNY 1972).

This array of disparate approaches and the absence of any generally accepted standard for testing the constitutionality of prisoner mail censorship regulations disserve both the competing interests at stake. On the one hand, the First Amendment interests implicated by censorship of inmate correspondence are given only haphazard and inconsistent protection. On the other, the uncertainty of the constitutional standard makes it impossible for correctional officials to anticipate what is required of them and invites repetitive, piecemeal litigation on behalf of inmates. The result has been unnecessarily to perpetuate the involvement of the federal courts in affairs of prison administration. Our task is to formulate a standard of review for prisoner mail censorship that will be responsive to these concerns.

B

We begin our analysis of the proper standard of review for constitutional challenges to censorship of prisoner mail with a somewhat different premise from that taken

[416 US 408]

by the other federal courts that have considered the question. For the most part, these courts have dealt with challenges to censorship of prisoner mail as involving broad questions of "prisoners' rights." This case is no exception. The District Court stated the issue in general terms as "the applicability of First Amendment rights to prison inmates . . . ," 354 F Supp, at 1096, and the arguments of the parties reflect the assumption that the resolution of this case requires an assessment of the extent to which prisoners may claim First Amendment freedoms. In our view this inquiry is unnecessary. In determining the proper standard of review for prison restrictions on inmate correspondence, we have no occasion to consider the extent to which an individual's right to free speech survives incarceration, for a narrower basis of decision is at hand. In the case of direct personal correspondence between inmates and those who have a particularized interest in communicating with them, mail censorship implicates more than the right of prisoners.

Communications by letter is not accomplished by the act of writing words on paper. Rather, it is effected only when the letter is read by the addressee. Both parties to the correspondence have an interest in securing that result, and censorship of the communication between them necessarily impinges on the interest of each. Whatever the status of a prisoner's claim to uncensored correspondence with an outsider, it is plain that the latter's interest is grounded in the First Amendment's guarantee of freedom of speech. And this does not depend on whether the nonprisoner correspondent is the author or intended recipient of a particular letter, for the addressee as well as the sender of direct personal correspondence

[416 US 409]

derives from the First and Fourteenth Amendments a protection against unjustified governmental interference with the intended communication. Lamont v Postmaster General, 381 US 301, 14 L Ed 2d 398, 85 S Ct 1493 (1965). Accord Kleindienst v Mandel, 408 US 753, 762-765, 33 L Ed 2d 683, 92 S Ct 2576 (1972); Martin v City of Struthers, 319 US 141, 143, 87 L Ed 1313, 63 S Ct 862 (1943). We do not deal here with difficult questions of the so-called "right to hear" and third-party standing but with a particular means of communication in which the interests of both parties are inextricably meshed. The wife of a prison inmate who is not permitted to read all that her husband wanted to say to her has suffered an abridgment of her interest in communicating with him as plain as that which results from censorship of her letter to him. In either event, censorship of prisoner mail works a consequential restriction on the First and Fourteenth Amendments rights of those who are not prisoners.

Accordingly, we reject any attempt to justify censorship of inmate correspondence merely by reference to certain assumptions about the legal status of prisoners. Into this category of argument falls appellants' contention that "an inmate's rights with reference to social correspondence are something fundamentally different than those enjoyed by his free brother." Brief for Appellants 19. This line of argument and the undemanding standard of review it is intended to support fail to recognize that the First Amendment liberties of free citizens are implicated in censorship of prisoner mail. We therefore turn for guidance, not to cases involving questions of "prisoners' rights," but to decisions of this Court dealing with the general problem of incidental restrictions on First Amendment liberties imposed in furtherance of legitimate governmental activities.

As the Court noted in Tinker v Des Moines School District, 393 US 503, 506, 21 L Ed 2d 731, 89 S Ct 733 (1969), First Amendment

[416 US 410]

guarantees must be "applied in light of the special characteristics of the . . . environment." Tinker concerned the interplay between the right to freedom of speech of public high school students and "the need for affirming the comprehensive authority of the States and of school officials, consistent with fundamental constitutional safeguards, to prescribe and control conduct in the schools." Id., at 508, 21 L Ed 2d 731. In overruling a school regulation prohibiting the wearing of antiwar armbands, the Court undertook a careful analysis of the legitimate requirements of orderly school administration in order to ensure that the students were afforded maximum freedom of speech consistent with those requirements. The same approach was followed in Healy v James, 408 US 169, 33 L Ed 2d 266, 92 S Ct 2338 (1972), where the Court considered the refusal of a state college to grant official recognition to a group of students who wished to organize a local chapter of the Students for a Democratic Society (SDS), a national student organization noted for political activism and campus disruption. The Court found that neither the identification of the local student group with the national SDS, nor the purportedly dangerous political philosophy of the local group, nor the college administration's fear of future, unspecified disruptive activities by the students could justify the incursion on the right of free association. The Court also found, however, that this right could be limited if necessary to prevent campus disruption, id., at 189-190, n 20, 33 L Ed 2d 266, and remanded the case for determination of whether the students had in fact refused to accept reasonable regulations governing student conduct.

In United States v O'Brien, 391 US 367, 20 L Ed 2d 672, 88 S Ct 1673 (1968), the Court dealt with incidental restrictions on free speech occasioned by the exercise of the governmental power to conscript men for military service. O'Brien had burned his Selective Service registration certificate on the steps

[416 US 411]

of a courthouse in order to dramatize his opposition to the draft and to our country's involvement in Vietnam. He was convicted of violating a provision of the Selective Service law that had recently been amended to prohibit knowing destruction or mutilation of registration certificates. O'Brien argued that the purpose and effect of the amendment were to abridge free expression and that the statutory provision was therefore unconstitutional, both as enacted and as applied to him. Although O'Brien's activity involved "conduct" rather than pure "speech," the Court did not define away the First Amendment concern, and neither did it rule that the presence of a communicative intent necessarily rendered O'Brien's actions immune to governmental regulation. Instead, it enunciated the following four-part test:

"[A] government regulation is sufficiently justified if it is within the constitutional power of the Government; if it furthers an important or substantial governmental interest; if the governmental interest is unrelated to the suppression of free expression; and if the incidental restriction on alleged First Amendment freedoms is no greater than is essential to the furtherance of that interest." Id., at 377, 20 L Ed 2d 672.

Of course, none of these precedents directly controls the instant case. In O'Brien the Court considered a federal statute which on its face prohibited certain conduct having no necessary connection with freedom of speech. This led the Court to differentiate between "speech" and "nonspeech" elements of a single course of conduct, a

distinction that has little relevance here. Both Tinker and Healy concerned First and Fourteenth Amendment liberties in the context of state educational institutions, a circumstance involving rather different governmental interests than are at stake here. In broader terms, however, these precidents involved inci-

[416 US 412]

dental restrictions on First Amendment liberties by governmental action in furtherance of legitimate and substantial state interest other than suppression of expression. In this sense these cases are generally analogous to our present inquiry.

The case at hand arises in the context of prisons. One of the primary functions of government is the preservation of societal order through enforcement of the criminal law, and the maintenance of penal institutions is an essential part of that task. The identifiable governmental interests at stake in this task are the preservation of internal order and discipline, the maintenance of institutional security against escape or unauthorized entry, and the rehabilitation of the prisoners. While the weight of professional opinion seems to be that inmate freedom to correspond with outsiders advances rather than retards the goal of rehabilitation, the legitimate governmental

[416 US 413]

interest in the order and security of penal institutions justifies the imposition of certain restraints on inmate correspondence. Perhaps the most obvious example of justifiable censorship of prisoner mail would be refusal to send or deliver letters concerning escape plans or containing other information concerning proposed criminal activity, whether within or without the prison. Similarly, prison officials may properly refuse to transmit encoded messages. Other less obvious possibilities come to mind, but it is not our purpose to survey the range of circumstances in which particular restrictions on prisoner mail might be warranted by the legitimate demands of prison administration as they exist from time to time in the various kinds of penal institutions found in this country. Our task is to determine the proper standard for deciding whether a particular regulation or practice relating to inmate correspondence constitutes an impermissible restraint of First Amendment liberties.

Applying the teachings of our prior decisions to the instant context, we hold that censorship of prisoner mail is justified if the following criteria are met. First, the regulation or practice in question must further an important or substantial governmental interest unrelated to the suppression of expression. Prison officials may not censor inmate correspondence simply to eliminate unflattering or unwelcome opinions or factually inaccurate statements. Rather, they must show that a regulation authorizing mail censorship furthers one or more of the substantial governmental interests of security, order, and rehabilitation. Second, the limitation of First Amendment freedoms must be no greater than is necessary or essential to the protection of the particular governmental interest involved. Thus a restriction on inmate correspondence

[416 US 414]

that furthers an important or substantial interest of penal administration will nevertheless be invalid if its sweep is unnecessarily broad. This does not mean, of course, that prison administrators may be required to show with certainty that adverse consequences would flow from the failure to censor a particular letter. Some latitude in anticipating the probable consequences of allowing certain speech in a prison environment is essential to the proper discharge of an administrator's duty. But any regulation or practice that restricts inmate correspondence must be generally necessary to protect one or more of the legitimate governmental interests identified above.

[416 US 415]
C

On the basis of this standard, we affirm the judgment of the District Court. The regulations invalidated by that court authorized, inter alia, censorship of statements that "unduly complain" or "magnify grievances," expression of "inflammatory political, racial, religious or other views," and matter deemed "defamatory" or "otherwise inappropriate." These regulations fairly invited prison officials and employees to apply their own personal prejudices and opinions as standards for prisoner mail censorship. Not surprisingly, some prison officials used the extraordinary latitude for discretion authorized by the regulations to suppress unwelcome criticism. For example, at one institution under the Department's jurisdiction, the checklist used by the mailroom staff authorized rejection of letters "criticizing policy, rules or officials," and the mailroom sergeant stated in a deposition that he would reject as "defamatory" letters "belittling staff or our judicial system or anything connected with the Department of Corrections." Correspondence was also censored for "disrespectful comments," "derogatory remarks," and the like.

Appellants have failed to show that these broad restrictions on prisoner mail were in any way necessary to the furtherance of a governmental interest unrelated to the suppression of expression. Indeed, the heart of appellants' position is not that the regulations are justified by a legitimate governmental interest but that they do not need to be. This misconception is not only stated affirmatively; it also underlies appellants' discussion of the particular regulations under attack. For example, appellants' sole defense of the prohibition against matter that is "defamatory" or "otherwise inappropriate" is that

[416 US 416]

it is "within the discretion of prison administrators." Brief for Appellants 21. Appellants contend that statements that "magnify grievances" or "unduly complain" are censored "as a precaution against flash riots and in the furtherance of inmate rehabilitation." Brief for Appellants 22. But they do not suggest how the magnification of grievances or undue complaining, which presumably occur in outgoing letters, could possibly lead to flash riots, nor do they specify what contribution the suppression of complaints makes to the rehabilitation of criminals. And, appellants defend the ban against "inflammatory political, racial, or religious or other views" on the ground that "[s]uch matter clearly presents a danger to prison security..." Brief for Appellants 21. The regulation, however, is not narrowly drawn to reach only material that might be thought to encourage

violence nor is its application limited to incoming letters. In short, the Department's regulations authorized censorship of prison mail far broader than any legitimate interest of penal administration demands and were properly found invalid by the District Court.

[416 US 417]
D

We also agree with the District Court that the decision to censor or withhold delivery of a particular letter must be accompanied by minimum procedural safeguards.

[416 US 418]
The interest of prisoners and their correspondents in uncensored communication by letter, grounded as it is in the First Amendment, is plainly a "liberty" interest within the meaning of the Fourteenth Amendment even though qualified of necessity by the circumstance of imprisonment. As such, it is protected from arbitrary governmental invasion. See Board of Regents v Roth, 408 US 564, 33 L Ed 2d 548, 92 S Ct 2701 (1972); Perry v Sindermann, 408 US 593, 33 L Ed 2d 570, 92 S Ct 2694 (1972). The District Court required that an inmate be notified of the rejection of a letter written by or addressed to him, that the author of that letter be given a reasonable opportunity to protest that decision, and that complaints be referred to a prison official other than

[416 US 419]
the person who originally disapproved the correspondence. These requirements do not appear to be unduly burdensome, nor do appellants so contend. Accordingly, we affirm the judgment of the District Court with

respect to the Department's regulations relating to prisoner mail.

II

The District Court also enjoined continued enforcement of Administrative Rule MV-IV-02, which provides in pertinent part:

"Investigators for an attorney-of-record will be confined to not more than two. Such investigators must be licensed by the State or must be members of the State Bar. Designation must be made in writing by the Attorney."

By restricting access to prisoners to members of the bar and licensed private investigators, this regulation imposed an absolute ban on the use by attorneys of law students and legal paraprofessionals to interview inmate clients. In fact, attorneys could not even delegate to such persons the task of obtaining prisoners' signatures on legal documents. The District Court reasoned that this rule constituted an unjustifiable restriction on the right of access to the courts. We agree.

The constitutional guarantee of due process of law has as a corollary the requirement that prisoners be afforded access to the courts in order to challenge unlawful convictions and to seek redress for violations of their constitutional rights. This means that inmates must have a reasonable opportunity to seek and receive the assistance of attorneys. Regulations and practices that unjustifiably obstruct the availability of professional representation or other aspects of the right of access to the courts are invalid. Ex parte Hull, 312 US 546, 85 L Ed 1034, 61 S Ct 640 (1941).

[416 US 420]
The District Court found that the rule restricting attorney-client interviews to members of the bar and licensed private investigators inhibited adequate professional representation of indigent inmates. The remoteness of many California penal institutions makes a personal visit to an inmate client a time consuming undertaking. The court reasoned that the ban against the use of law students or other paraprofessionals for attorney-client interviews would deter some lawyers from representing prisoners who could not afford to pay for their traveling time or that of licensed private investigators. And those lawyers who agree to do so would waste time that might be employed more efficaciously in working on the inmates' legal problems. Allowing law students and paraprofessionals to interview inmates might well reduce the cost of legal representation for prisoners. The District Court therefore concluded that the regulation imposed a substantial burden on the right of access to the courts.

As the District Court recognized, this conclusion does not end the inquiry, for prison administrators are not required to adopt every proposal that may be thought to facilitate prisoner access to the courts. The extent to which that right is burdened by a particular regulation or practice must be weighed against the legitimate interests of penal administration and the proper regard that judges should give to the expertise and discretionary authority of correctional officials. In this case the ban against the use of law students and other paraprofessional personnel was absolute. Its prohibition was not limited to prospective interviewers who posed some colorable threat to security or to those inmates thought to be especially dangerous. Nor was it shown that a less restrictive regulation would unduly burden the administrative task of screening and monitoring visitors.

[416 US 421]

Appellants' enforcement of the regulation in question also created an arbitrary distinction between law students employed by practicing attorneys and those associated with law school programs providing legal assistance to prisoners. While the Department flatly prohibited interviews of any sort by law students working for attorneys, it freely allowed participants of a number of law school programs to enter the prisons and meet with inmates. These largely unsupervised students were admitted without any security check other than verification of their enrollment in a school program. Of course, the fact that appellants have allowed some persons to conduct attorney-client interviews with prisoners does not mean that they are required to admit others, but the arbitrariness of the distinction between the two categories of law students does reveal the absence of any real justification for the sweeping prohibition of Administrative Rule MV-IV-02. We cannot say that the District Court erred in invalidating this regulation.

This result is mandated by our decision in Johnson v Avery, 393 US 483, 21 L Ed 2d 718, 89 S Ct 747 (1969). There the Court struck down a prison regulation prohibiting any inmate from advising or assisting another in the preparation of legal documents. Given the inadequacy of alternative sources of legal assistance, the rule had the effect of denying to illiterate or poorly educated inmates any opportunity to vindicate possibly valid constitutional claims. The Court found that the regulation impermissibly burdened the right of access to the courts despite the not insignificant state interest in preventing the establishment of personal power structures by unscrupulous jailhouse lawyers and the attendant problems of prison discipline that

[416 US 422]

follow. The countervailing state interest in Johnson is, if anything, more persuasive than any interest advanced by appellants in the instant case.

The judgement is

Affirmed.

[Concurring opinions omitted.]

WOLFF v McDONNELL

418 US 539, 41 L Ed 2d 935, 94 S Ct 2963 (1974)

OPINION OF THE COURT
[Footnotes omitted]

[418 US 542]

Mr. Justice **White** delivered the opinion of the Court.

We granted the petition for writ of certiorari in this case, 414 US 1156, 39 L Ed 2d 108, 94 S Ct 913 (1974), because it raises important questions concerning the administration of a state prison.

Respondent, on behalf of himself and other inmates of the Nebraska Penal and Correctional Complex, Lincoln, Nebraska, filed a complaint under 42 USC § 1983 [42 USCS § 1983] challenging several of the practices, rules and regulations of the Complex. For present purposes, the pertinent

[418 US 543]

allegations were that disciplinary proceedings did not comply with the Due Process Clause of the Fourteenth Amendment to the Federal Constitution; that the inmate legal assistance program did not meet constitutional standards, and that the regulations governing the inspection of mail to and from attorneys for inmates were unconstitutionally restrictive. Respondent requested damages and injunctive relief.

After an evidentiary hearing, the District Court granted partial relief. 342 F Supp 616 (Neb 1972). Considering itself bound by prior Circuit authority, it rejected the procedural due process claim; but it went on to hold that the prison's policy of inspecting all incoming and outgoing mail to and from attorneys violated prisoners' rights of access to the courts and that the restrictions placed on inmate legal assistance were not constitutionally defective.

[418 US 544]

The Court of Appeals reversed, 483 F2d 1059 (CA8 1973), with respect to the due process claim, holding that the procedural requirements outlined by this Court in Morrissey v Brewer, 408 US 471, 33 L Ed 2d 484, 92 S Ct 2593 (1972), and Gagnon v Scarpelli, 411 US 778, 36 L Ed 2d 656, 93 S Ct 1756 (1973), decided after the District Court's opinion in this case, should be generally followed in prison disciplinary hearings but left the specific requirements, including the circumstances in which counsel might be required, to be determined by the District Court on remand. With respect to a remedy, the court further held that Preiser v Rodriguez, 411 US 475, 36 L Ed 2d 439, 93 S Ct 1827 (1973), forbade the actual restoration of good-time credits in this § 1983 suit but ordered expunged from prison records any determinations of misconduct arrived at in proceedings that failed to comport with due process as defined by the court. The court generally affirmed the judgment of the District Court with respect to correspondence with attorneys, but ordered further proceedings to determine whether the State was meeting its burden under Johnson v Avery, 393 US 483, 21 L Ed 2d 718, 89 S Ct 747 (1969), to provide legal assistance to prison inmates, the court holding that the State's duty extended to civil rights cases as well as to habeas corpus proceedings.

I

We begin with the due process claim. An understanding of the issues involved requires a detailing of the prison disciplinary regime set down by Nebraska statutes and prison regulations.

[418 US 545]

Section 16 of the Nebraska Treatment and Corrections Act, as amended, Neb Rev Stat § 83-185 (Cum Supp 1972), provides that the chief executive officer of each penal facility is responsible for the discipline of inmates

[418 US 546]

in a particular institution. The statute provides for a range of possible disciplinary action. "Except in flagrant or serious cases, punishment for misconduct shall consist of deprivation of privileges. In cases of flagrant or serious misconduct, the chief executive officer may order that a person's reduction of term as provided in section 83-1,107 [good-time credit] be forfeited or withheld and

[418 US 547]

also that the person be confined in a disciplinary cell." Each breach of discipline is to be entered in the person's file together with the disposition or punishment therefor.

As the statute makes clear, there are basically two kinds of punishment for flagrant or serious misconduct. The first is the forfeiture or withholding of good-time credits, which affects the term of confinement, while the second, confinement in a disciplinary cell, involves alteration of the conditions of confinement. If the misconduct is less than flagrant or serious, only deprivation of privileges results.

[418 US 548]

The only statutory provision establishing procedures for the imposition of disciplinary sanctions which pertains to good time, § 38 of the Nebraska Treatment and Corrections Act, as amended, Neb Rev Stat § 83-1,107 (Cum Supp 1972), merely requires that an inmate be "consulted regarding the charges of misconduct" in connection with the forfeiture, withholding, or restoration of credit. But prison authorities have framed written regulations dealing with procedures and policies for controlling inmate misconduct. By regulation, misconduct is

[418 US 549]

classified into two categories: major misconduct is a "serious violation" and must be formally reported to an Adjustment Committee, composed of the Associate Warden

[418 US 550]

Custody, the Correctional Industries Superintendent, and the Reception Center Director. This Committee is directed to "review and evaluate all misconduct reports"

[418 US 551]

and, among other things, to "conduct investigations, make findings, [and] impose disciplinary actions." If only minor misconduct, "a less serious violation," is involved,

[418 US 552]

the problem may either be resolved informally by the inmate's supervisor or it can be formally reported for action to the Adjustment Committee. Repeated minor misconduct must be reported. The Adjustment Committee has available a wide range of sanctions. "Disciplinary action taken and recommended may include but not necessarily be limited to the following: reprimand, restrictions of various kinds, extra duty, confinement in the Adjustment Center [the disciplinary cell], withholding the statutory good time and/or extra earned good time, or a combination of the elements listed herein."

Additional procedures have been devised by the Complex governing the actions of the Adjustment Committee. Based on the testimony, the District Court found, 342 F Supp, at 625-626, that the following procedures were in effect when an inmate is written up or charged with a prison violation:

"(a) The chief correction supervisor reviews the 'write-ups' on the inmates by the officers of the Complex daily;

[418 US 553]

"(b) the convict is called to a conference with the chief correction supervisor and the charging party;

"(c) following the conference, a conduct report is sent to the Adjustment Committee;

"(d) there follows a hearing before the Adjustment Committee and the report is read to the inmate and discussed;

"(e) if the inmate denies charge he may ask questions of the party writing him up;

"(f) the Adjustment Committee can conduct additional investigations if it desires;

"(g) punishment is imposed."

II

This class action brought by respondent alleged that the rules, practices, and procedures at the Complex which might result in the taking of good time violated the Due Process Clause of the Fourteenth Amendment. Respondent sought three types of relief: (1) the restoration of good time; (2) submission of a plan by the prison authorities for a hearing procedure in connection with withholding and forfeiture of good time which complied with the requirements of due process; and (3) damages for the deprivation of civil rights resulting from the use of the allegedly unconstitutional procedures. [Portion of opinion re: appropriateness of Civil Rights Action omitted.]

III

Petitioners assert that the procedure for disciplining prison inmates for serious misconduct is a matter of policy raising no constitutional issue. If the position implies that prisoners in state instutitions are wholly without the protections of the Constitution and the Due Process Clause, it is plainly untenable. Lawful imprisonment necessarily makes unavailable many rights and privileges of the ordinary citizen, a "retraction justified by the considerations underlying our penal system." Price v Johnston, 334 US 266, 285, 92 L Ed 1356, 68 S Ct 1049 (1948). But though his rights may be diminished by the needs and exigencies of the institutional environment, a prisoner is not wholly stripped of constitutional protections when he is imprisoned for crime. There is no iron curtain

[418 US 556]

drawn between the Constitution and the prisons of this country. Prisoners have been held to enjoy substantial religious freedom under the First and Fourteenth Amendments. Cruz v Beto, 405 US 319, 31 L Ed 2d 263, 92 S Ct 1079 (1972); Cooper v Pate, 378 US 546, 12 L Ed 2d 1030, 84 S Ct 1733 (1964). They retain right of access to the courts. Younger v Gilmore, 404 US 15, 30 L Ed 2d 142, 92 S Ct 250 (1971), affg Gilmore v Lynch, 319 F Supp 105 (ND Cal 1970); Johnson v Avery, 393 US 483, 21 L Ed 2d 718, 89 S Ct 747 (1969); Ex parte Hull, 312 US 546, 85 L Ed 1034, 61 S Ct 640 (1941). Prisoners are protected under the Equal Protection Clause of the Fourteenth Amendment from invidious discrimination based on race. Lee v Washington, 390 US 333, 19 L Ed 2d 1212, 88 S Ct 994 (1968). Prisoners may also claim the protections of the Due Process Clause. They may not be deprived of life, liberty, or property without due process of law. Haines v Kerner, 404 US 519, 30 L Ed 2d 652, 92 S Ct 594 (1972); Wilwording v Swenson, 404 US 249, 30 L Ed 2d 418, 92 SCt 407 (1971); Screws v United States, 325 US 91, 89 L Ed 1495, 65 S Ct 1031, 162 ALR 1330 (1945).

Of course, as we have indicated, the fact that prisoners retain rights under the Due Process Clause in no way implies that these rights are not subject to restrictions imposed by the nature of the regime to which they have been lawfully committed. Cf. CSC v Letter Carriers, 413 US 548, 37 L Ed 2d 796, 93 S Ct 2880 (1973); Broadrick v Oklahoma, 413 US 601, 37 L Ed 2d 830, 93 S Ct 2908 (1973); Parker v Levy, 417 US 733, 41 L Ed 2d 439, 94 S Ct 2547 (1974). Prison disciplinary proceedings are not part of a criminal prosecution, and the full panoply of rights due a defendant in such proceedings does not apply. Cf. Morrissey v Brewer, 408 US, at 488, 33 L Ed 2d 484. In sum, there must be mutual accommodation between institutional needs and objectives and the provisions of the Constitution that are of general application.

We also reject the assertion of the State that whatever may be true of the Due Process Clause in general or of other rights protected by that Clause against state infringement, the interest of prisoners in disciplinary procedures

[418 US 557]

is not included in that "liberty" protected by the Fourteenth Amendment. It is true that the Constitution itself does not guarantee good time credit for satisfactory behavior while in prison. But here the State itself has not only provided a statutory right to good-time but also specifies that it is to be forfeited only for serious misbehavior. Nebraska may have the authority to create, or not, a right to a shortened prison sentence through the accumulation of credits for good behavior, and it is true that the Due Process Clause does not require a hearing "in every conceivable case of government impairment of private interest." Cafeteria Workers v McElroy, 367 US 886, 894, 6 L Ed 2d 1230, 81 S Ct 1743 (1961). But the State having created the right to good time and itself recognizing that its deprivation is a sanction authorized for major misconduct, the prisoner's interest has real substance and is sufficiently embraced within Fourteenth Amendment "liberty" to entitle him to those minimum procedures appropriate under the circumstances and required by the Due Process Clause to insure that the state-created right is not arbitrarily abrogated. This is the thrust of recent cases in the prison disciplinary context. In Haines v Kerner, supra, the state prisoner asserted a "denial of due process in the steps leading to [disciplinary] confinement." 404 US, at 520, 30 L Ed 2d 652. We reversed the dismissal of the § 1983 complaint for failure to state a claim. In Preiser v Rodriguez, supra, the prisoner complained that he had been deprived of good-time credits without notice or hearing and without due process of law. We considered the claim a proper subject for a federal habeas corpus proceeding.

This analysis as to liberty parallels the accepted due process analysis as to property. The Court has consistently held that some kind of hearing is required at some time before a person is finally deprived of his property

[418 US 558]

interests. Anti-Fascist Committee v McGrath, 341 US 123, 168, 95 L Ed 817, 71 S Ct 624 (1951) (Frankfurter, J., concurring). The requirement for some kind of a hearing applies to the taking of private property, Grannis v Ordean, 234 US 385, 58 L Ed 1363, 34 S Ct 779 (1914), the revocation of licenses, In re Ruffalo, 390 US 544, 20 L Ed 2d 117, 88 S Ct 1222 (1968), the operation of state dispute settlement mechanisms, when one person seeks to take property from another, or to government-created jobs held absent "cause" for termination, Board of Regents v Roth, 408 US 564, 33 L Ed 2d 548, 92 S Ct 2701 (1972); Arnett v Kennedy, 416 US 134, 164, 40 L Ed 2d 15, 94 S Ct 1633 (1974) (Powell, J., concurring); id., at 171, 40 L Ed 2d, at 15 (White, J., concurring in part and dissenting in part); id., 206, 40 L Ed 2d 15 (Marshall, J., dissenting). Cf. Stanley v Illinois, 405 US 645, 652-654, 31 L Ed 2d 551, 92 S Ct 1208 (1972); Bell v Burson, 402 US 535, 29 L Ed 2d 90, 91 S Ct 1586 (1971).

We think a person's liberty is equally protected, even when the liberty itself is a statutory creation of the State. The touchstone of due process is protection of the individual against arbitrary action of government, Dent v West Virginia, 129 US 114, 123, 32 L Ed 623, 9 S Ct 231 (1899). Since prisoners in Nebraska can only lose good-time credits if they are guilty of serious misconduct, the determination of whether such behavior has occurred becomes critical, and the minimum requirements of procedural due process appropriate for the circumstances must be observed.

IV

As found by the District Court, the procedures employed are: (1) a preliminary conference with the chief corrections supervisor and the charging party, where the prisoner is informed of the misconduct charge and engages in preliminary discussion on its merits; (2) the preparation of a conduct report and a hearing held before the Adjustment Committee, the disciplinary body of the prison, where the report is read to the inmate; and

[418 US 559]

(3) the opportunity at the hearing to ask questions of the charging party. The State contends that the procedures already provided are adequate. The

Court of Appeals held them insufficient and ordered that the due process requirements outlined in Morrissey and Scarpelli be satisfied in serious disciplinary cases at the prison.

Morrissey held that due process imposed certain minimum procedural requirements which must be satisfied before parole could finally be revoked. These procedures were:

"(a) written notice of the claimed violations of parole; (b) disclosure to the parolee of evidence against him; (c) opportunity to be heard in person and to present witnesses and documentary evidence; (d) the right to confront and cross-examine adverse witnesses (unless the hearing officer specifically finds good cause for not allowing confrontation); (e) a 'neutral and detached' hearing body such as a traditional parole board, members of which need not be judicial officers or lawyers; and (f) a written statement by the factfinders as to the evidence relied on and reasons for revoking parole." 408 US, at 489, 33 L Ed 2d 484.

The Court did not reach the question as to whether the parolee is entitled to the assistance of retained counsel or to appointed counsel, if he is indigent. Following the decision in Morrissey, in Gagnon v Scarpelli, 411 US 778, 36 L Ed 2d 656, 93 S Ct 1756 (1973), the Court held the requirements of due process established for parole revocation were applicable to probation revocation proceedings. The Court added to the required minimum procedures of Morrissey the right to counsel, where a probationer makes a request, "based on a timely and colorable claim (i) that he has not committed the alleged violation of the conditions upon which he is at liberty;

or (ii) that, even if the violation

[418 US 560]

is a matter of public record or is uncontested, there are substantial reasons which justified or mitigated the violation and make revocation inappropriate, and that the reasons are complex or otherwise difficult to develop or present." Id., at 790, 36 L Ed 2d 656. In doubtful cases, the agency was to consider whether the probationer appeared to be capable of speaking effectively for himself, id., at 790-791, 36 L Ed 2d 656, and a record was to be made of the grounds for refusing to appoint counsel.

We agree with neither petitioners nor the Court of Appeals: the Nebraska procedures are in some respects constitutionally deficient but the Morrissey-Scarpelli procedures need not in all respects be followed in disciplinary cases in state prisons.

We have often repeated that "[t]he very nature of due process negates any concept of inflexible procedures universally applicable to every imaginable situation." Cafeteria Workers v McElroy, 367 US, at 895, 6 L Ed 2d 1230. "[C]onsideration of what procedures due process may require under any given set of circumstances must begin with a determination of the precise nature of the government function involved as well as of the private interest that has been affected by governmental action." Ibid.; Morrissey, 408 US, at 481, 33 L Ed 2d 484, 92 S Ct 2593. Viewed in this light it is immediately apparent that one cannot automatically apply procedural rules designed for free citizens in an open society, or for parolees or probationers under only limited restraints, to the very different situation presented by a disciplinary proceeding in a state prison.

Revocation of parole may deprive the parolee of only conditional liberty, but it nevertheless "inflicts a 'grievous loss' on the parolee and often on others." Id., at 482, 33 L Ed 2d 484. Simply put, revocation proceedings determine whether the parolee will be free or in prison, a matter of obvious great moment to him. For the prison inmate,

[418 US 561]

the deprivation of good time is not the same immediate disaster that the revocation of parole is for the parolee. The deprivation, very likely, does not then and there work any change in the conditions of his liberty. It can postpone the date of eligibility for parole and extend the maximum term to be served, but it is not certain to do so, for good time may be restored. Even if not restored, it cannot be said with certainty that the actual date of parole will be affected; and if parole occurs, the extension of the maximum term resulting from loss of good time may affect only the termination of parole, and it may not even do that. The deprivation of good time is unquestionably a matter of considerable importance. The State reserves it as a sanction for serious misconduct, and we should not unrealistically discount its significance. But it is qualitatively and quantitatively different from the revocation of parole or probation.

In striking the balance that the Due Process Clause demands, however, we think the major consideration militating against adopting the full range of procedures suggested by Morrissey for alleged parole violators is the very different stake the State has in the structure and content of the prison disciplinary hearing. That the revocation

of parole be justified and based on an accurate assessment of the facts is a critical matter to the State as well as the parolee; but the procedures by which it is determined whether the conditions of parole have been breached do not themselves threaten other important state interests, parole officers, the police, or witnesses — at least no more so than in the case of the ordinary criminal trial. Prison disciplinary proceedings, on the other hand, take place in a closed, tightly controlled environment peopled by those who have chosen to violate the criminal law and who have been lawfully incarcerated for doing so. Some are first offenders, but many are recidivists who

[418 US 562]

have repeatedly employed illegal and often very violent means to attain their ends. They may have little regard for the safety of others or their property or for the rules designed to provide an orderly and reasonably safe prison life. Although there are very many varieties of prisons with different degrees of security, we must realize that in many of them the inmates are closely supervised and their activities controlled around the clock. Guards and inmates co-exist in direct and intimate contact. Tension between them is unremitting. Frustration, resentment, and despair are commonplace. Relationships among the inmates are varied and complex and perhaps subject to the unwritten code that exhorts inmates not to inform on a fellow prisoner.

It is against this background that disciplinary proceedings must be structured by prison authorities; and it is against this background that we must make our constitutional judgments, realizing that we are dealing with the maximum security institution as well as those where security considerations are not so paramount. The reality is that disciplinary hearings and the imposition of disagreeable sanctions necessarily involve confrontations between inmates and authority and between inmates who are being disciplined and those who would charge or furnish evidence against them. Retaliation is much more than a theoretical possibility; and the basic and unavoidable task of providing reasonable personal safety for guards and inmates may be at stake, to say nothing of the impact of disciplinary confrontations and the resulting escalation of personal antagonisms on the important aims of the correctional process.

Indeed, it is pressed upon us that the proceedings to ascertain and sanction misconduct themselves play a major role in furthering the institutional goal of modifying the behavior and value systems of prison inmates

[418 US 563]

sufficiently to permit them to live within the law when they are released. Inevitably there is a great range of personality and character among those who have transgressed the criminal law. Some are more amenable to suggestion and persuasion than others. Some may be incorrigible and would merely disrupt and exploit the disciplinary process for their own ends. With some, rehabilitation may be best achieved by simulating procedures of a free society to the maximum possible extent; but with others, it may be essential that discipline be swift and sure. In any event, it is argued, there would be great unwisdom in encasing the disci-

plinary procedures in an inflexible constitutional straitjacket that would necessarily call for adversary proceedings typical of the criminal trial, very likely raise the level of confrontation between staff and inmate, and make more difficult the utilization of the disciplinary process as a tool to advance the rehabilitative goals of the institution. This consideration, along with the necessity to maintain an acceptable level of personal security in the institution, must be taken into account as we now examine in more detail the Nebraska procedures that the Court of Appeals found wanting.

V

Two of the procedures that the Court held should be extended to parolees facing revocation proceedings are not, but must be, provided to prisoners in the Nebraska Complex if the minimum requirements of procedural due process are to be satisfied. These are advance written notice of the claimed violation and a written statement of the factfindings as to the evidence relied upon and the reasons for the disciplinary action taken. As described

[418 US 564]

by the Warden in his oral testimony, on the basis of which the District Court made its findings, the inmate is now given oral notice of the charges against him at least as soon as the conference with the chief correction officer and charging party. A written record is there compiled and the report read to the inmate at the hearing before the Adjustment Committee where the charges are discussed and pursued. There is no indication that the inmate is ever given a written statement by the Committee as to the evidence or informed in writing or otherwise as to the reasons for the disciplinary action taken.

Part of the function of notice is to give the charged party a chance to marshal the facts in his defense and to clarify what the charges are, in fact. See In re Gault, 387 US 1, 33-34, and n 54, 18 L Ed 2d 527, 87 S Ct 1428 (1967). Neither of these functions was performed by the notice described by the Warden. Although the charges are discussed orally with the inmate somewhat in advance of the hearing, the inmate is sometimes brought before the Adjustment Committee shortly after he is orally informed of the charges. Other times, after this initial discussion, further investigation takes place which may reshape the nature of the charges or the evidence relied upon. In those instances, under procedures in effect at the time of trial, it would appear that the inmate first receives notice of the actual charges at the time of the hearing before the Adjustment Committee. We hold that written notice of the charges must be given to the disciplinary-action defendant in order to inform him of the charges and to enable him to marshal the facts and prepare a defense. At least a brief period of time after the notice, no less than 24 hours, should be allowed to the inmate to prepare for the appearance before the Adjustment Committee.

We also hold that there must be a "written statement by the factfinders as to the evidence relied on and reasons" for the disciplinary action. Morrissey, 408 US, at

[418 US 565]

489, 33 L Ed 2d 484. Although Nebraska does not seem to provide administrative review of the action taken by the Adjustment Committee, the actions taken at such proceedings may involve review by other bodies. They might furnish the basis of a decision by the Director of Corrections to transfer an inmate to another institution because he is considered "to be incorrigible by reason of frequent intentional breaches of discipline," Neb Rev Stat § 83-185 (4) (Cum Supp 1972), and are certainly likely to be considered by the state parole authorities in making parole decisions. Written records of proceedings will thus protect the inmate against collateral consequences based on a misunderstanding of the nature of the original proceeding. Further, as to the disciplinary action itself, the provision for a written record helps to insure that administrators, faced with possible scrutiny by state officials and the public, and perhaps even the courts, where fundamental constitutional rights may have been abridged, will act fairly. Without written records, the inmate will be at a severe disadvantage in propounding his own cause to or defending himself from others. It may be that there will be occasions when personal or institutional safety are so implicated, that the statement may properly exclude certain items of evidence, but in that event the statement should indicate the fact of the omission. Otherwise, we perceive no conceivable rehabilitative objective or prospect of prison disruption that can flow from the requirement of these statements.

[418 US 566]

We are also of the opinion that the inmate facing disciplinary proceedings should be allowed to call witnesses and present documentary evidence in his defense when permitting him to do so will not be unduly hazardous to institutional safety or correctional goals. Ordinarily, the right to present evidence is basic to a fair hearing; but the unrestricted right to call witnesses from the prison population carries obvious potential for disruption and for interference with the swift punishment that in individual cases may be essential to carrying out the correctional program of the institution. We should not be too ready to exercise oversight and put aside the judgment of prison administrators. It may be that an individual threatened with serious sanctions would normally be entitled to present witnesses and relevant documentary evidence; but here we must balance the inmate's interest in avoiding loss of good time against the needs of the prison, and some amount of flexibility and accommodation is required. Prison officials must have the necessary discretion to keep the hearing within reasonable limits and to refuse to call witnesses that may create a risk of reprisal or undermine authority, as well as to limit access to other inmates to collect statements or to compile other documentary evidence. Although we do not prescribe it, it would be useful for the Committee to state its reason for refusing to call a witness, whether it be for irrelevance, lack of necessity, or the hazards presented in individual cases. Any less flexible rule appears untenable as a constitutional matter, at least on the record made in this case. The operation of a correctional institution is at best an extraordinarily difficult undertaking. Many prison officials, on the spot and with the responsibility for the safety of inmates and staff, are reluctant to extend the unqualified right to call witnesses; and in our view, they must have the necessary discretion without being subject to unduly crippling constitutional

[418 US 567]

impediments. There is this much play in the joints of the Due Process Clause, and we stop short of imposing a more demanding rule with respect to witnesses and documents..

Confrontation and cross-examination present greater hazards to institutional interests. If confrontation and cross-examination of those furnishing evidence against the inmate were to be allowed as a matter of course, as in criminal trials, there would be considerable potential for havoc inside the prison walls. Proceedings would inevitably be longer and tend to unmanageability. These procedures are essential in criminal trials where the accused, if found guilty, may be subjected to the most serious deprivations, Pointer v Texas, 380 US 400, 13 L Ed 2d 923, 85 S Ct 1065 (1965), or where a person may lose his job in society, Greene v McElroy, 360 US 474, 496-497, 3 L Ed 2d 1377, 79 S Ct 1400 (1959). But they are not rights universally applicable to all hearings. See Arnett v Kennedy, 416 US 134, 40 L Ed 2d 15, 94 S Ct 1633 (1974). Rules of procedure may be shaped by consideration of the risks of error, In re Winship, 397 US 358, 368, 25 L Ed 2d 368, 90 S Ct 1068 (1970) (Harlan, J., concurring); Arnett v Kennedy, supra, p 171, 40 L Ed 2d 15, (White, J., concurring in part and dissenting in part), and should also be shaped by the consequences which will follow their adoption. Although some States do seem to allow cross-examination in disciplinary hearings, we are not apprised of the conditions under which

[418 US 568]

the procedure may be curtailed; and it does not appear that confrontation and cross-examination are generally required in this context. We think that the Constitution should not be read to impose the procedure at the present time and that adequate bases for decision in prison disciplinary cases can be arrived at without cross-examination.

Perhaps as the problems of penal institutions change and correctional goals are reshaped, the balance of interests involved will require otherwise. But in the current environment, where prison disruption remains a serious concern to administrators, we cannot ignore the desire and effort of many States, including Nebraska, and the Federal Government, to avoid situations that may trigger deep emotions and that may scuttle the disciplinary process as a rehabilitation vehicle. To some extent, the American adversary trial presumes contestants who are able to cope with the pressures and aftermath of the battle, and such may not generally be the case of those in the prisons of this country. At least, the Constitution, as we interpret it today, does not require the contrary assumption. Within the limits set forth in this opinion we are content for now to leave the continuing development of measures to review adverse actions affecting inmates to the sound discretion of corrections officials administering the scope of such inquiries.

We recognize that the problems of potential disruption may differ depending on whom the inmate proposes to cross-examine. If he proposes to examine an unknown fellow inmate, the danger may be the greatest, since the disclosure of the identity of the accuser, and the cross-examination which will follow, may pose a high risk of reprisal within the institution. Conversely, the inmate accuser, who might freely tell his story privately to prison officials, may refuse to testify or admit any knowledge of the situation in question. Although the dangers posed by

[418 US 569]

cross-examination of known inmate accusers, or guards, may be less, the resentment which may persist after confrontation may still be substantial. Also, even where the accuser or adverse witness is known, the disclosure of third parties may pose a problem. There may be a class of cases where the facts are closely disputed, and the character of the parties minimizes the dangers involved. However, any constitutional rule tailored to meet these situations would undoubtedly produce great litigation and attendant costs in a much wider range of cases. Further, in the last analysis, even within the narrow range of cases where interest balancing may well dictate cross-examination, courts will be faced with the assessment of prison officials as to the dangers involved, and there would be a limited basis for upsetting such judgments. The better course at this time, in a period where prisons practices are diverse and somewhat experimental, is to leave these matters to the sound discretion of the officials of state prisons.

As to the right to counsel, the problem as outlined in Scarpelli with respect to parole and probation revocation proceedings is even more pertinent here:

"The introduction of counsel into a revocation proceeding will alter significantly the nature of the proceeding. If counsel is provided for the probationer or parolee, the State in turn will normally provide its own counsel; lawyers, by training and disposition, are advocates and bound by professional duty to present all available evidence and arguments in support of their clients' positions and to contest with vigor all adverse evidence and views. The role of the hearing body itself, aptly described in Morrissey as being 'predictive and discretionary' as well as factfinding, may become more akin to that of a judge at a trial, and less attuned to the rehabilitative

[418 US 570]

needs of the individual probationer or parolee. In the greater self-consciousness of its quasi-judicial role, the hearing body may be less tolerant of marginal deviant behavior and feel more pressure to reincarcerate than to continue nonpunitive rehabilitation. Certainly, the decision-making process will be prolonged, and the financial cost to the State — for appointed counsel, counsel for the State, a longer record, and the posibility of judicial review — will not be insubstantial." 411 US, at 787-788, 36 L Ed 2d 656 (footnote omitted).

The insertion of counsel into the disciplinary process would inevitably give the proceedings a more adversary cast and tend to reduce their utility as a means to further correctional goals. There would also be delay and very practical problems in providing counsel in sufficient numbers at the time and place where hearings are to be held. At this stage of the development of these procedures we are not prepared to hold that inmates have a right to either retained or appointed counsel in disciplinary proceedings.

Where an illiterate inmate is involved, however, or where the complexity of the issue makes it unlikely that the inmate will be able to collect and present the evidence necessary for an adequate comprehension of the case, he should be free to seek the aid of a fellow inmate, or if that is forbidden, to have adequate substitute aid in the form of help from the staff or from a sufficiently competent inmate designated by the staff. We need not pursue the matter further here, however, for there is no claim that respondent McDonnell, is within the class of inmates entitled to advice or help from others in the course of a prison disciplinary hearing.

Finally, we decline to rule that the Adjustment Committee which conducts the required hearings at the Nebraska

[418 US 571]

Prison Complex and determines whether to revoke good time is not sufficiently impartial to satisfy the Due Process Clause. The Committee is made up of the Associate Warden Custody as chairman, the Correctional Industries Superintendent, and the Reception Center Director. The Chief Corrections Officer refers cases to the Committee after investigation and an initial interview with the inmate involved. The Committee is not left at large with unlimited discretion. It is directed to meet daily and to operate within the principles stated in the controlling regulations, among which is the command that "[f]ull consideration must be given to the causes for the adverse behavior, the setting and circumstances in which it occurred, the man's accountability, and the correctional treatment goals," as well as the direction that "disciplinary measures will be taken only at such times and to such degrees as are necessary to regulate and control a man's behavior within acceptable limits and will never be rendered capriciously or in the nature of retaliation or revenge." We find no warrant in the record presented here for concluding that the Adjustment Committee presents such a hazard of arbitrary decisionmaking that it should be held violative of due process of law.

Our conclusion that some, but not all, of the procedures specified in Morrissey and Scarpelli must accompany the deprivation of good time by state prison authorities is

[418 US 572]

not graven in stone. As the nature of the prison disciplinary process changes in future years, circumstances may then exist which will require further consideration and reflection of this Court. It is our view, however, that the procedures we have now required in prison disciplinary proceedings represent a reasonable accommodation between the interests of the inmates and the needs of the institution.

[418 US 573]

VI

The Court of Appeals held that the due process requirements in prison disciplinary proceedings were to apply retroactively so as to require that prison records containing determinations of misconduct, not in accord with required procedures, be expunged. We disagree and reverse on this point.

The question of retroactivity of new procedural rules affecting inquiries into infractions of prison discipline is effectively foreclosed by this Court's ruling in Morrissey that the due process requirements there announced were to be "applicable to *future* revocations of parole," 408 US, at 490, 33 L Ed 2d 484 (emphasis supplied). Despite the fact that procedures are related to the integrity of the factfinding

[418 US 574]

process, in the context of disciplinary proceedings, where less is generally at stake for an individual than at a criminal trial, great weight should be given to the significant impact a retroactivity ruling would have on the administration of all prisons in the country, and the reliance prison officials placed, in good faith, on prior law not requiring such procedures. During 1973, the Federal Government alone conducted 19,000 misconduct hearings, as compared with 1,173 parole revocation hearings, and 2,023 probation revocation hearings. If Morrissey-Scarpelli rules are not retroactive out of consideration for the burden on federal and state officials, this case is a fortiori. We also note that a contrary holding would be very troublesome for the parole system since performance in prison is often a relevant criterion for parole. On the whole, we do not think that error was so pervasive in the system under the old procedures as to warrant this cost or result.

VII

The issue of the extent to which prison authorities can open and inspect incoming mail from attorneys to inmates, has been considerably narrowed in the course of this litigation. The prison regulation under challenge provided that "[a]ll incoming and outgoing mail will be read and inspected," and no exception was made for attorney-prisoner mail. The District Court held that incoming mail from attorneys might be opened if normal contraband detection techniques failed to disclose contraband, and if there was a reasonable possibility that contraband would be included in the mail. It further held that if an incoming letter was marked "privileged," thus identifying it as from an attorney, the letter could not be opened except in the presence of the inmate. Prison authorities were not to read the mail from attorneys. The Court of Appeals affirmed the District Court order,

[418 US 575]

but placed additional restrictions on prison authorities. If there was doubt that a letter was actually from an attorney, "a simple telephone call should be enough to settle the matter," 483 F2d, at 1067, the court thus implying that officials might have to go beyond the face of the envelope, and the "privileged" label, in ascertaining what kind of communication was involved. The court further stated that "the danger that a letter from an attorney, an officer of the court, will contain contraband is ordinarily too remote and too speculative to justify the [petitioners'] regulation permitting the opening and inspection of all legal mail." Ibid. While methods to detect contraband could be employed, a letter was to be opened only "in the appropriate circumstances" in the presence of the inmate.

Petitioners now concede that they cannot open and *read* mail from attorneys to inmates, but contend that they may open all letters from attorneys as long as it is done in the presence of the

prisoners. The narrow issue thus presented is whether letters determined or found to be from attorneys may be opened by prison authorities in the presence of the inmate or whether such mail must be delivered unopened if normal detection techniques fail to indicate contraband.

Respondent asserts that his First, Sixth, and Fourteenth Amendment rights are infringed, under a procedure whereby the State may open mail from his attorney, even though in his presence and even though it may not be read. To begin with, the constitutional status of the rights asserted, as applied in this situation, is far from clear. While First Amendment rights of correspondents with prisoners may protect against the censoring of inmate mail, when not necessary to protect legitimate governmental interests, see Procunier v Martinez, 416 US 396, 40 L Ed 2d 224, 94 S Ct 1800 (1974), this Court has not yet recognized First

[418 US 576]

Amendment rights of prisoners in this context, cf. Cruz v Beto, 405 US 319, 31 L Ed 2d 263, 92 S Ct 1079 (1972); Cooper v Pate, 378 US 546, 12 L Ed 2d 1030, 84 S Ct 1733 (1964). Furthermore, freedom from censorship is not equivalent to freedom from inspection or perusal. As to the Sixth Amendment, its reach is only to protect the attorney-client relationship from intrusion in the criminal setting, see Black v United States, 385 US 26, 17 L Ed 2d 26, 87 S Ct 190 (1966); O'Brien v United States, 386 US 345, 18 L Ed 2d 94, 87 S Ct 1158 (1967); see also Coplon v United States, 89 US App DC 103, 191 F2d 749 (1951), while the claim here would insulate all mail from inspection, whether related to civil or criminal matters. Finally, the

Fourteenth Amendment due process claim based on access to the courts, Ex parte Hull, 312 US 546, 85 L Ed 1034, 61 S Ct 640 (1941); Johnson v Avery, 393 US 483, 21 L Ed 2d 718, 89 S Ct 747 (1969); Younger v Gilmore, 404 US 15, 30 L Ed 2d 142, 92 S Ct 250 (1971), has not been extended by this Court to apply further than protecting the ability of an inmate to prepare a petition or complaint. Moreover, even if one were to accept the argument that inspection of incoming mail from an attorney placed an obstacle to access to the court, it is far from clear that this burden is a substantial one. We need not decide, however, which, if any, of the asserted rights are operative here, for the question is whether, assuming some constitutional right is implicated, it is infringed by the procedure now found acceptable by the State.

In our view, the approach of the Court of Appeals is unworkable and none of the above rights is infringed by the procedures petitioners now accept. If prison officials had to check in each case whether a communication was from an attorney before opening it for inspection, a near-impossible task of administration would be imposed. We think it entirely appropriate that the State require any such communications to be specially marked as originating from an attorney, with his name and address being given, if they are to receive special treatment. It would also certainly be permissible that prison authorities require

[418 US 577]

that a lawyer desiring to correspond with a prisoner, first identify himself and his client to the prison officials, to assure that the letters marked privileged are actually from members of the bar. As

to the ability to open the mail in the presence of inmates, this could in no way constitute censorship, since the mail would not be read. Neither could it chill such communications, since the inmate's presence insures that prison officials will not read the mail. The possibility that contraband will be enclosed in letters, even those from apparent attorneys, surely warrants prison officials' opening the letters. We disagree with the Court of Appeals that this should only be done in "appropriate circumstances." Since a flexible test, besides being unworkable, serves no arguable purpose in protecting any of the possible constitutional rights enumerated by respondent, we think that petitioners, by acceding to a rule whereby the inmate is present when mail from attorneys is inspected, have done all, and perhaps even more, than the Constitution requires.

VIII

The last issue presented is whether the Complex must make available, and if so has made available, adequate legal assistance, under Johnson v Avery, supra, for the preparation of habeas corpus petitions and civil rights actions by inmates. The issue arises in the context of a challenge to a regulation providing, in pertinent part:

"Legal Work
"A legal advisor has been appointed by the Warden for the benefit of those offenders who are in need of legal assistance. This individual is an offender who has general knowledge of the law procedure. He is not an attorney and can not represent you as such.
"No other offender than the legal ad-

visor is permitted to assist you in the preparation of legal documents

[418 US 578]

unless with the specific written permission of the Warden."

Respondent contended that this regulation was invalid because it failed to allow inmates to furnish assistance to one another. The District Court assumed that the Warden freely gave permission to inmates to give assistance to each other, and that Johnson v Avery, supra, was thereby satisfied. The Court of Appeals found that the record did not support the assumption and that permission has been denied soley because of the existence of the inmate legal advisor, one of the inmates specially approved by the prison authorities. It decided, therefore, to remand the case to decide whether the one advisor satisfied the requirements of Johnson v Avery. In so doing, the court stated that in determining the need for legal assistance, petitioners were to take into account the need for assistance in civil rights actions as well as habeas corpus suits.

In Johnson v Avery, an inmate was disciplined for violating a prison regulation which prohibited inmates from assisting other prisoners in preparing habeas corpus petitions. The Court held that "unless and until the State provides some reasonable alternative to assist inmates in the preparation of petitions for post-conviction relief," inmates could not be barred from furnishing assistance to each other. 393 US, at 490, 21 L Ed 2d 718. The court emphasized that the writ of habeas corpus was of fundamental importance in our constitutional scheme, and since the basic purpose of the writ

"is to enable those unlawfully incarcerated to obtain their freedom, it is fundamental that access of prisoners to the courts for the purpose of presenting their complaints may not be denied or obstructed." Id., at 485, 21 L Ed 2d 718. Following Avery, the Court, in Younger v Gilmore, supra, affirmed a three-judge court judgment which required state officials to provide indigent

[418 US 579]

inmates with access to a reasonably adequate law library for preparation of legal actions.

Petitioners contend that Avery is limited to assistance in the preparation of habeas corpus petitions and disputes the direction of the Court of Appeals to the District Court that the capacity of the inmate adviser be assessed in light of the demand for assistance in civil rights actions as well as in the preparation of habeas writs. Petitioners take too narrow a view of that decision.

First, the demarcation line between civil rights actions and habeas petitions is not always clear. The Court has already recognized instances where the same constitutional rights might be redressed under either form of relief. Cf. Preiser v Rodriguez, 411 US 475, 36 L Ed 2d 439, 93 S Ct 1827 (1973); Haines v Kerner, 404 US 519, 30 L Ed 2d 652, 92 S Ct 594 (1972); Wilwording v Swenson, 404 US 249, 30 L Ed 2d 418, 92 S Ct 407 (1971). Second, while it is true that only in habeas actions may relief be granted which will shorten the term of confinement, Preiser, supra, it is more pertinent that both actions serve to protect basic constitutional rights. The right of access to the courts, upon which Avery was premised, is founded in the Due Process Clause and assures that no person will be denied the opportunity to present to the judiciary allegations concerning violations of fundamental constitutional rights. It is futile to contend that the Civil Rights Act of 1871 has less importance in our constitutional scheme than does the Great Writ. The recognition by this Court that prisoners have certain constitutional rights which can be protected by civil rights actions would be diluted if inmates, often "totally or functionally illiterate," were unable to articulate their complaints to the courts. Although there may be additional burdens on the Complex, if inmates may seek help from other inmates, or from the inmate adviser if he proves adequate, in both habeas and civil rights actions, this should not prove overwhelming. At

[418 US 580]

present only one inmate serves as legal adviser and it may be expected that other qualified inmates could be found for assistance if the Complex insists on naming the inmates from whom help may be sought.

Finding no reasonable distinction between the two forms of actions, we affirm the Court of Appeals on this point, and as the Court of Appeals suggested, the District Court will assess the adequacy of legal assistance under the reasonable-alternative standard of Avery.

Affirmed in part, reversed in part, and remanded.

[Concurring and dissenting opinions omitted.]

BELL v WOLFISH

441 US 000, 60 L Ed 2d 447, 99 S Ct 1861 (1979)

OPINION OF THE COURT
[Footnotes omitted]

Mr. Justice Rehnquist delivered the opinion of the Court.

Over the past five Terms, this Court has in several decisions considered constitutional challenges to prison conditions or practices by convicted prisoners. This case requires us to examine the constitutional rights of pretrial detainees — those persons who have been charged with a crime but who have not yet been tried on the charge. The parties concede that to ensure their presence at trial, these persons legitimately may be incarcerated by the Government prior to a determination of their guilt or innocence, *infra*, at 12-13 and n. 15; see 18 U. S. C. §§ 3146, 3148, and it is the scope of their rights during this period of confinement prior to trial that is the primary focus of this case.

This lawsuit was brought as a class action in the United States District Court for the Southern District of New York to challenge numerous conditions of confinement and practices at the Metropolitan Correctional Center (MCC), a federally operated short term custodial facility in New York City designed primarily to house pretrial detainees. The District Court, in words of the Court of Appeals for the Second Circuit, "intervened broadly into almost every facet of the institution" and enjoined no fewer than 20 MCC practices on constitutional and statutory grounds. The Court of Appeals largely affirmed the District Court's constitutional rulings and in the process held that under the Due Process Clause of the Fifth Amendment, pretrial detainees may "be subjected to only those 'restrictions and privations' which 'inhere in their confinement itself or which are justified by compelling necessities of jail administration.'" *Wolfish* v. *Levi*, 573 F. 2d 118, 124 (1978), quoting *Rhem* v. *Malcolm*, 507 F. 2d 333, 336 (CA2 1974). We granted certiorari to consider the important constitutional questions raised by these decisions and to resolve an apparent conflict among the circuits. — U.S. — (1978). We now reverse.

I

The MCC was constructed in 1975 to replace the converted waterfront garage on West Street that had served as New York City's federal jail since 1928. It is located adjacent to the Foley Square federal courthouse and has as its primary objective the housing of persons who are being detained in custody prior to trial for federal criminal offenses in the United States District Courts for the Southern and Eastern Districts of New York and for the District of New Jersey. Under the Bail Reform Act, 18 U. S. C. § 3146, a person in the federal system is committed to a detention facility only because no other less drastic means can reasonably ensure his presence at trial. In addition to pretrial detainees, the MCC also houses some convicted inmates who are awaiting sentencing or transportation to federal prison or who are serving generally relatively short sentences in a service capacity at the MCC, convicted prisoners who have been lodged at the facility under writs of habeas corpus *ad prosequendum* or *ad testificandum* issued to ensure their presence at upcoming trials, witnesses in protective custody and persons incarcerated for contempt.

The MCC differs markedly from the familiar image of a jail; there are no barred cells, dank, colorless corridors, or clanging steel gates. It was intended to include the most advanced and innovative features of modern design of detention facilities. As the Court of Appeals stated: "[I]t represented the architectural embodiment of the best and most progressive penological planning." 573 F. 2d, at 121. The key design element of the 12-story structure is the "modular" or "unit" concept, whereby each floor designed to house inmates has one or two largely self-contained residential units that replace the traditional cellblock jail construction. Each unit in turn has several clusters or corridors of private rooms or dormitories radiating from a central 2-story "multipurpose" or common

room, to which each inmate has free access approximately 16 hours a day. Because our analysis does not turn on the particulars of the MCC concept or design, we need not discuss them further.

When the MCC opened in August 1975, the planned capacity was 449 inmates, an increase of 50% over the former West Street facility. *Id.*, at 122. Despite some dormitory accomodations, the MCC was designed primarily to house these inmates in 389 rooms, which orginally were intended for single occupancy. While the MCC was under construction, however, the number of persons committed to pretrial detention began to rise at an "unprecedented rate." *Ibid.* The Bureau of Prisons took several steps to accommodate this unexpected flow of persons assigned to the facility, but despite these efforts, the inmate population at the MCC rose above its planned capacity within a short time after its opening. To provide sleeping space for this increased population, the MCC replaced the single bunks in many of the individual rooms and dormitories with double bunks. Also, each week some newly arrived inmates had to sleep on cots in the common areas until they could be transferred to residential rooms as space became available. See 573 F. 2d, at 127-128.

On November 28, 1975, less than four months after the MCC had opened, the named respondents initiated this action by filing in the District Court a petition for a writ of habeas corpus. The District Court certified the case as a class action on behalf of all persons confined at the MCC, pretrial detainees and sentenced prisoners alike. The petition served up a veritable potpourri of complaints that implicated virtually every facet of the institution's conditions and practices. Respondents charged, *inter alia*, that they had been deprived of their statutory and constitutional rights because of overcrowded conditions, undue length of confinement, improper searches, inadequate recreational, educational and employment opportunities, insufficient staff and objectionable restrictions on the purchase and receipt of personal items and books.

In two opinions and a series of orders, the District Court enjoined numerous MCC practices and conditions. With respect to pretrial detainees, the court held that because they are "presumed to be innocent and held only to ensure their presence at trial, 'any deprivation or restriction of . . . rights beyond those which are necessary for confinement alone, must be justified by a compelling necessity.'" 439 F. Supp., at 124, quoting *Detainees of Brooklyn House of Detention* v. *Malcolm*, 520 F. 2d 392, 397 (CA2 1975). And while acknowledging that the rights of sentenced inmates are to be measured by the different standard of the Eighth Amendment, the court declared that to house "an inferior minority of persons . . . in ways found unconstitutional for the rest" would amount to cruel and unusual punishment. 428 F. Supp., at 399.

Applying these standards on cross-motions for partial summary judgment, the District Court enjoined the practice of housing two inmates in the individual rooms and prohibited enforcement of the so-called "publisher-only" rule, which at the time of the court's ruling prohibited the receipt of all books and magazines mailed from outside the MCC except those sent directly from a publisher or a book club. After a trial on the remaining issues, the District Court enjoined, *inter alia*, the doubling of capacity in the dormitory areas, the use of the common rooms to provide temporary sleeping accomodations, the prohibition against inmates' receipt of packages containing food and items of personal property, and the practice of requiring inmates to expose their body cavities for visual inspection following contact visits. The court also granted relief in favor of pretrial detainees, but not convicted inmates, with respect to the requirement that detainees remain outside their rooms during routine inspections by MCC officials.

The Court of Appeals largely affirmed the District Court's rulings, although it rejected that court's Eighth Amendment analysis of conditions of confinement for convicted prisoners because the "parameters of judicial intervention into . . . conditions . . . for sentenced prisoners are more restrictive than in the case of pretrial detainees." 573 F. 2d, at 125. Accordingly, the court remanded the matter to the District Court for it to determine whether the housing for sentenced inmates at the MCC was constitutionally "adequate." But the Court of Appeals approved the due process standard employed by the District Court in enjoining the conditions of pretrial confinement. It therefore held that the MCC had failed to make a showing of "compelling necessity" sufficient to justify housing two pretrial detainees in the individual rooms. 573 F. 2d, at 126-127. And for purposes of our review (since petitioners challenge only some of the Court of Appeals' rulings), the court affirmed the District Court's granting of relief against the "publisher-only" rule, the practice of conducting body cavity searches after contact visits, the prohibition against receipt of packages of food and personal items from outside the institution, and the requirement that detainees remain outside their rooms during routine searches of rooms by MCC officials. *Id.*, at 129-132.

II

As a first step in our decision, we shall address "double-bunking" as it is referred to by the parties, since it is a condition of confinement that is alleged only to deprive pretrial detainees of their liberty without due process of law in contravention of the Fifth Amendment. We will treat in order the Court of Appeals' standard of review, the analysis which we believe the Court of Appeals should have employed, and the conclusions to which our analysis leads us in the case of double-bunking.

A

The Court of Appeals did not dispute that the Government may permissibly incarcerate a person charged with a crime but not yet convicted to ensure his presence at trial. However, reasoning from the "premise that an individual is to be treated as innocent until proven guilty," the court concluded that pretrial detainees retain the "rights afforded unincarcerated individuals," and that therefore it is not sufficient that the conditions of confinement for pretrial detainees "merely comport with contemporary standards of decency prescribed by the cruel and unusual punishment clause of the eighth amendment." 573 F. 2d, at 124. Rather, the court held, the Due Process Clause requires that pretrial detainees "be subjected to only those 'restrictions and privations' which 'inhere in their confinement itself or which are justified by compelling necessities of jail administration.'" *Ibid.*, quoting *Rhem* v. *Malcolm*, 507 F. 2d, at 336. Under the Court of Appeals' "compelling necessity" standard, "deprivation of the rights of detainees cannot be justified by the cries of fiscal necessity, . . . administrative convenience, . . . or by the cold comfort that conditions in other jails are worse." 573 F. 2d, at 124 (citations omitted). The court acknowledged, however, that it could not "ignore" our admonition in *Procunier* v. *Martinez*, 416 U. S. 396, 405 (1974), that "courts are ill-equipped to deal with the increasingly urgent problems of prison administration," and concluded that it would "not [be] wise for [it] to second-guess the expert administrators on matters on which they are better informed." 573 F. 2d, at 124.

Our fundamental disagreement with the Court of Appeals is that we fail to find a source in the Constitution for its compelling necessity standard. Both the Court of Appeals and the District Court seem to have relied on the "presumption of innocence" as the source of the detainee's substantive right to be free from conditions of confinement that are not justified by compelling necessity. 573 F. 2d, at 124; 439 F. Supp., at 124; accord, *Campbell* v. *Magruder*, — U. S. App. D. C. —, 580 F. 2d 521, 529 (1978); *Detainees of Brooklyn House of Detention* v. *Malcolm*, 520 F. 2d 392, 397 (CA2 1975); *Rhem* v. *Malcolm*, 507 F. 2d 333, 336 (CA2 1974). But see *Feeley* v. *Sampson*,

570 F. 2d 364, 369 n. 4 (CA1 1978); *Hampton* v. *Holmesburg Prison Officials*, 546 F. 2d 1077, 1080 n. 1 (CA3 1976). But the presumption of innocence provides no support for such a rule.

The presumption of innocence is a doctrine that allocates the burden of proof in criminal trials; it also may serve as an admonishment to the jury to judge an accused's guilt or innocence solely on the evidence adduced at trial and not on the basis of suspicions that may arise from the fact of his arrest, indictment or custody or from other matters not introduced as proof at trial. *Taylor* v. *Kentucky*, 436 U. S. 478, 485 (1978); see *Estelle* v. *Williams*, 425 U. S. 501 (1976); *In re Winship*, 397 U. S. 358 (1970); 9 J. Wigmore, Evidence § 2511 (3d ed. 1940). It is "an inaccurate, shorthand description of the right of the accused to 'remain inactive and secure, until the prosecution has taken up its burden and produced evidence and effected persuasion . . .' [an] 'assumption' that is indulged in the absence of contrary evidence." *Taylor* v. *Kentucky, supra,* at 483-484, n. 12. Without question, the presumption of innocence plays an important role in our criminal justice system. "The principle that there is a presumption of innocence in favor of the accused is the undoubted law, axiomatic and elementary, and its enforcement lies at the foundation of the administration of our criminal law." *Coffin* v. *United States*, 156 U. S. 432, 453 (1895). But it has no application to a determination of the rights of a pretrial detainee during confinement before his trial has even begun.

The Court of Appeals also relied on what it termed the "indisputable rudiments of due process" in fashioning its compelling necessity test. We do not doubt that the Due Process Clause protects a detainee from certain conditions and restrictions of pretrial detainment. See *infra,* at 13-19. Nonetheless, that clause provides no basis for application of a compelling necessity standard to conditions of pretrial confinement that are not alleged to infringe any other, more specific guarantee of the Constitution.

It is important to focus on what is at issue here. We are not concerned with the initial decision to detain an accused and the curtailment of liberty that such a decision necessarily entails. See *Gerstein* v. *Pugh*, 420 U. S. 103, 114 (1975); *United States* v. *Marion*, 404 U. S. 307, 320 (1971). Neither respondents nor the courts below question that the Government may permissibly detain a person suspected of committing a crime prior to a formal adjudication of guilt. See *Gerstein* v. *Pugh, supra,* at 111-114. Nor do they doubt that the Government has a substantial interest in ensuring that persons accused of crimes are available for trials and ultimately, for service of their sentences, or that confinement of such persons pending trial is a legitimate means of furthering that interest. Tr. of Oral Arg. 27; see *Stack* v. *Boyle*, 342 U. S. 1, 4 (1951). Instead, what *is* at issue when an aspect of pretrial detention that is not alleged to violate any express guarantee of the Constitution is challenged, is the detainee's right to be free from punishment, see *infra,* at 13-14, and his understandable desire to be as comfortable as possible during his confinement, both of which may conceivably coalesce at some point. It seems clear that the Court of Appeals did not rely on the detainee's right to be free from punishment, but even if it had that right does not warrant adoption of that court's compelling necessity test. See *infra*, at 13-19. And to the extent the court relied on the detainee's desire to be free from discomfort, it suffices to say that this desire simply does not rise to the level of those fundamental liberty interests delineated in cases such as *Roe* v. *Wade*, 410 U. S. 113 (1973); *Eisenstadt* v. *Baird*, 405 U. S. 438 (1972); *Stanley* v. *Illinois*, 405 U. S. 645 (1972); *Griswold* v. *Connecticut*, 381 U. S. 479 (1965); *Meyer* v. *Nebraska*, 262 U. S. 390 (1923).

B

In evaluating the constitutionality of conditions or restrictions of pretrial detention that implicate only the protection against deprivation of liberty without due process of law, we think that the proper inquiry is whether those conditions amount to punishment of the detainee. For under the Due Process Clause, a detainee may not be punished prior to an adjudication of guilt in accordance with due process of law. See *Ingraham* v. *Wright*, 430 U. S. 651, 671-672 n. 40, 674 (1977); *Kennedy* v. *Mendoza-Martinez*, 372 U. S. 144, 165-167, 186 (1963); *Wong Wing* v. *United States*, 163 U. S. 228, 237 (1896). A person lawfully committed to pretrial detention has not been adjudged guilty of any crime. He has had only a "judicial determination of probable cause as a prerequisite to [the] extended restraint of [his] liberty following arrest." *Gerstein* v. *Pugh*, 420 U. S., at 114; see *Virginia* v. *Paul*, 148 U. S. 107, 119 (1893). And, if he is detained for a suspected violation of a federal law, he also has had a bail hearing. See 18 U. S. C. §§ 3146, 3148. Under such circumstances, the Government concededly may detain him to ensure his presence at trial and may subject him to the restrictions and conditions of the detention facility so long as those conditions and restrictions do not amount to punishment, or otherwise violate the Constitution.

Not every disability imposed during pretrial detention amounts to "punishment" in the constitutional sense, however. Once the Government has exercised its conceded authority to detain a person pending trial, it obviously is entitled to employ devices that are calculated to effectuate this detention. Traditionally, this has meant confinement in a facility which, no matter how modern or how antiquated, results in restricting the movement of a detainee in a manner in which he would not be restricted if he simply were free to walk the streets pending trial. Whether it be called a jail, a prison, or custodial center, the purpose of the facility is to detain. Loss of freedom of choice and privacy are inherent incidents of confinement in such a facility. And the fact that such detention interferes with the detainee's understandable desire to live as comfortably as possible and with as little restraint as possible during confinement does not convert the conditions or restrictions of detention into "punishment."

This Court has recognized a distinction between punitive measures that may not constitutionally be imposed prior to a determination of guilt and regulatory restraints that may. See, e. g., *Kennedy* v. *Mendoza-Martinez, supra*, at 168; *Flemming* v. *Nestor*, 363 U. S. 603, 613-614 (1960); cf. *DeVeau* v. *Braisted*, 363 U. S. 144, 160 (1960). In

Kennedy v. *Mendoza-Martinez, supra,* the Court examined the automatic forfeiture of citizenship provisions of the immigration laws to determine whether that sanction amounted to punishment or a mere regulatory restraint. While it is all but impossible to compress the distinction into a sentence or a paragraph, the Court there described the tests traditionally applied to determine whether a governmental act is punitive in nature:

"Whether the sanction involves an affirmative disability or restraint, whether it has historically been regarded as a punishment, whether it comes into play only on a finding of *scienter,* whether its operation will promote the traditional aims of punishment — retribution and deterrence, whether the behavior to which it applies is already a crime, whether an alternative purpose to which it may rationally be connected is assignable for it, and whether it appears excessive in relation to the alternative purpose assigned are all relevant to the inquiry, and may often point in differing directions." 372 U. S., at 168-169 (footnotes omitted).

Because forfeiture of citizenship traditionally had been considered punishment and the legislative history of the forfeiture provisions "conclusively" showed that the measure was intended to be punitive, the Court held that forfeiture of citizenship in such circumstances constituted punishment that could not constitutionally be imposed without due process of law. *Id.,* 167-170, 186.

The factors identified in *Mendoza-Martinez* provide useful guideposts in determining whether particular restrictions and conditions accompanying pretrial detention amount to punishment in the constitutional sense of that word. A court must decide whether the disability is imposed for the purpose of punishment or whether it is but an incident of some other legitimate governmental purpose. See *Flemming* v. *Nestor, supra,* at 613-617. Absent a showing of an expressed intent to punish on the part of detention facility officials, that determination generally will turn on "[w]hether an alternative purpose to which [the restriction] may rationally be connected is assignable for it, and whether it appears excessive in relation to the alternative purpose assigned [to it]." *Kennedy* v. *Mendoza-Martinez, supra,* at 168-169; see *Flemming* v. *Nestor, supra,* at 617. Thus, if a particular condition or restriction of pretrial detention is reasonably related to a legitimate governmental objective, it does not, without more, amount to "punishment." Conversely, if a restriction or condition is not reasonably related to a legitimate goal — if it is arbitrary or purposeless — a court permissibly may infer that the purpose of the governmental action is punishment that may not constitutionally be inflicted upon detainees *qua* detainees. See *Flemming* v. *Nestor, supra,* at 617. Courts must be mindful that these inquiries spring from constitutional requirements and that judicial answers to them must reflect that fact rather than a court's idea of how best to operate a detention facility. Cf. *United States* v. *Lovasco,* 431 U. S. 783, 790 (1977); *United States* v. *Russell,* 411 U. S. 423, 435 (1973).

One further point requires discussion. The Government asserts, and respondents concede, that the "essential objective of pretrial confinement is to insure the detainees' presence at trial." Brief for Petitioners 43; see Brief for

Respondents 33. While this interest undoubtedly justifies the original decision to confine an individual in some manner, we do not accept respondent's argument that the Government's interest in ensuring a detainee's presence at trial is the *only* objective that may justify restraints and conditions once the decision is lawfully made to confine a person. "If the government could confine or otherwise infringe the liberty of detainees only to the extent necessary to ensure their presence at trial, house arrest would in the end be the only constitutionally justified form of detention." *Campbell* v. *Magruder, supra,* at 529. The Government also has legitimate interests that stem from its need to manage the facility in which the individual is detained. These legitimate operational concerns may require administrative measures that go beyond those that are, strictly speaking, necessary to ensure that the detainee shows up at trial. For example, the Government must be able to take steps to maintain security and order at the institution and make certain no weapons or illicit drugs reach detainees. Restraints that are reasonably related to the institution's interest in maintaining jail security do not, without more, constitute unconstitutional punishment, even if they are discomforting and are restrictions that the detainee would not have experienced had he been released while awaiting trial. We need not here attempt to detail the precise extent of the legitimate governmental interests that may justify conditions or restrictions of pretrial detention. It is enough simply to recognize that in addition to ensuring the detainees' presence at trial, the effective management of the detention facility once the individual is confined is a valid objective that may justify imposition of conditions and restrictions of pretrial detention and dispel any inference that such restrictions are intended as punishment.

C

Judged by this analysis, respondents' claim that double-bunking violated their due process rights fails. Neither the District Court nor the Court of Appeals intimated that it considered double-bunking to constitute punishment; instead, they found that it contravened the compelling necessity test, which today we reject. On this record, we are convinced as a matter of law that double-bunking as practiced at the MCC did not amount to punishment and did not, therefore, violate respondents' rights under the Due Process Clause of the Fifth Amendment.

The rooms at the MCC that housed pretrial detainees have a total floor space of approximately 75 square feet. Each of them designated for double-bunking, see n. 4, *supra,* contains a double bunkbed, certain other items of furniture, a wash basin and an uncovered toilet. Inmates generally are locked into their rooms from 11 p. m. to 6:30 a. m. and for brief periods during the afternoon and evening head counts. During the rest of the day, they may move about freely between their rooms and the common areas.

Based on affidavits and a personal visit to the facility, the District Court concluded that the practice of double-bunking was unconstitutional. The court relied on two factors for its conclusion: (1) the fact that the rooms were designed to house only one inmate, 428 F. Supp., at 336-337; and (2) its judgment that confining two persons in one room or cell of this size constituted a "fundamental denial[] of decency, privacy, personal security, and, simply, civilized humanity. . . ." *Id.*, at 339. The Court of Appeals agreed with the District Court. In response to petitioners' arguments that the rooms at the MCC were larger and more pleasant than the cells involved in the cases relied on by the District Court, the Court of Appeals stated:

"[W]e find the lack of privacy inherent in double-celling in rooms intended for one individual a far more compelling consideration than a comparison of square footage or the substitution of doors for bars, carpet for concrete, or windows for walls. The Government has simply failed to show any substantial justification for double-celling." 573 F. 2d., at 127.

We disagree with both the District Court and the Court of Appeals that there is some sort of "one man, one cell" principle lurking in the Due Process Clause of the Fifth Amendment. While confining a given number of people in a given amount of space in such a manner as to cause them to endure genuine privations and hardship over an extended period of time might raise serious questions under the Due Process Clause as to whether those conditions amounted to punishment, nothing even approaching such hardship is shown by this record.

Detainees are required to spend only seven or eight hours each day in their rooms, during most or all of which they presumably are sleeping. The rooms provide more than adequate space for sleeping. During the remainder of the time, the detainees are free to move between their rooms and the common area. While double-bunking may have taxed some of the equipment or particular facilities in certain of the common areas, *United States ex rel. Wolfish* v. *United States*, 428 F. Supp., at 337, this does not mean that the conditions at the MCC failed to meet the standards required by the Constitution. Our conclusion in this regard is further buttressed by the detainees' length of stay at the MCC. See *Hutto* v. *Finney*, 437 U. S. 678, 686-687 (1978). Nearly all of the detainees are released within 60 days. See n. 3, *supra.* We simply do not believe that requiring a detainee to share toilet facilities and this admittedly rather small sleeping place with another person for generally a maximum period of 60 days violates the Constitution.

III

Respondents also challenged certain MCC restrictions and practices that were designed to promote security and order at the facility on the ground that these restrictions violated the Due Process Clause of the Fifth Amendment, and certain other constitutional guarantees, such as the First and Fourth Amendments. The Court of Appeals seemed to approach the challenges to security restrictions in a fashion different from the other contested conditions and restrictions. It stated that "once it has been determined that the mere fact of confinement of the detainee justifies the restrictions, the institution must be permitted to use reasonable means to insure that its legitimate interests in security are safeguarded." 573 F. 2d, at 124. The court might disagree with the choice of means to effectuate those interests, but it should not "second-guess the expert administrators on matters on which they are better informed. . . . Concern with minutiae of prison administration can only distract the court from detached consideration of the one overriding question presented to it: does the practice or condition violate the Constitition?" *Id.*, at 124-125. Nonetheless, the court affirmed the District Court's injunction against several security restrictions. The Court rejected the arguments of petitioners that these practices served the MCC's interest in security and order and held that the practices were unjustified interferences with the retained constitutional rights of *both* detainees and convicted inmates. *Id.*, at 129-132. In our view, the Court of Appeals failed to heed its own admonition not to "second-guess" prison administrators.

Our cases have established several general principles that inform our evaluation of the constitutionality of the restrictions at issue. First, we have held that convicted prisoners do not forfeit all constitutional protections by reason of their conviction and confinement in prison. See *Jones v. North Carolina Prisoners' Labor Union*, 433 U. S. 119, 129 (1977); *Meachum v. Fano*, 427 U. S. 215, 225 (1976); *Wolff v. McDonnell*, 418 U. S. 539, 555-556 (1974); *Pell v. Procunier*, 417 U. S. 817, 822 (1974). "There is no iron curtain drawn between the Constitution and the prisons of this country." *Wolff v. McDonnell, supra*, at 555-556. So, for example, our cases have held that sentenced prisoners enjoy freedom of speech and religion under the First and Fourteenth Amendments, see *Pell v. Procunier, supra, Cruz v. Beto*, 405 U. S. 319 (1972); *Cooper v. Pate*, 378 U. S. 546 (1964), that they are protected against invidious discrimination on the basis of race under the Equal Protection Clause of the Fourteenth

Amendment, see *Lee v. Washington*, 390 U. S. 333 (1968), and that they may claim the protection of the Due Process Clause to prevent additional deprivation of life, liberty or property without due process of law, see *Meachum v. Fano, supra; Wolff v. McDonnell, supra*. A *fortiori*, pretrial detainees, who have not been convicted of any crimes, retain at least those constitutional rights that we have held are enjoyed by convicted prisoners.

But our cases also have insisted on a second proposition: simply because prison inmates retain certain constitutional rights does not mean that these rights are not subject to restrictions and limitations. "Lawful incarceration brings about the necessary withdrawal or limitation of many privileges and rights, a retraction justified by the considerations underlying our penal system." *Price v. Johnston*, 334 U. S. 266, 285 (1948); see *Jones v. North Carolina Prisoners' Labor Union, supra*, at 125; *Wolff v. McDonnell, supra*, at 555; *Pell v. Procunier, supra*, at 822. The fact of confinement as well as the legitimate goals and policies of the penal institution limit these retained constitutional rights. *Jones v. North Carolina Prisoners' Labor Union, supra*, at 125; *Pell v. Procunier, supra*, at 822. There must be a "mutual accommodation between institutional needs and objectives and the provisions of the Constitution that are of general application." *Wolff v. McDonnell, supra*, at 556. This principle applies equally to pretrial detainees and convicted prisoners. A detainee simply does not possess the full range of freedoms of an unincarcerated individual.

Third, maintaining institutional security and preserving internal order and discipline are essential goals that may require limitation or retraction of the retained constitutional rights of both convicted prisoners and pretrial detainees. "Central to all other corrections goals is the institutional consideration of internal security within the corrections facilities themselves." *Pell* v. *Procunier, supra,* at 823; see *Jones* v. *North Carolina Prisoners' Labor Union, supra,* at 129; *Procunier* v. *Martinez,* 416 U. S. 396, 412 (1974). Prison officials must be free to take appropriate action to ensure the safety of inmates and corrections personnel and to prevent escape or unauthorized entry. Accordingly, we have held that even when an institutional restriction infringes a specific constitutional guarantee, such as the First Amendment, the practice must be evaluated in the light of the central objective of prison administration, safeguarding institutional security. *Jones* v. *North Carolina Prisoners' Labor Union, supra,* at 129; *Pell* v. *Procunier, supra,* at 822, 826; *Procunier* v. *Martinez, supra,* at 412-414.

Finally, as the Court of Appeals correctly acknowledged, the problems that arise in the day-to-day operation of a corrections facility are not susceptible of easy solutions. Prison administrators therefore should be accorded wide-ranging deference in the adoption and execution of policies and practices that in their judgment are needed to preserve internal order and discipline and to maintain institutional security. *Jones* v. *North Carolina Prisoners' Labor Union, supra,* at 128; *Procunier* v. *Martinez, supra,* at 404-405; *Cruz* v. *Beto,* 405 U. S., at 321; see *Meachum* v. *Fano,* 427 U. S., at 228-229. "Such considerations are peculiarly within the province and professional expertise of corrections officials, and, in the absence of substantial evidence in the record to indicate that the officials have exaggerated their response to these considerations, courts should ordinarily defer to their expert judgment in such matters." *Pell* v. *Procunier, supra,* at 827. We further observe that on occasion, prison administrators may be "experts" only by Act of Congress or of a state legislature. But judicial deference is accorded not merely because the administrator ordinarily will, as a matter of fact in a particular case, have a better grasp of his domain than the reviewing judge, but also because the operation of our correctional facilities is peculiarly the province of the Legislative and Executive Branches of our Government, not the Judicial. *Procunier* v. *Martinez, supra,* at 405; cf. *Meachum* v. *Fano, supra,* at 229. With these teachings of our cases in mind, we turn to an examination of the MCC security practices that are alleged to violate the Constitution.

A

At the time of the lower courts' decisions, the Bureau of Prisons' "publisher-only" rule, which applies to all Bureau facilities, permitted inmates to receive books and magazines from outside the institution only if the materials were mailed directly from the publisher or a book club. 573 F. 2d, at 129-130. The warden of the MCC stated in an affidavit that "serious" security and administrative problems were caused when bound items were received by inmates from unidentified sources outside the facility. App. 24. He noted that in order to make a "proper and thorough" inspection of such items, prison officials would have to remove the covers of hardback books and to leaf through every page of all books and magazines to ensure that drugs, money, weapons or other contraband were not secreted in the material. "This search process would take a substantial and inordinate amount of available staff time." *Ibid.* However, "there is relatively little risk that material received directly from the publisher or book club would contain contraband, and therefore, the security problems are significantly reduced without a drastic drain on staff resources." *Ibid.*

The Court of Appeals rejected these security and administrative justifications and affirmed the District Court's order enjoining enforcement of the "publisher-only" rule at the MCC. The Court of Appeals held that the rule "severely and impermissibly restricts the reading material available to inmates" and therefore violates their First Amendment and due process rights. 573 F. 2d, at 130.

It is desirable at this point to place in focus the precise question that now is before this Court. Subsequent to the decision of the Court of Appeals, the Bureau of Prisons amended its "publisher-only" rule to permit the receipt of books and magazines from bookstores as well as publishers and book clubs. 43 Fed. Reg. 30576 (July 17, 1978). In addition, petitioners have informed the Court that the Bureau proposes to amend the rule further to allow receipt of paperback books, magazines and other soft-covered materials from any source. Brief for Petitioners 66 n. 49, 69, and n. 51. The Bureau regards hardback books as the "more dangerous source of risk to institutional security," however, and intends to retain the prohibition against receipt of hardback books unless they are mailed directly from publishers, book clubs or bookstores. *Id.*, at 69 n. 51. Accordingly, petitioners request this Court to review the District Court's injunction only to the extent it enjoins petitioners from prohibiting receipt of hardcover books that are not mailed directly from publishers, book clubs or bookstores. *Id.*, at 69; Tr. of Oral Arg. 59-60.

We conclude that a prohibition against receipt of hardback books unless mailed directly from publishers, book clubs or bookstores does not violate the First Amendment rights of MCC inmates. That limited restriction is a rational response by prison officials to an obvious security problem. It hardly needs to be emphasized that hardback books are especially serviceable for smuggling contraband into an institution; money, drugs and weapons easily may be secreted in the bindings. *E. g., Woods v. Daggett,* 541 F. 2d 237 (CA10 1976). They also are difficult to search effectively. There is simply no evidence in the record to indicate that MCC officials have exaggerated their response to this security problem and to the administrative difficulties posed by the necessity of carefully inspecting each book mailed from unidentified sources. Therefore, the considered judgment of these experts must control in the absence of prohibitions far more sweeping than those involved here. See *Jones* v. *North Carolina Prisoners' Labor Union, supra,* at 128; *Pell* v. *Procunier, supra,* at 827.

Our conclusion that this limited restriction on receipt of hardback books does not infringe the First Amendment rights of MCC inmates is influenced by several other factors. The rule operates in a neutral fashion, without regard to the content of the expression. *Pell* v. *Procunier, supra,* at 828. And there are alternative means of obtaining reading material that have not been shown to be burdensome or insufficient. "We regard the available 'alternative means of [communication as] a relevant factor' in a case such as this where 'we [are] called upon to balance First Amendment rights against [legitimate] govermental . . . interests.'" *Id.,* at 824, quoting *Kliendienst* v. *Mandel,* 408 U. S. 753, 765 (1972); see *Cruz* v. *Beto,* 405 U. S., at 321, 322 n. 2. The restriction, as it is now before us, allows soft bound books and magazines to be received from any source and hardback books to be received from publishers, bookstores and book clubs. In addition, the MCC has a "relatively large" library for use by inmates. *United States ex rel. Wolfish* v. *United States,* 428 F. Supp., at 340. To the limited extent the rule might possibly increase the cost of obtaining published materials, this Court has held that where "other avenues" remain available for the receipt of materials by inmates, the loss of "cost advantages does not fundamentally implicate *free speech* values." See *Jones* v. *North Carolina Prisoners' Labor Union, supra,* at 130-131. We are also influenced in our decision by the fact that the rule's impact on pretrial detainees is limited to a maximum period of approximately 60 days. See n. 3, *supra.* In sum, considering all the circumstances, we view the rule, as we now find it, to be a "reasonable 'time, place and manner' regulation[   ] . . . [that is] necessary to further significant govern mental interests. . . . " *Grayned* v. *City of Rockford,* 408 U. S. 104, 115 (1972); see *Cox* v. *New Hampshire,* 312 U. S. 569, 575-576 (1941); *Cox* v. *Louisiana,* 379 U. S. 536, 554-555 (1965); *Adderley* v. *Florida,* 385 U. S. 39, 46-48 (1966).

B

Inmates at the MCC were not permitted to receive packages from outside the facility containing items of food or personal property, except for one package of food at Christmas. This rule was justified by MCC officials on three grounds. First, officials testified to "serious" security problems that arise from the introduction of such packages into the institution, the "traditional file in the cake kind of situation" as well as the concealment of drugs "in heels of shoes [and] seams of clothing." App. 80; see *id.,* at 24, 84-85. As in the case of the "publisher-only" rule, the warden testified that if such packages were allowed, the inspection process necessary to ensure the security of the institution would require a "substantial and inordinate amount of available staff time." *Id.,* at 24. Second, officials were concerned that the introduction of personal property into the facility would increase the risk of thefts, gambling and inmate conflicts, the "age-old problem of you have it and I don't." *Id.,* at 80; see *id.,* at 85. Finally, they noted storage and sanitary problems that would result from inmates' receipt of food packages. *Id.,* at 67, 80. Inmates are permitted, however, to purchase certain items of food and personal property from the MCC commissary.

The District Court dismissed these justifications as "dire predictions." It was unconvinced by the asserted security problems because other institutions allow greater ownership of personal property and receipt of packages than does the MCC. And because the MCC permitted inmates to purchase items in the commissary, the court could not accept official fears of increased theft, gambling or conflicts if packages were allowed. Finally, it believed that sanitation could be assured by proper housekeeping regulations. Accordingly, it ordered the MCC to promulgate regulations to permit receipt of at least items of the kind that are available in the commissary. 439 F. Supp., at 152-153. The Court of Appeals accepted the District Court's analysis and affirmed, although it noted that the MCC could place a ceiling on the permissible dollar value of goods received and restrict the number of packages. 573 F. 2d, at 132.

Neither the District Court nor the Court of Appeals identified which provision of the Constitution was violated by this MCC restriction. We assume, for present purposes, that their decisions were based on the Due Process Clause of the Fifth Amendment, which provides protection for convicted prisoners and pretrial detainees alike against the deprivation of their property without due process of law. See *supra*, at 23. But as we have stated, these due process rights of prisoners and pretrial detainees are not absolute; they are subject to reasonable limitation or retraction in light of the legitimate security concerns of the institution.

We think the District Court and the Court of Appeals have trenched too cavalierly into areas that are properly the concern of MCC officials. It is plain from their opinions, that the lower courts simply disagreed with the judgment of MCC officials about the extent of the security interests affected and the means required to further those interests. But our decisions have time and again emphasized that this sort of unguided substitution of judicial judgment for that of the expert prison administrators on matters such as this is inappropriate. See *Jones* v.

North Carolina Prisoners' Labor Union, supra; Pell v. *Procunier, supra; Procunier* v. *Martinez, supra.* We do not doubt that the rule devised by the District Court and modified by the Court of Appeals may be a reasonable way of coping with the problems of security, order and sanitation. It simply is not, however, the only constitutionally permissible approach to these problems. Certainly, the Due Process Clause does not mandate a "lowest common denominator" security standard, whereby a practice permitted at one penal institution must be permitted at all institutions.

Corrections officials concluded that permitting the introduction of packages of personal property and food would increase the risks of gambling, theft and inmate fights over that which the institution already experienced by permitting certain items to be purchased from its commissary. "It is enough to say that they have not been conclusively shown to be wrong in this view." *Jones* v. *North Carolina Prisoners' Labor Union, supra,* at 132. It is also all too obvious that such packages are handy devices for smuggling of contraband. There simply is no basis in this record for concluding that MCC officials have exaggerated their response to these serious problems or that this restriction is irrational. It does not therefore deprive the convicted inmates or pretrial detainees of the MCC of their property without due process of law in contravention of the Fifth Amendment.

C

The MCC staff conducts unannounced searches of inmate living areas at irregular intervals. These searches generally are formal unit "shakedowns" during which all inmates are cleared of the residential units, and a team of guards searches each room. Prior to the District Courts' order, inmates were not permitted to watch the searches. Officials testified that permitting inmates to observe room inspections would lead to friction between the inmates and security guards and would allow the inmates to attempt to frustrate the search by distracting personnel and moving contraband from one room to another ahead of the search team.

The District Court held that this procedure could not stand as applied to pretrial detainees because MCC officials had not shown that the restriction was justified by "compelling necessity." The court stated that "[a]t least until or unless [petitioners] can show a pattern of violence or other disruptions taxing the powers of control — a kind of showing not remotely approached by the Warden's expressions — the security argument for banishing inmates while their rooms are searched must be rejected." 439 F. Supp., at 149. It also noted that in many instances inmates suspected guards of thievery. *Id.*, at 148-149. The Court of Appeals agreed with the District Court. It saw "no reason whatsoever not to permit a detainee to observe the search of his room and belongings from a reasonable distance," although the court permitted the removal of any detainee who became "obstructive." 573 F. 2d, at 132.

The Court of Appeals did not identify the constitutional provision on which it relied in invalidating the room search rule. The District Court stated that the rule infringed the detainee's interest in privacy and indicated that this interest in privacy was founded on the Fourth Amendment. 439 F. Supp., at 149-150. It may well be argued that a person confined in a detention facility has no reasonable expectation of privacy with respect to his room or cell and that therefore the Fourth Amendment provides no protection for such a person. Cf. *Lanza* v. *New York*, 370 U. S. 139, 143-144 (1962). In any case, given the realities of institutional confinement, any reasonable expectation of privacy that a detainee retained necessarily would be of a diminished scope. *Id.*, at 143. Assuming, *arguendo*, that a pretrial detainee retains such a diminished expectation of privacy after commitment to a custodial facility, we nonetheless find that the room search rule does not violate the Fourth Amendment.

It is difficult to see how the detainee's interest in privacy is infringed by the room search rule. No one can rationally doubt that room searches represent an appropriate security measure and neither the District Court nor the Court of Appeals prohibited such searches. And even the most zealous advocate of prisoners' rights would not suggest that a warrant is required to conduct such a search. Detainees' drawers and beds and personal items may be searched, even after the lower courts' rulings. Permitting detainees to observe the searches does not lessen the invasion of their privacy; its only conceivable beneficial effect would be to prevent theft or misuse by those conducting the search. The room search rule simply facilitates the safe and effective performance of the search which all concede may be conducted. The rule itself, then, does not render the searches "unreasonable" within the meaning of the Fourth Amendment.

D

Inmates at all Bureau of Prisons facilities, including the MCC, are required to expose their body cavities for visual inspection as a part of a strip search conducted after every contact visit with a person from outside the institution. Corrections officials testified that visual cavity searches were necessary not only to discover but also to deter the smuggling of weapons, drugs and other contraband into the institution. App. 70-72, 83-84. The District Court upheld the strip search procedure but prohibited the body cavity searches, absent probable cause to believe that the inmate is concealing contraband. 439 F. Supp., at 147-148. Because petitioners proved only one instance in the MCC's short history where contraband was found during a body cavity search, the Court of Appeals affirmed. In its view, the "gross violation of personal privacy inherent in such a search cannot be outweighed by the government's security interest in maintaining a practice of so little actual utility." 573 F. 2d, at 131.

Admittedly, this practice instinctively gives us the most pause. However, assuming for present purposes that inmates, both convicted prisoners and pretrial detainees, retain some Fourth Amendment rights upon commitment to a corrections facility, see *Lanza* v. *New York, supra; Stroud* v. *United States,* 251 U. S. 15, 21 (1919), we nonetheless conclude that these searches do not violate that Amendment. The Fourth Amendment prohibits only unreasonable searches, *Carroll* v. *United States,* 267 U. S. 132, 147 (1925), and under the circum-

stances, we do not believe that these searches are unreasonable.

The test of reasonableness under the Fourth Amendment is not capable of precise definition or mechanical application. In each case it requires a balancing of the need for the particular search against the invasion of personal rights that the search entails. Courts must consider the scope of the particular intrusion, the manner in which it is conducted, the justification for initiating it and the place in which it is conducted. *E.g., United States* v. *Ramsey,* 431 U. S. 606 (1977); *United States* v. *Martinez-Fuerte,* 428 U. S. 543 (1976); *United States* v. *Brignoni-Ponce,* 422 U. S. 873 (1975); *Terry* v. *Ohio,* 392 U. S. 1 (1968); *Katz* v. *United States,* 389 U. S. 347 (1967); *Schmerber* v. *California,* 384 U. S. 757 (1966). A detention facility is a unique place fraught with serious security dangers. Smuggling of money, drugs, weapons and other contraband is all too common an occurrence. And inmate attempts to secrete these items into the facility by concealing them in body cavities are documented in this record, App. 71-76, and in other cases. *E. g., Ferraro* v. *United States,* — F. 2d — (CA6, filed Dec. 15, 1978) (No. 78-5250); *United States* v. *Park,* 521 F. 2d 1381, 1382 (CA9 1975). That there has been only one instance where an MCC inmate was discovered attempting to smuggle contraband into the institution on his person may be more a testament to the effectiveness of this search technique as a deterrent than to any lack of interest on part of the inmates to secrete and import such items when the opportunity arises.

We do not underestimate the degree to which these searches may invade the personal privacy of inmates. Nor do we doubt, as the District Court noted, that on occasion a security guard may conduct the search in an abusive fashion. 439 F. Supp., at 147. Such abuse cannot be condoned. The searches must be conducted in a reasonable manner. *Schmerber* v. *California, supra,* at 771-772. But we deal here with the question whether visual body cavity inspections as contemplated by the MCC rules can *ever* be conducted on less than probable cause. Balancing the significant and legitimate security interests of the institution against the privacy interests of the inmates, we conclude that they can.

IV

Nor do we think that the four MCC security restrictions and practices described in Part III, *supra,* constitute "punishment" in violation of the rights of pretrial detainees under the Due Process Clause of the Fifth Amendment. Neither the District Court not the Court of Appeals suggested that these restrictions and practices were employed by MCC officials with an intent to punish the pretrial detainees housed there. Respondents do not even make such a suggestion; they simply argue that the restrictions were greater than necessary to satisfy petitioners' legitimate interest in maintaining security. Brief for Respondents 51-53. Therefore, the determination whether these restrictions and practices constitute punishment in the constitutional sense depends on whether they are rationally related to a legitimate nonpunitive governmental purpose and whether they appear excessive in relation to that purpose. See *supra,* at 16-17. Ensuring security and order at the institution is a permissible nonpunitive objective, whether the facility houses pretrial detainees, convicted inmates, or both. *Supra,* at 18; see *id.,* at 24-25, and n. 28. For the reasons set forth in Part III, *supra,* we think that these particular restrictions and practices were reasonable responses by MCC officials to legitimate security concerns. Respondents simply have not met their heavy burden of showing that these officials have exaggerated their response to the genuine security considerations that actuated these restrictions and practices. See n. 23, *supra.* And as might be expected of restrictions applicable to pretrial detainees, these restrictions were of only limited duration so far as the MCC pretrial detainees were concerned. See n. 3, *supra.*

V

There was a time not too long ago when the federal judiciary took a completely "hands-off" approach to the problem of prison administration. In recent years, however, these courts largely have discarded this "hands-off" attitude and have waded into this complex arena. The deplorable conditions and draconian restrictions of some of our Nation's prisons are too well known to require recounting here, and the federal courts rightly have condemned these sordid aspects of our prison systems. But many of these same courts have, in the name of the Constitution, become increasingly enmeshed in the minutiae of prison operations. Judges, after all, are human. They, no less than others in our society, have a natural tendency to believe that their individual solutions to often intractable problems are better and more workable than those of the persons who are actually charged with and trained in the running of the particular institution under examination. But under the Constitution, the first question to be answered is not whose plan is best, but in what branch of the Government is lodged the authority to initially devise the plan. This does not mean that constitutional rights are not to be scrupulously observed. It does mean, however, that the inquiry of federal courts into prison management must be limited to the issue of whether a particular system violates any prohibition of the Constitution, or in the case of a federal prison, a statute. The wide range of "judgment calls" that meet constitutional and statutory requirements are confided to officials outside of the Judicial Branch of Government.

The judgment of the Court of Appeals is, accordingly, reversed and the case is remanded for proceedings consistent with this opinion.

It is so ordered.

[Concurring and dissenting opinions omitted.]

Appendix D

MAJOR AND MINOR MISCONDUCT

Following are descriptions of resident behavior which is prohibited and subject to disciplinary sanctions. The left-hand column lists and defines the violations—any behavior that fits the definition is misconduct. In the right-hand column are specific common examples of behavior fitting under the rule violation. These are just *examples*; other actions that fit the violation definition are also misconduct even though they are not mentioned in the right-hand column. The violations are divided into major and minor misconduct. However, repeated misconduct will always be handled as major.

In addition to the violations which follow, three other kinds of charges are possible: accomplice, attempt, or conspiracy to commit a specific violation.

1) ACCOMPLICE - A resident who assists another to commit a specific misconduct or, after it is committed, conceals the violation from the authorities. The charge should be "accomplice to assault," etc. then describe what the resident allegedly did. *Examples* of this include: "jiggering," lookout, holding down a victim, allowing use of cell/room for commission of a violation.

2) ATTEMPT - A resident intends to commit a specific rule violation *and* does something towards committing it, even though he or she may not have succeeded.

3) CONSPIRACY - A resident intends to commit a specific violation *and* agrees with at least one other person to commit the violation. No action is necessary.

Many rule violations necessarily include other less serious violations. This is where the violations are similar and have common facts or elements. For example, the "lesser included" violations of *escape* are: attempted escape, out of place, missing count and late furlough return. Being insolent to an officer is a lesser included violation of threatening an officer; fighting may be a "lesser included" of assault. When a resident is charged with misconduct and the evidence does not support the particular violation charged but does establish a lesser included violation, the hearing officer or committee does have the authority to find the resident guilty of the lesser included violation.

MAJOR RULE VIOLATIONS	COMMON EXAMPLES

Escape; Attempt to Escape
Leaving or failing to return to lawful custody without authorization. Failure to return within two hours after designated time from furlough or pass will be charged as ESCAPE. ESCAPE is a felony and will always be referred to the prosecutor.

Leaving from hospital trip or while housed at hospital; hiding from authorities even if still on prison property.

Any act that would be a felony if prosecuted under Michigan law is also a major misconduct violation.

Extortion; receiving stolen property; fraud.

ASSAULTIVE OR VIOLENT VIOLATION

Homicide
Causing the death of another person by any means.

Assault
Physical confrontation where one party is the victim and the other is the assailant. Injury is not necessary, but contact is.

Attack by one or more persons; striking with feces or other objects; physical resistance of, or interference with, an employee.

Intimidating or threatening behavior
Words, actions, or other behavior expressing an intent to injure, which place another in fear of being physically harmed or assaulted. Includes attempted assault.

Sexual Assault
Physical confrontation for sexual purposes, where one party is the victim and the other is the assailant. Non-consensual physical contact for sexual purposes.

Fighting
Mutual physical confrontation, including a swing and miss, even where not done in anger.

Fight between residents, whether with fists, broom handles or other weapons.

ACTS OF SERIOUS INSUBORDINATION

Disobey a direct order
Refusal or failure to follow a valid, reasonable order.

Refusal to obey an order or instruction; failure to answer call; failure to report to assignment.

Possession of Forged Documents; Forgery
Knowingly possessing a falsified document; altering or falsifying a document with the intent to deceive or defraud.

A fake pass, application, furlough papers, etc. which is represented to be true.

Incite to Riot or Strike;
Rioting or Striking
Encouragement of action to disrupt or endanger the institution, persons or property. Participation in such action.

Interference with the Administration of Rules.
Acts intending to impede, disrupt or mislead the institutional disciplinary processes.

Intimidating or tampering with an informant or witness; tampering with evidence; destroying or discarding a disciplinary action (flimsey); interfering with an employee writing a misconduct report.

Bribery of an Employee
Offering to give or withhold anything to persuade an employee to neglect duties or perform favors.

Lying to an Employee
Providing false information to an employee under any circumstances.

Insolence
Behavior, including touching, gestures and language, which intends to harrass, annoy, show disrespect, or cause alarm in an employee.

Cursing; abusive language, writing or gesture directed at an employee.

Destruction or Misuse of State Property
Any destruction, removal, alteration, tampering, or other misuse of state property, including state clothing and food.

Alteration of earphones; tampering with locking device; door plug; throwing brakes; burning mattress.

THREATS TO THE GOOD ORDER AND SECURITY OF THE INSTITUTION

Dangerous contraband
Possession of weapon, explosives, acids, caustics, materials for incendiary devices, escape materials. Possession of "critical" tools.

Gasoline, sulphuric acid, lye, prison-made knives, pipe bomb, rope and grappling hook.

Possession of money
Any money other than 50 pennies is contraband.

Creating a Disturbance
Actions of a resident resulting in disruption or disturbance, but not endangering persons or property.

Excessive noise.

Sexual Misconduct
Consensual touching of the sexual or other intimate parts of another person, done for the purpose of gratifying the sexual desire of either party. ALSO, imitating the appearance of the opposite sex. (NOTE: the embrace authorized at the beginning of a visit is not misconduct.)

Kissing, hugging, intercourse, sodomy. Clothing of the opposite sex; men wearing make-up.

Substance Abuse
Possession, selling or providing to others, or under the influence of, any intoxicant, inhalant, controlled substance or marijuana.

Two in a Cell/Room
No resident may be in another's cell or room unless specifically authorized.

Out of place or bounds/AWOL
Being anywhere without the proper authorization; being absent from where required to be. ("Skating" in own housing unit during the day is a minor.)

"Skating" in another block; no pass or I.D. card; misuse of pass; missing count; failure to return on time from furlough, but returned within two hours of deadline.

Theft
Any unauthorized taking of another person's property.

Cell theft

Gambling; Possession of Gambling Paraphernalia
Playing games or making bets for money or anything of value.

Betting slips

MINOR RULE VIOLATIONS [1]	COMMON EXAMPLES

Misdemeanor
Any act that would be a misdemeanor of prosecuted under Michigan law is also a minor misconduct violation, unless specified elsewhere as a major.

Abuse of privileges
Intentional violation of any department or institutional regulation dealing with resident privileges, unless it is specified elsewhere as a major.

Violations of rules or regulations, regarding visits, mail or telephone; improper fund transfer; unauthorized legal assistance.

Contraband
Possession or use of non-dangerous property which a resident has no authorization to have, where there is no suspicion of theft or fraud.

Unauthorized items; anything with someone else's name or number on it; Excessive store items.

Health, Safety or Fire Hazard
Creating one of the above dangers by act or omission.

Dirty cell; smoking in unauthorized areas; lack of personal hygiene.

Temporary out of place/bounds
In own housing unit, during the day. Out of place for a brief time or adjacent to where supposed to be.

Tardy for count or assignment; on gallery outside own cell.

Unauthorized Communications
Any contact, by letter, gesture or verbally, with an unauthorized person or in an unauthorized manner.

Love letters to another resident; passing property on a visit either directly or through a third person.

Violation of Posted Rules
For example, of housing unit, dining room, work or school assignment which are not covered elsewhere.

Violation of kitchen sanitary regulations wasting food; excessive noise in housing unit, playing TV or radio without earphone.

---

[1] The second violation within 30 days or 4th within a year's time (from the 3rd preceding violation, not calendar year) shall be charged and processed as a MAJOR.

Appendix E

REPORTING AND REVIEWING
OFFICERS MISCONDUCT VIOLATION CHECKLIST

To be properly and completely charged, each misconduct report must contain specific basic information. Some kinds of information should be included no matter what the charge. For example, the reporting officer must always give the name and number of *all* residents involved in a misconduct incident on *each* report that is written. A reporting officer must make clear what he/she personally witnessed that is, describe what you personally saw or heard (e.g., heard arguing but did not see blows being struck).

Other types of information are unique to the misconduct being charged; therefore, a "checklist" of necessary questions to be answered for every charge follows. ("R" means the resident who is being charged with misconduct.)

MINOR MISCONDUCT

ABUSE OF PRIVILEGES
1. What is the privilege or rule?
2. What did "R" do?

CONTRABAND
1. What is the item?
2. Where was it found?
3. Who has control of that area?
*4. Where is the item now?

HEALTH, SAFETY OR FIRE HAZARD
1. What did "R" do?
2. How was that a hazard? OR What rule did it violate?

TEMPORARY OUT OF
PLACE/BOUNDS
1. Where was "R"?
2. Where was "R" supposed to be?
3. How long was "R" out of place/bounds?

UNAUTHORIZED COMMUNICATIONS
1. Did "R" contact someone? By what means?
2. Who did "R" contact?
*3. If a written communication, where is it now?

VIOLATION OF POSTED RULES
1. What is the rule?
2. Where is it posted?
3. How did "R" violate it? (exactly what did "R" do?)

MAJOR MISCONDUCT

ESCAPE: ATTEMPT TO ESCAPE
1. Where was "R" required to be?
2. Was "R" absent? OR When did "R" leave?
3. Did "R" call or return? When?
4. Where was "R" apprehended? When?

HOMICIDE
1. Did someone die?
2. What did "R" do?

ASSAULT
1. Did "R" strike someone? If so, who?
2. Was there some kind of physical assault or interference? If so, with whom?
*3. Was a weapon involved? What was it? Where is it now?

INTIMIDATING OR THREATENING
BEHAVIOR
1. What were "R's" words or actions?
2. To whom were they said or directed?

SEXUAL ASSAULT
1. Did "R" touch or assault someone? Who?
2. On what part of the body?
*3. Was a weapon involved? Where is it now? What was it?

MAJOR MISCONDUCT (continued)

FIGHTING
1. Was there an exchange of blows?
2. Who was involved?
3. Did the reporting officer see the exchange? Hear it? Come upon the aftermath?
*4. Were weapons involved? What were they? Where are they now?

DISOBEY A DIRECT ORDER
1. What was the order? Who gave it?
2. Who was it given to?
3. In what way was it disobeyed?

POSSESSION OF FORGED
DOCUMENTS; FORGERY
1. Who possessed or forged the document?
2. What did the document appear to be?
3. What was the document in fact (in what way falsified)?
*4. Where is the document now (should be attached as evidence)?

INCITE TO RIOT OR STRIKE;
PARTICIPATE
1. What were "R's" words or actions?
2. How many other residents were present?
3. Did a riot or strike develop? Any reaction?

INTERFERENCE WITH
ADMINISTRATION OF RULES
1. What was "R's" action?
2. How did that interfere?

BRIBERY OF AN EMPLOYEE
1. What did "R" offer. To whom?
2. What did "R" say it was for?

LYING TO AN EMPLOYEE
1. What did "R" say?
2. How was that false?

INSOLENCE
1. What did "R" say or do?
2. Who was it directed at?

DESTRUCTION OR MISUSE OF
STATE PROPERTY
1. What was the state property?
2. How was it misused?
3. Who did it?
*4. Where is the property now?

DANGEROUS CONTRABAND
1. What was the item?
2. Exactly where was it found?
3. Who has control of that area?
*4. Where is the item now?

POSSESSION OF MONEY
1. What was the item?
2. Exactly where was it found?
3. Who has control of that area?
*4. Where is the item now?

CREATING A DISTURBANCE
1. What did "R" say or do?
2. How many other residents were nearby?
3. What reaction was there?

SEXUAL MISCONDUCT
1. Was "R" touching another resident? Who?
2. What part of the body was being touched?
3. Where were they?
4. Were they fully clothed?
                    OR
1. What clothing or makeup was "R" wearing?

SUBSTANCE ABUSE
If possession:
1. What was the substance? Was it tested?
2. Where was it found?
3. Who has control of that area?
*4. Where is it now?
If under the influence:
1. Specifically describe "R's" condition/ behavior.
2. Was any prohibited substance found? (If so, answer questions 1-4 above)

MAJOR MISCONDUCT (continued)

TWO IN A CELL/ROOM
  1. Where was "R"?
  2. Where does "R" lock?
  3. Who else was in the cell/room?

OUT OF PLACE/BOUNDS
  1. Where was "R"?
  2. Where was "R" supposed to be?
  3. Did "R" have a pass or I.D.?
  4. How long was "R" out of place?

THEFT
  1. What was the property?
  2. Who does it belong to?
  3. Where was it found?
  4. Who has control of that area?
*5. Where is it now?

GAMBLING; PARAPHERNALIA
  1. Did officer witness a game?
  2. Did officer witness "R" betting?
  3. What was being bet?
  4. Who else was in game?
*5. Is there physical evidence of the game? Where is it now?
                    OR
  1. What paraphernalia was found?
  2. Exactly where was it found?
  3. Who has control of that area?
*4. Where is it now?

* The reporting officer must always seize weapons and property believed to be contraband or stolen and retain it for evidence. These charges cannot be established without the evidence.

*HEARING AND APPELLATE OFFICER
MAJOR MISCONDUCT CHECKLIST*

Each major misconduct violation has specific elements which must be present to establish guilt. Some of these apply no matter what the charge; for example, to be found guilty, a resident must have committed the violation (1) voluntarily–not forced into it by someone else, and (2) either intentionally, recklessly or negligently–not accidentally or by mistake.

Other elements are unique to the misconduct being charged; therefore, a "checklist" of the elements necessary to establish guilt for every major misconduct follows. To determine whether the necessary elements are present, the hearing officer must consider and weigh all the evidence presented, including its specificity, whether it is the product of direct observation or hearsay, and the credibility of witnesses.

ESCAPE; ATTEMPT TO ESCAPE
1. R voluntarily removed self from custody without authorization.
2. R intended to leave or not return
3. R did not act under duress
(This is a defense for R to raise.)

HOMICIDE
1. R did something that caused X's death (did not have to intend death).
*2. R did not act in self-defense

ASSAULT
1. There was a physical confrontation
2. The confrontation was intentional, reckless or negligent (not accidental)
3. The confrontation was not mutual (if mutual=fighting)
4. R was not the victim (if victim=not guilty)
*5. R did not act in self-defense (if self-defense=not guilty)

INTIMIDATING AND
THREATENING BEHAVIOR
1. There was specific action by R expressing the intent to physically injure X.
2. R intended to cause *fear* of harm in X (even though may not have actually intended to harm X). The imminence of the threatened harm should be considered in deciding intent to cause fear.

SEXUAL ASSAULT
1. There was touching for sexual purposes
2. The touching was not consensual
3. R was the aggressor

FIGHTING
1. There was a physical confrontation (including "horseplay")
2. The confrontation was not accidental
3. The confrontation was mutual (if not, may be an assault case.)
*4. R did not act in self-defense (if self-defense=not guilty)

DISOBEY A DIRECT ORDER
1. A reasonable order was given to R.
2. R knew the order was given to him/her.
3. R voluntarily failed to follow the order

POSSESSION OF
FORGED DOCUMENTS; FORGERY
1. R had possession of the document
**2. The document was falsified
3. R *knew* it was a fake document
        OR
1. R falsified a document.

MAJOR MISCONDUCT (continued)

INCITE TO RIOT OR STRIKE; PARTICIPATE

1. R's actions/words were intended to encourage others to disrupt the institution or endanger persons or property (if intent is not present, the violation may be "creating a disturbance.")

OR

1. R participated in such action

INTERFERENCE WITH THE ADMINISTRATION OF RULES

R attempted to interfere with the institutional disciplinary process (need not have succeeded in interfering).

BRIBERY OF AN EMPLOYEE

1. R offered something to an employee
2. R intended that the employee do something in exchange for that which was offered.

LYING TO AN EMPLOYEE

1. R gave false information to an employee
2. R knew the information was false

INSOLENCE

1. R said or did something which harrassed, annoyed, insulted or alarmed an employee
2. R intended his or her behavior to so affect the employee. (If the behavior was not directed at the employee, intent is probably not present.)

DESTRUCTION OR MISUSE OF STATE PROPERTY

**1. State property was altered, destroyed or misused
2. R did it.

DANGEROUS CONTRABAND

**1. The item fits the *dangerous* contraband category.
2. It was in R's possession or area of control.
3. R knew or should have known, the item was there (consider access by others). R "should have known" the item was there if R had the responsibility to search own quarters upon arrival, had exclusive control of the area, etc.

POSSESSION OF MONEY

1. Money other than 50 pennies was found
2. It was in R's possession or area of control.
3. R knew, or should have known, it was there.

CREATING A DISTURBANCE

1. R did something that caused a disturbance among other residents (no intent is necessary).

SEXUAL MISCONDUCT

1. There was sexual touching between R and someone else
2. It was consensual (if not consensual, may be sexual assault).

OR

**1. The clothing or makeup was clearly that of the opposite sex.

SUBSTANCE ABUSE

**1. The substance fits this category.
2. It was found in R's possession or area of control.

OR

1. R's condition was specifically described and is characteristic of being under the influence of alcohol or a prohibited drug.
2. The condition was not due to a handicap or legitimate medication (this is a defense for R to raise.)

TWO IN A CELL/ROOM

1. R was in another resident's cell/room
2. R had no authorization to be there.
3. R allowed another resident into his or her cell/room (must find that R voluntarily permitted the second resident in).

OUT OF PLACE/BOUNDS

1. R had no authorization to be where he was
2. Does not fit minor misconduct of "temporary".

MAJOR MISCONDUCT (continued)

THEFT

**1. Property found in R's possession or area of control does not belong to R.

2. R had no permission from owner (if had permission=minor misconduct of contraband, because still unauthorized by the institution.)

GAMBLING; POSSESSION OF GAMBLING PARAPHERNALIA

1. R was making bets or arranging for others to do so.

OR

**1. Items known to be gambling paraphernalia at this institution were found.

2. They were in R's possession or area of control

*SELF-DEFENSE: R can use the amount of force reasonably necessary to prevent the threatened harm. The following conditions must be met to justify using force in self-defense (and therefore, being found not guilty.)

a. R reasonably believed that X imminently would use physical force against him/her.

b. R was not the original aggressor.

c. R did not provoke X.

d. The use of force was not by mutual agreement.

e. R had no reasonable alternative to the use of force (*e.g.* was retreat a reasonable possibility?)

AND

f. R did not use more force than was reasonably necessary to defend self.

An incident may have begun as an assault on R but R fought back harder than was necessary for defense. In these situations, R should be found guilty of "fighting."

** The hearing officer must have the physical evidence to make a decision in these cases. This may be either the item itself, a photograph or drawing. In the case of "substance abuse" a description of the substance plus field or laboratory test results are necessary if the resident denies guilt.

MICHIGAN DEPARTMENT OF CORRECTIONS
NOTICE OF VISITOR RESTRICTION   CSO-315   Rev. 7/77

Date________________________

Dear_________________________________:
            (Resident)
Your visitor(s)____

____

(has, have) been restricted from visiting:

☐ Any department facility permanently.
☐ Any department facility until _________________________________.
☐ This institution for ____.
☐ Unless the following conditions are met:_______________________

____

____

because on ____
            (Date and Reason)

____

____

If you have reasons why your visitor(s) should not be restricted and wish to request a hearing, **WITHIN TEN DAYS** fill out the back of this form and send it to the Deputy Supt./Deputy Warden who will schedule a hearing with a hearing officer. A copy of this is also being sent to the visitor(s) for any response they may have regarding this matter.

____
Deputy Warden/Deputy Supt.

____
Institution

cc: Resident
     Visitor(s)
     RO Folder
     Information Desk
     Lansing

2-1

☐ I request a hearing on this matter.

You may have a hearing investigator if you need one to interview witnesses or gather other evidence for your hearing.

☐ I need a hearing investigator because ___________________________________

____

OR

☐ I do not need a hearing investigator.

DATE   RESIDENT'S SIGNATURE & NUMBER

INDEX

A

Access
 to courts, 93-108
 to prisons and jails by media, 32
Adjustment committee, *see* Disciplinary
  hearing
Assault
 protection from, 74-75
 self-defense, 132, Appendix D
Attorney
 for employees, 10
 jailhouse lawyers as, 99, 101
 mail, 24, 96
 visits, 34-35
 Wolff v. McDonnell, 24, Appendix B
Attorney fees
 bad faith, ordered when, 78

B

Bad faith
 civil rights violation, 12
 damages, test for, 11-13
 Hutto v. Finney, 78
Bail, 148
Balancing test
 access to courts, alternative means, 97
 due process, 112, 115-116
 explanation of, 6, 8
 jailhouse lawyers, restrictions on, 100
 law libraries, 104
 manner of search, 65-67
 parole revocation, 116
 restrictions generally, 38
 strip search, applicability to, 64-65
Baxstrom v. Herold, 142, 147
Baxter v. Palmigiano, 117, 135
Beards
 as expression, 28
 as religious belief, 30
Beliefs

political, 37
religious, 40, 41
sincerity of, 44
Bell v. Wolfish, see Appendix C for full
 text
cell search, procedures for, 62
citation for, 38, 67, 153
double bunking, 76
pretrial detention conditions, 145-146,
 148-151
publisher-only rule, 27, 102
role of courts, 154
strip searches, 65
Black Muslims
case citations, 50
equal treatment of, 47
religious beliefs, 45
Books, *see* Law library
Bounds v. Smith, 104, 105-107, 108

C

Capital punishment
case citations, 92
Coker v. Georgia, 89
constitutionality of, 88
excessiveness of, 88-89
Furman v. Georgia, 87
mandatory, 90
procedures for imposition, 88, 89-90
Censorship, *see* Mail
Charges, disciplinary
duplicate, 130
lesser included, 130
list, Appendix D
notice required, 121
Civil Rights Action (1983)
against individual employee, 11
bad faith, 11-13
excessive force, 71
generally, 11
guidelines, acting under as defense, 13